Beethoven

String Quartets
Op. 59 Nos. 1–3 (*Razumovsky*)
Op. 74, (*The Harp*)
Op. 95 (*Quartetto Serioso*)

Their Creation, Origins and Reception History
Incorporating
Contextual Accounts of Beethoven and His Contemporaries

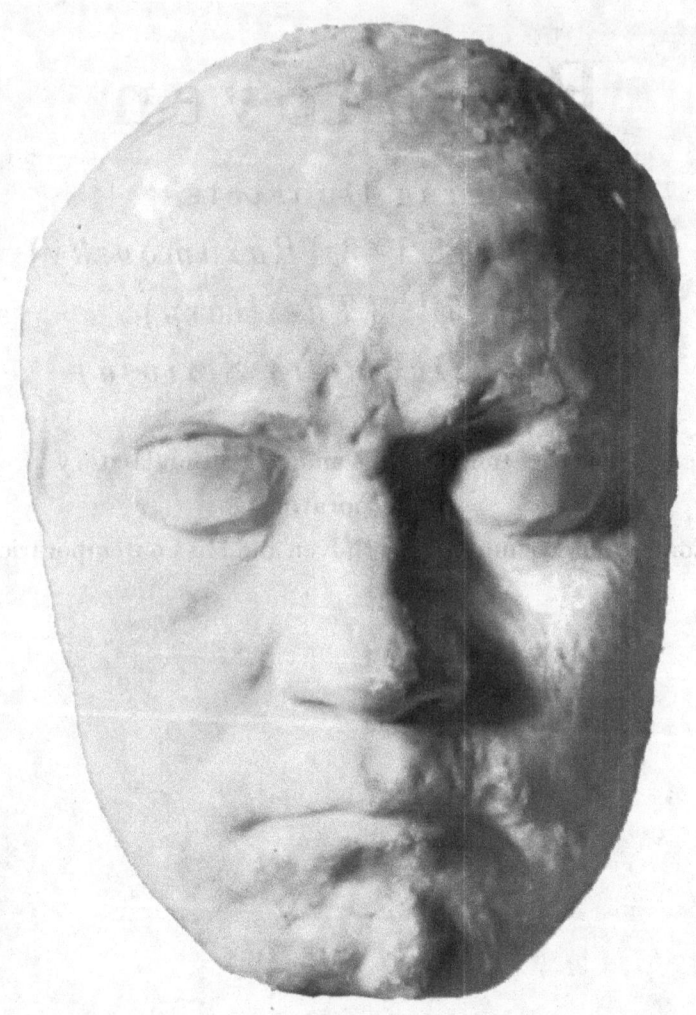

BEETHOVEN
As depicted by the life mask taken by Franz Klein in 1812
(derived from a copy in the author's possession)

BEETHOVEN
STRING QUARTETS
OP. 59 NOS. 1–3
OP. 74, OP. 95

THEIR
CREATION ORIGINS
AND
RECEPTION HISTORY

Incorporating contextual accounts of
Beethoven and his contemporaries

Terence M. Russell

Jelly Bean Books

The right of Terence Russell to be identified as the
Author of the Work has been asserted by him in accordance
with the Copyright, Designs and Patents Act 1988.

Copyright © Terence M. Russell 2022

Published by
Jelly Bean Books
136 Newport Road
Cardiff
CF24 1DJ

ISBN: 978-1-915439-13-0

www.candyjarbooks.co.uk

All rights reserved.
No part of this publication may be reproduced, stored in a
retrieval system, or transmitted at any time or by any means,
electronic, mechanical, photocopying, recording or otherwise
without the prior permission of the copyright holder. This book is
sold subject to the condition that it shall not by way of trade or
otherwise be circulated without the publisher's prior consent in any
form of binding or cover other than that in which it is published.

CONTENTS

AUTHOR'S NOTE	I
INTRODUCTION	IX
EDITORIAL PRINCIPLES	XVIII
BEETHOVEN'S FINANCIAL TRANSACTIONS	XX
BEETHOVEN STRING QUARTETS, THEIR CREATION ORIGINS AND RECEPTION	1
String Quartets Op. 59, Nos. 1–3 *Razumovsky*	56
In F major, Op. 59, No. 1	79
In E minor, Op. 59, No. 2	93
In C major, Op. 59, No. 3	115
String Quartet in E-flat major, Op. 74, *The Harp*	176
String Quartet in F minor, Op. 95, *Quartetto Serioso*	239
BIBLIOGRAPHY	275
INDEX	281
ABOUT THE AUTHOR	

AUTHOR'S NOTE

I have cherished the idea of making a study of the life and work of Beethoven for many years. This statement requires a few words of personal reflection. I first encountered Beethoven in my early piano lessons – Minuet in G major, WoO 10, No. 2. At the same time I became acquainted with his piano pupil Carl Czerny – *Book One, Piano Studies.* My heart sank when I discovered the rear cover advertised a further *99* books in the same series – scales, arpeggios studies for the left hand, studies for the right hand – all the way to his Op. 824! By coincidence, my *Czerny Book One* was edited by Alec Rowley – who had the same surname as my music teacher. In my childish innocence, I often wondered why *he himself* never appeared to give me a lesson!

In my teenage years I found myself drawn ever closer to Beethoven's music in the manner that ferromagnetic materials are ineluctably held captive in the sway of a magnetic field. The impulse to which I yielded is well described in words the conductor Bruno Walter gave in one of his rare public addresses: 'It is my belief that young people at that age are more easily impressed by what is heroic and grandiose; that they more easily understand works of art in which passionate feelings are violently uttered in raised accents, and that the lighter sounds of cheerfulness are less impressive to them.' I do indeed recall the stirring effect made on me on first hearing the Overture *Egmont*, the unfolding drama of the Fifth Symphony and the declamatory opening chords of the *Emperor* Piano Concerto.

I resolved to read everything I could about Beethoven, starting with Marion Scott's pioneering English-language study of the composer in the *Master Musicians series*. My father took out a subscription for me for *The Gramophone* magazine, enabling me to read reviews of the new 'LP' recordings — none of which though I could afford! The LP was then — 1950s — beginning to supplant the 78 rpm shellac records, stacks of which could be purchased for as little as six pence each in 'old' money. At this same time I had the privilege of hearing Beethoven's music performed by the *Hallé Orchestra* under the baton of Sir John Barbirolli, and experienced the *Carl Rosa Opera Company* perform the composer's only opera *Fidelio*; I borrowed the piano-reduction score from the City Library to become better acquainted with this moving work — only to find the score's fists full of notes were well beyond my capabilities. Nonetheless, since then *Fidelio's* every note has been woven into my DNA. I also recall the period when the *London Promenade Concerts* were designated 'Friday night is Beethoven night'.

Through these influences I resolved to visit Vienna to see where Beethoven had lived and worked. But how? The support for such travel was beyond the means of my family. Fortunately in my final year at school (1959) an opportunity presented itself. I saw a poster that stated *WUS — World University Service* — required volunteers to work in the Austrian town of Linz to help relocate refugees who were living there in improvised wooden shacks — displaced and dispossessed victims of the Second World War. To those participating all expenses would be paid together with free accommodation — in one of the crumbling wooden shacks! From Linz, I planned to make my way to Vienna.

I applied to *WUS* and, despite being a mere school-leaver, I was accepted. The *WUS* authorities doubtless reasoned the building-trade skills I had acquired during my secondary education in the building department of a technical school would be useful. This proved to be the case. At the refugee camp I dug trenches and was allowed to assist as a bricklayer. All about me were wide-eyed children eager to help but mostly getting in the way. I recall one afternoon when a reporter from *The Observer* newspaper paid a visit to our construction site to gather material for an article he was writing on European post-war recovery — he generously admired my trenches and brickwork!

Of lasting significance was another visit, this time from a Belgian priest. He took a group of us to the nearby *Mauthausen* Concentration Camp, recently opened as a silent and solemn memorial to those who had perished there. It was a deeply moving experience. Years later I learned of the views of the ardent Beethovenian Sir Michael Tippet. After the horrors of the *Holocaust*, he posed the question for mankind: 'What price Beethoven now?' He posited: 'Could we any longer find solace in Beethoven's setting of Schiller's *Ode to Joy* and its utopian vision — "Be embraced you Millions"?'

My refugee contribution duly came to end and Vienna beckoned. On arrival there I found scenes reminiscent of *The Third Man* and *Harry Lime*. I recall, for example, encountering cobblestones piled high in the streets waiting to be replaced after having been disturbed by the heavy armoured vehicles that had so recently passed over them. But Vienna was welcoming. I visited the houses where Beethoven had lived and worked and paused outside others associated with him that were identified by a commemorative plaque and the Austrian flag. A particularly memorable occasion was attending a recital in the great salon within the palace of Beethoven's noble patron Prince Lobkowitz — the very one where the *Eroica* Symphony had been premiered. Ultimately, my steps led me to the composer's first resting place in the *Währinger Ortsfriedhof*. I paid silent homage to the great man and, as I did so, discovered nearby the resting place of Franz Schubert to whom Beethoven was an endless source of admiration and inspiration.

I felt a youthful impulse to discover yet more about Beethoven and his music. But absorption in musicology would have to take second place. My chosen career beckoned in the guise of architecture — 'the mother of the arts' and 'the handmaid of society'. There was room though for Beethoven's music and from that time on it has been my constant companion through attendance at recitals, in concerts and music-making in the home. And at home a reproduction of Franz Kline's 1812 study of the composer has greeted me each day for more than half a century.

On my retirement from a career in architectural practice, research and university teaching, the opportunity finally presented itself for me to devote time to researching Beethoven musicology. Having attained my eightieth year also emboldened me to make progress with my good intentions!

With these autobiographical remarks outlined I will say a few remarks about my working method — see also the comments made in *Editorial Principles*.

As a member of staff of The University of Edinburgh, I had the good fortune to have access to the *Reid Music Library*, formed from a nucleus of books bequeathed by General John Reid and augmented over the years by such custodians as Sir Donald Francis Tovey, sometime *Reid Professor of Music* and renowned Beethoven scholar. Over a period of three years, I made a survey of the many works in the Reid collection. I consulted each item in turn making records on paper slips — many hundreds — that I deemed to be relevant for my researches. I confined my searches to book-publications, as reflected in my accompanying bibliography. All of this was quite some years ago, the cut-off date for my researches being 2007. Beyond this date I have not surveyed any further works. I am mindful though that Beethoven musicology and related publication continue to be a major field of endeavour in the manner of the proverbial 'ever rolling stream'.

In the intervening years since completing my archival researches, personal tribulations associated with family illness and bereavement slowed my progress in giving expression to my projected intentions. Latterly, however, with renewed energy, and more time at my disposal, I have been able to make progress. My studies take the form of a set of monographs. These trace the creation origins and reception history of each of Beethoven's piano sonatas and string quartets. The resulting texts also incorporate contextual accounts of Beethoven and his contemporaries. Also included in my musicological surveys are two related Beethoven anthologies. The set of monographs in question, identified by short title, are:

Beethoven: An anthology of selected writings.
Beethoven: The piano sonatas: An anthology of selected writings.

The Piano Sonatas:
Op. 2–Op. 28
Op. 31–Op. 81A
Op. 90–Op. 111

The String Quartets:
Op. 18, Nos. 1–6
Op. 59, Nos. 1–3 (Razumovsky); Op. 74 (The Harp);
   Op. 95 (Quartetto Serioso)
Op. 127, Op. 132 and Op. 130 (Galitzin)
Op. 131, Op. 135; Grosse Fuge, Op. 133 and Op. 134
   (Fugue transcription)

I provide further information about these studies in the introduction to each individual monograph. Suffice it for me to state here the basic premise upon which my work is founded. I believe it is rewarding, concerning the life of a great artist, to find connections between who he *was* and what he *did*; in Martin Cooper's words 'between his personality, as expressed on the one hand in human relationships, and on the other in artistic creation'. (*Beethoven, The Last Decade*) That is not to say I consider it essential to the enjoyment of Beethoven's music to know this or that fact about it. His music can be enjoyed, as millions do, with — in Robert Simpson's apt phrase —'an innocent ear', for what it is and how it reaches out to us in purely musical terms without any prejudging of its merits based upon extra-musicological facts.

I must make a further point. I am mindful that a scholar who ventures into a field of study that is not rightly his may be regarded with some suspicion. In this regard I can but ask the reader to place his or her trust in me in the following way. I have attempted to bring to my work the care which publishers and their desk editors have required of me in my book writings relating to architecture — listed elsewhere.

As inferred, it is now more than sixty years since I paid homage to Beethoven in Vienna's *Währinger Ortsfriedhof* and my warmth of feeling towards the composer and his music have grown with the passing of the years. My studies are not intended to be propaedeutic — that would be pretentious. However, if in sharing with others what I have to say contributes to their knowledge and understanding of the composer, and thereby increases their own feelings towards him and his works, my own pleasure in bringing my work to completion will be all the more enhanced.

It is perhaps fitting that my studies should appear in Beethoven's 250th Anniversary Year — I must confess more by chance than design!

When Beethoven arrived in Vienna, he was unknown. He was armed though with a note of encouragement from his youthful friend and benefactor Count Ferdinand Waldstein. It contained the often-quoted words: 'Receive Mozart's spirit from Haydn's hands.' Some forty years later Beethoven passed away in the House of the black-robed Spaniards at 200 *Alservorstädter*, the *Glacis* where he had lived since the autumn of 1825. Soldiers had to be called to secure the doors to the inner courtyard of the house from the pressure of onlookers. His body was blessed in the *Alservorsttädt Parish Church*, schools were closed and perhaps as many as 10,000 people formed a funeral procession — an honour ordinarily reserved for monarchs. The *Marcia Funebre* from the composer's Op. 26 Piano Sonata was performed at the funeral ceremony. Franz Grillparzer read the funeral oration. Franz Schubert, who, as remarked in life so admired Beethoven, was one of the pallbearers. The composer's mortal remains were lowered into a simple vault. Beethoven now belonged to history.

Dr Terence M. Russell
Edinburgh 2020

INTRODUCTION

The subjects of this study are the creation origins and reception history of Beethoven's string quartets. It is one of three that broadly correspond with the generally accepted periods into which the composer's compositions are held to conform and which have been described as 'early', 'middle', and 'late' and their counterparts, 'imitative', 'heroic' and 'introspective'. In our first study the string quartets Op. 18, Nos. 1–6 are considered alongside the transcription for string quartet of the Piano Sonata in E major, Op. 14. In the second part are the string quartets Op. 59, Nos. 1–3 (*Razumowsky*), Op. 74 in E-flat major, (*The Harp*) and Op. 95 in F minor (*Quartetto serioso*). In the third part are the string quartets Op. 127, Op. 130, Op. 131, Op. 132, Op. 135 and the *Great Fugue*, Op. 133 together with Beethoven's four-hand keyboard transcription Op. 134.

The collection of writings presented here, derive from the string quartet compositions of Beethoven's so-called second period. They take the form of extended essays that may serve the reader as a source of reference — in the manner of programme notes to a recital. Accordingly, the remarks relating to each string quartet are 'free standing' and can be read independently. That said they are also interlinked by the events unfolding in the composer's life. An attempt has been made, therefore, to interrelate the individual essays so that they may be read as a continuous narrative — in typical book fashion. A summary outline of this narrative is provided in the Index for each individual string quartet. Thereby, the reader is provided not only with a guide to the contents discussed in each quartet-text but also has an over-arching time-line of the principal events bearing on Beethoven's life and work. By way of an introduction to the individual essays in this part of our survey, we provide the following summary-outline bearing upon the compositions to which we make reference.

In our first study of Beethoven's writing for the medium of the string quartet, we have seen how he not only absorbed the legacy of his great predecessors Haydn and Mozart but also gave expression to his own singular and independent style of writing for four string instruments — his first contribution to the genre, the String Quartets Op. 18, having their creation origins in the period 1799—1800. Notwithstanding his newfound confidence in writing string quartets, it would be another six years before Beethoven turned his attention once more to the medium in the form of the three *Razumovsky* String Quartets. He showed no similar reticence in writing other works. For example: from 1800 we have the Piano Concerto No. 3, Op. 37; from 1802 Symphony No. 2, Op. 36; from 1803 the epochal Symphony No. 3, Op. 55; from 1804 the Opera *Leonora-Fidelio*; and from 1805 the Piano Concerto No. 4, Op. 58. Alongside these compositions came a steady flow of works for solo piano including the *Moonlight* Sonata, Op. 27, the *Eroica* Piano Variations, Op. 35, and the *Waldstein* Sonata, Op. 55. Later, but still within the proximity of the Quartets Op. 74 and Op. 95 came the Fourth, Fifth and Sixth Symphonies, the Violin Concerto and the music to Goethe's drama *Egmont.*

From the foregoing we can see that whereas when Beethoven embarked on the Op. 18 set he was a novitiate, in a manner of speaking, when he eventually returned to the composition of string quartets he had at his disposal a formidable array of newly acquired skills combined with new ideas regarding time-scale in music and an awareness of the largeness of its possibilities. In the words of music critic Conrad Wilson (2003): 'Beethoven's middle quartets, by their very nature, have qualities not only of progress but also of consolidation about them. Intense, idiomatic, original, they are the work of a composer who has found his style and developed it to a high level of technical assurance and emotional expression. Drawn-out string chords, leaping melodies, violent rhythms, rapt slow movements conceived to perfection in quartet terms — these are among the features of the music which players have to contend with, recognising that the works originally demanded something new and special.'

Beethoven inherited a tradition of string quartet writing whose format was governed by universally accepted conventions. Four movements followed in sequence, the outer movements adopting a fast tempo, the inner movements a slower tempo typically in the manner of a minuet or scherzo. Moreover, quartet playing was central to social music-making that was within the reach of the more accomplished amateur. The instruments had equal status and the players could engage in a form of musical conversation. Writing in the music journal *Allgemeine musikalische Zeitung* (*AmZ*) of 1800, the Italian composer Giuseppe Cambini remarked: '[If] music should not stir up or soothe the emotions, then it should at least draw our attention to itself and so divert us from the cares and griefs of our everyday life.'

In due course Beethoven progressively stamped his authority on the quartet medium by enhancing its stature and transforming it almost beyond recognition, confronting both performers and listeners he challenged their expectations of easy music-making and straightforward comprehension. The quartets of his second period heighten the drama, impart new dynamic impulse and, in the words of musicologist Bernhard Jacobson, 'expand development sections to fearsome new proportions and equally fearsome new levels of constructive ingenuity'. Beethoven's string quartet writing thereby removed the genre from the domain of the amateur and the social gathering to the concert hall and the custodianship of such professional string players as the composer's friend and associate Ignaz Schuppanzigh — founder of the string quartet that bore his name and arguably the very first professional string quartet.

The French musicologist Joseph de Marliave likened the three *Razumovsky* String Quartets to *quartet-symphonies* in which he discerned the composer 'striving towards the symphonic idiom, with orchestral effects that sometimes seem to burst the slender framework of the quartet genre'. A review of the three Op. 59 Quartets was published in the *AmZ* on 18 March 1807, based probably on a private performance when the compositions were still in manuscript. The reviewer commented: 'Three new, very long and difficult violin quartets by Beethoven, dedicated to the Russian ambassador, Count [later Prince] Razumovsky, also attract the attention of all connoisseurs. They are deep in conception and marvellously worked out, but are not universally comprehensible, with the possible exception of the third one, in C major, which by virtue of its individuality, melody, and harmonic power must win over every educated friend of music.'

Beethoven's String Quartet in E-flat major, Op. 74 is the tenth in the sequence of his sixteen works composed for the genre. The work is familiarly known by its nickname *The Harp* arising from the use made by the composer of a sequence of arpeggiated *pizziacati* that are heard near the start of the first movement. The soubriquet was not sanctioned by Beethoven who conferred few titles on his compositions. The piece was composed soon after the *Razumovsky* Quartets. To quote de Marliave once more: 'Here one sees mirrored in the music the dark places of the artist's soul; here at last Beethoven finds expression for all the pent-up love and sorrow, plumbing the depths of his unsatisfied longings, laying bare the secret beauty of his inmost thoughts.' Many authorities consider the Op. 74 Quartet to be an underrated masterpiece 'of deep, consummate beauty of thought and execution' (Robert Simpson) and one that of all his quartets 'is the most subjective' (Basil Lam).

The music critic, writing in the 1811 issue of the *AmZ*, was concerned to advocate that the medium of the string quartet should adhere to the established and accepted norms of 'classical decorum'; he was disturbed by Beethoven's overt preoccupation with 'rhetorical subject matter'. He perceived the Quartet, Op. 74 to be a powerful blend of the 'bizarre and the fantastic' and 'an amalgam of heterogeneous elements pervaded by a sombre and even lugubrious spirit'. He reproached Beethoven for trying to express in this Quartet sentiments alien to what he conceived to be the nature of the genre. He considered the quartet more generally to be better suited to the expression of 'sweet earnestness' rather than 'lamenting melancholy' and should not have the goal of 'celebrating the dead or picturing feelings of despair'; rather, 'it should gladden the heart through the mild, comforting play of the imagination' — with acknowledgment to Maynard Solomon.

Such misgivings as those expressed by the *AmZ* music critic have long been set aside. In the words of the American musicologist Lewis Lockwood (2005): 'We can reckon this Quartet among the most remarkable products of the years from 1808 to 1812, the romantic twilight of Beethoven's second maturity ... From the beginning of Op. 74 we are in a new world of Beethoven's quartet writing, and as the work progresses it reveals an increasingly complex aesthetic profile.'

Much of the character of the String Quartet in F minor, Op. 95 is implicit in its sub-title *Quartetto serioso*. This is one of the few occasions when the composer conferred an interpretative title on one of his compositions. Others of the period include the *Pathétique* Sonata, the *Eroica* Symphony, and the *Pastoral* Symphony; later on such expressions appear in the *Farewell* and *Hammerklavier* Piano Sonatas. Of interest is that *serioso* is a Beethoven-invented word, albeit a derivative of the more correct Italian *sèrio*. Also unique to the composition is that its dedicatee was not a member of a noble family. Beethoven dedicated the work to his close friend, Nicholas Zmeskall von Domanovez (Domanovecz) who was employed as a civil servant in the Hungarian Court Chancellery in Vienna. He became acquainted with the composer in the 1790s, soon after Beethoven's arrival in Vienna, following which the two became close friends. Zmeskall was an excellent cellist and regularly performed in the string quartet sessions convened by Beethoven's patron Prince Karl Lichnowsky.

Extra-musical influences may have conditioned aspects of the character of Op. 95. The Quartet belongs to the period in the composer's life when he was coming to terms with the realization of the irretrievable loss of his hearing, the death of two of his closest teachers and his personal physician, the pain of unrequited love, the insecurity of his financial position — and with it the prospect of leaving Vienna for good — and the harrowing experience of the French bombardment followed by the occupation of Vienna with its attendant upheavals and deprivations. Basil Lam (1975) has likened Beethoven's suffering to that of Goethe's *Werthe*, as set forth in *The sorrows of young Werthe* in which a sensitive artist of romantic and passionate temperament gives expression to his innermost feelings. That said, Lam cautions against attaching too much significance to the extra-musical circumstances of the composer's life and their bearing on the music itself. He writes: 'Any attempt to relate a composer's work to what is known of his life is bound to be a crude over-simplification, if only because music has a complex life of its own that resists verbalisation.'

A clue to the reason why Beethoven included the epithet *serioso* in the title to the F minor Quartet was doubtless his realisation that, for the period in question, it was out of character with his audiences' expectations. His audiences, and for that matter those of his composer-contemporaries, can be arranged into three groups. First and foremost were the aristocracy who held musical soirees in their great salons; next came the wealthy class of bankers, manufacturers and professionals; and thirdly was the rising class of the less affluent such as musicians, civil servants and shop keepers (Beethoven's older brother was an apothecary) who would in course of time dominate the musical scene — especially when hearing string quartets played in public became more common with the inception of such professional string quartets as that of Ignaz Schuppanzigh to which we have made reference.

When Beethoven was planning the publication of the F minor Quartet in England, he wrote to Sir George Smart, a founder member of the (Royal) Philharmonic Society. He informed Smart that 'the Quartet was not to be played in public', further testimony to his awareness that his new musical style was too in advance of the musical conventions of the day — judged even by his own daring standards. In this work he was beginning to explore compositional techniques that he would develop even further in his last string quartets such as, discordant outbursts of sound juxtaposed with silence pregnant with meaning, quirky tempos and metric ambiguity, unorthodox groupings of movements, and even greater freedom with tonality. Writing about these innovations Joseph Kerman (1967) observes: '[The] Quartet in F minor seems to foreshadow aspects of the technique of the last quartets in its dominant qualities of conciseness, directness, and instant confrontation of contrast.' For these reasons, he describes the Op. 95 as 'The chief signpost to the third period'.

The Quartet is as violent as it is serious; everything is concise, rapid and without respite or relaxation. With a playing time of scarcely twenty minutes — only about half that of Op. 59, No. 1 — it is the shortest and most compressed of all of the composer's string quartets. In his *Beethoven: A critical biography* (1913) Vincent d'Indy characterised the F minor Quartet as 'a drama that looms through the symphonic warp and woof'. In his pioneering study of the composer and his music, Romain Rolland (1917) maintained the composition 'stood on the borderline between Beethoven's second and third styles' within which was to be discerned 'the gruff and brooding Beethoven'. Writing twenty years later, the American musician-musicologist Arthur Shepherd proclaimed the Op. 95 to be 'a compound of defiant power and tender pathos'. Gerald

Abraham's insights, as expressed in his *Beethoven's second-period quartets*, (1944) provide a fitting summation: 'Never before in the history of chamber music can so much power and passion have been packed into so small a space, and without once overstepping the ill-guarded boundary into the territory of the symphonic. The greatness of Beethoven's music is a greatness *sui generis* ['of its own kind'].'

TMR

EDITORIAL PRINCIPLES

By its very nature a study of this kind draws extensively on the work of others. Every effort has been made to acknowledge this in the text by indicating words quoted or adapted with single quotation marks. Wherever possible, for the sake of consistency, I have retained the orthography of quoted texts making only occasional silent changes of spelling and capitalization. Deleted words are identified by means of three ellipsis points ... and interpolations are encompassed within square brackets [ ]. Quoted words, phrases and longer cited passages of text remain the intellectual property of their copyright holders.

I address the reader in the second person notwithstanding that the work is my own. It follows that I must bear the responsibility for any errors of misunderstanding or misinterpretation for which I ask the reader's forbearance. A collaboration I must acknowledge is the help I received from the librarians of the Reid Music Library at the University of Edinburgh. Over the three-year period it took me to compile my reference sources, they served me with unfailing courtesy, often supplying me with twenty or more books at a time. In converting my manuscript into book format, I wish to thank my editorial coordinator, William Rees, for his support and painstaking care. I would also like to thank Shaun Russell for his work designing the cover for each of the twelve volumes.

My admiration for Beethoven provided the initial impulse to commence this undertaking and has sustained me over the several years it has taken to bring my enterprise to completion. That said, I am no Beethoven idolater. I am mindful of the danger that awaits one who ventures to chronicle the work of a great artist. I believe it was Sigmund Freud who suggested that biographers may become so disposed to their subject, and their emotional involvement with their hero, that their work becomes an exercise in idealisation. In response to such a charge let me say. First, I am no biographer. I do however make occasional reference to Beethoven's personal life and his relationships with his contemporaries. Second, I acknowledge Beethoven has his detractors. Accordingly, I have not shrunk from allowing dissentient voices, critical of Beethoven and his work, to be heard. These, however, are few and are silenced amidst the adulation that awaits the reader in support of the endeavours of one of humanity's great creators and one who courageously showed the way in overcoming personal adversity.

TMR

BEETHOVEN'S FINANCIAL TRANSACTIONS

Beethoven's negotiations with his music publishers make many references to his compositions. Today they are recognised for what they are — enduring works of art — but referred to in his business correspondence they appear almost as though they were mere everyday commodities — for which he required an appropriate remuneration. Beethoven resented the time he had to devote to the business-side of his affairs. He believed an agency should exist, for fellow artists such as himself, from which a reasonable sum could be paid for the work (composition) submitted, leaving more time for creative enterprises. In the event Beethoven, like Mozart before him, had to deal with publishers largely on his own. Beethoven, though, did benefit in his business dealings from the help he received from his younger brother Kasper Karl (Caspar Carl). From

1800, Carl worked as a clerk in Vienna's Department of Finance in which capacity he found time to correspond with publishers to offer his brother's works for sale and – importantly – to secure the best prices he could. In April 1802 Beethoven wrote to the Leipzig publishers Breitkopf & Härtel: '[You] can rely entirely on my brother who, in general, attends to my affairs.' Whilst Carl promoted Beethoven's interests with determination, he appears to have lacked tact and made enemies. For example, Beethoven's piano pupil Ferdinand Ries – who for a while also helped the composer with his business negotiations – is on record as describing Carl as being 'the biggest skinflint in the world'. The currencies most referred to in Beethoven's correspondence are as follows:

- silver gulden and florin: these were interchangeable and had a value of about two English/British shillings
- ducat: 4 1/2 gulden/florins: valued at about nine shillings
- louis d'or: This gold coin was adopted during the Napoleonic wars and the French occupation of Vienna and Austria more widely. It had a value of about two ducats or approximately twenty shillings or one-pound sterling.

Beethoven was never poor – in the romantic sense of 'an artist starving in a garret'. On arriving in Vienna in 1792, he was fortunate to receive financial support from his patron Prince Karl Lichnowsky who conferred on him an annuity of 600 florins that he maintained for several years. Between the months of February and July of 1796, Beethoven undertook a concert tour taking in Prague, Dresden, Leipzig and Berlin. He was well received and wrote to his other younger brother Nikolaus Johann: 'My art is winning me friends and what more do I want? ... I shall make a good deal of money.' Later on, in 1809, Napoleon Bonaparte's youngest brother Jérôme Bonaparte offered Beethoven an appointment at his Court with the promise of an income of 4,000 florins. Alarmed at the prospect of losing Beethoven — now the most celebrated composer in Europe — three of Vienna's most notable citizens, namely, the Archduke Rudolph (Beethoven's only composition pupil), Prince Kinsky and Prince Lobkowitz settled on the composer the same sum of 4,000 florins. Inflation, however, brought about by the Napoleonic wars, soon eroded its value; personal misfortune to Lobkowitz and Kinsky also took its toll.

Beethoven undoubtedly had to work hard to secure a reasonable standard of living. Notwithstanding, despite his occasional straitened circumstances, he contributed generously to the needs of others. For example, he allowed his works to be performed free of charge at charitable concerts; in 1815 his philanthropy earned for him the honour of Bürgerrecht — 'freedom of the City'.

Beethoven earned a great deal of money when his music was performed, to considerable acclaim, at several concerts held in association with the Congress of Vienna (1814-15). He did not though benefit from it personally; he invested it on behalf of his nephew Karl. It is one of the misfortunes of Beethoven's life that in money-matters he was culpably improvident. This is poignantly evident in a letter he wrote on 18 March 1827 to the Philharmonic Society of London just one week before his death; the Society had made him a gift of £100. He sent the Society 'his most heartfelt thanks for their particular sympathy and support'.

TMR

'Beethoven's middle quartets, by their very nature, have qualities not only of progress but also of consolidation about them. Intense, idiomatic, original, they are the work of a composer who has found his style and developed it to a high level of technical assurance and emotional expression. Drawn-out string chords, leaping melodies, violent rhythms, rapt slow movements conceived to perfection in quartet terms — these are among the features of the music which players have to contend with, recognising that the works originally demanded something new and special.'

Conrad Wilson, *Notes on Beethoven: 20 crucial works*, Edinburgh: Saint Andrew Press, 2003.

STRING QUARTETS OP. 59, NOS. 1-3
RAZUMOVSKY

'The three quartets dedicated to Count Rasoumowsky [Razumovsky] are the natural fulfilment of the promise of the symphonies and the piano sonatas, but a greater achievement, since the form of the quartet is less adapted to innovation of style than either the sonata or the symphony ... The content of these quartets is as great as the content of the symphonies, only the medium is different.'

Wilhelm von Lenz, *Beethoven et ses Trois Styles*, 1855, pp. 144–5, quoted in: Joseph de Marliave, *Beethoven's quartets*, 1925 (reprint 1961), p. 142.

'The set of three quartets, Op. 59, dedicated to Prince [formerly *Count*] Rasoumoffsky [Razumovsky], are considered by many professors Beethoven's grandest of quartets; they are certainly not surpassed in terseness of part-writing, variety of ideas, and clearness of design. They are also totally beyond the skill of ordinary amateurs, and nothing short of a correct execution can render them satisfactorily intelligible.'

John Ella, *Musical Sketches, abroad and at home: with original music by Mozart, Czerny, Graun, etc., vocal cadenzas and other musical illustrations*, Vol. 1, 1869 p. 166.

'[The] three Op. 59 Quartets are not merely accidentally associated ... they have spiritual affinity. The closing movements of all three strike the same note of victory and each work marks an advance on the preceding; they are all three embodiments of a single poetic idea, variously presented, each time with increasing perfection. Exterior conflicts are first portrayed, then interior problems, while in the last three the strife of opposites becomes a thing of the past, and only a memory of past battles varies the final song of enduring triumph.'

Paul Bekker, *Beethoven*, 1925, p. 317.

'The first six quartets are the work of a young composer in the full enthusiasm of youth, eager to imitate the models he loves and admires: those to come are the work of an acknowledged master already famous for many triumphs of a great spirit ... If one may say that Haydn created the string quartet as an art form, Beethoven achieved even greater attainment than his predecessor in the Quartets Op. 59, revealing the expressive capacity latent in the genre to an extent never dreamed of by earlier musicians. It is for this reason primarily that these three quartets have so deep a significance.'

Joseph de Marliave, *Beethoven's quartets*, 1925 (reprint 1961), pp. 51–3.

'Interesting and loveable as are [the] first six quartets they pale before the new world opened to one by the three *Razumovsky* Quartets, Op. 59. In the five years' interval which separates them, Beethoven had grown enormously in stature; his hand is firmer, his character formed, and he now feels himself able to a large extent to dispense with the support hitherto given him by tradition.'

Rebecca Clarke, *The [Beethoven] quartets as a player sees them*, in: *Music & Letters, Beethoven*, Special Issue: Vol. VIII, No. 2, 1927, pp. 180–1.

'After the *Eroica*, one is tempted to say, it was inevitable for Beethoven's quartets to have grown to formidable proportions, taken a new look at their life's ambition, and stormed the threshold of the symphony. A new world was being explored, and if the string quartet was going to find a place in it at all, it had to smash the fragile, decorous boundaries set by the classic image of chamber music.'

Joseph Kerman, *The Beethoven Quartets*, 1967, p. 151.

'[The] *Razumovsky's* hold there own, partly — but only partly — because they do not compete with the late batch, are in fact so different as to offer few comparisons. No music more sounds in high spirits ... But these are hardly the first qualities to come to mind in connection with the late quartets; rather, by *Razumovsky* standards, the anomalies and unevennesses, just as, with the view the other way round, the *Razumovsky's* inevitably remind the listener of the developments — in depth and compression, in the conversion of form to new expressive ends, in stylistic refinement — that lay ahead.'

Igor Stravinsky, *Themes and Conclusions*, 1972, pp. 255–6.

'In Op. 59 [Beethoven] completed the removal of the string quartet from the private house to the concert hall. Spiritually and technically these quartets leave the sphere of the amateur musician and address themselves to the listener able to follow their intellectual processes.'

Heinz Becker, Liner notes to The Amadeus Quartet, *Beethoven: The string quartets*, 1974.

'There is one sense in which the *Razumovsky* Quartets represent a continuation of the heroic impulse: an application of the principles of composition elaborated in the *Eroica* Symphony to another genre, an expansion of the quartet form beyond its eighteenth-century traditional boundaries to a point where one may legiti-

> mately speak of these quartets as "symphonic quartets".'

Maynard Solomon, *Beethoven*, 1977, p. 201.

> 'With the Op. 59 Quartets Beethoven does for the string quartet medium what the *Eroica*, Op. 55, did for the symphony. There would be occasional looking back, but things would never be the same.'

Paul Yarbrough, Liner notes to The Alexander String Quartet, *Ludwig van Beethoven, The String Quartets,* Arte Nova Classics [undated, c. 1980].

> Shostakovich was invited to address the Pan-Slavonic Meeting at the height of the war in Moscow in April 1942. He had just been awarded the Stalin Prize for his Seventh Symphony and services to the arts in the Russian Federation. The occasion prompted him to affirm: 'As a musician I am proud of that my county's music occupies a most honourable position in world music culture.' He cited Glinka, Borodin, Mussorgsky and Tchaikovsky for the manner in which 'their melodies have always served as a source of inspiration for the greatest of musicians.' He concluded: 'Suffice it to mention Beethoven's *Russian* Quartets.'

Dmitry Shostakovich, Dmitry Shostakovich about himself and his times, Progress Publishers, 1981, pp. 95–6.

> 'Beethoven seems to have relished the challenge of using his new grand manner in an intimate

medium: the *Razumovsky* Quartets are notably less orchestral in sound than those of Op. 18, less dependent on brusque *sforzando* effects and more richly filled with textural inventions which, though quite new, are ideally suited to the quartet.'

Paul Griffiths, *The string quartet*, 1983, p. 86.

'The *Razumovskys* mark the opening of a new period in the history of the string quartet; they are the spiritual parents of all the quasi-orchestral string quartets of the later nineteenth century. Not that they themselves are orchestral, though they sometimes come near to overstepping the boundary-line of true chamber style (as in the last movement of No. 3); their *symphonic* character lies in their less intimate nature — they are emphatically chamber music for a hall and an audience — in their dimensions, and in the inner organization that expanded them to such dimensions. No quartets of such length can ever have been written before.'

Gerald Abraham, *Beethoven's Chamber Music*, in: *The Age of Beethoven, The New Oxford History of Music*, Vol. VIII, Gerald Abraham, editor, 1988, p. 288 and p. 340.

'The Op. 59 are a world apart from the Op. 18; they are post-*Eroica* works and exhibit many aspects of that great deepening of Beethoven's musical style which the composition of the *Eroica* Symphony seems to have affected. Most obviously, in the enormous size of the individual movements, the straining of the medium and the

> generally symphonic, orchestral character of the work, which have led some writers to dub Op. 59, No. 1 an *Eroica* for string quartet.'

Barry Cooper, *The Beethoven Compendium: a guide to Beethoven's life and music*, 1991, p. 234.

> 'There is no denying the unprecedented artistic ambition and scale of the three works [Op. 59] are the product of Beethoven's artistic imagination and of a musical society in Vienna that increasingly valued the connoisseurship associated with the medium.'

David Wyn Jones: *Beethoven and the Viennese Legacy* in: Robin Stowell, editor *The Cambridge Companion to the string quartet*, 2003, pp. 214–6.

> '[In] character the three works are contrasted rather than unified. The first, in F major, broad and swinging, the second in E minor plaintive and passionate, the third in C major brilliant and athletic. Together they could be said to form a kind of Beethovenian answer to Mozart's last three symphonies, equally clearly composed as a group.'

Conrad Wilson, *Notes on Beethoven: 20 Crucial Works*, 2003, p. 51.

> 'Much greater than their predecessors in his Op. 18, these quartets reflect his fixation around this time with experimentation and boundary-breaking. They leave behind his early dependence on

Haydn and Mozart, and move into the stormy world we more readily associate with Beethoven.'

Alison Bullock, *Notes to the BBC Radio Three Beethoven Experience*, Thursday 9 June 2005, www.bbc.co.uk/radio3/Beethoven

'These works embody a new concept of music as *process*, whereby the potential for development of basic musical elements is probed on a broad scale. As part of this new exploration of musical potential, Beethoven could begin with what seem to be mere fragments and enact a process of creative development within the work itself.'

William Kinderman, editor, *The String Quartets of Beethoven*, 2005, p. 4.

'One of the most astonishing exploratory aspects of the *Razumovsky* Quartets, Op. 59, is their innovative treatment of register as a structural and expressive resource. Beethoven deployed different registers not only for sonorous or colouristic effect but also to create coherent large-scale structures by means of long-range linear patterns. Particularly in the linear progressions of the highest registers, the Op. 59 Quartets exhibit exciting narrative processes, which correlate with tonal and formal design ... Beethoven's innovative structural deployment of the highest register ... distinguishes these masterpieces as peaks of heroic musical inspiration.'

Malcolm Miler *Peak Experience* in: William Kinderman, editor, *The String Quartets of Beethoven*, 2005, p. 60.

In his *Beethoven et ses trois styles* (Paris 1855), the composer's early biographer Wilhelm von Lenz describes the *Razumovsky* Quartets as 'three miracles dropped from Heaven'. He elaborates: 'This work is the very stronghold of chamber music ... It throws down a triumphant challenge to the past, the present and the future ... creating a whole world of new conceptions and new styles, no one could ever aspire to the achievement of three such masterpieces, uniting to form a perfect whole in an entirely new form.'[i] On the occasion of Beethoven's Death Centenary (1927), the English composer, violist and writer on music Rebecca Clarke was moved to remark in similar fashion: 'There are passages, it is true, in the early quartets [Op. 18] that in some measure presage the power of the late ones; but the contrast between the two styles is the more striking because there is no work for this combination to mark the transition, the Beethoven of the *Razumovskys* appearing to have sprung full-grown and almost unheralded into existence.'[ii]

The *Razumovsky* Quartets Op. 59, No. 1 in F major, No. 2 in E minor and No. 3 in C major did not, of course, descend like manna from Heaven. By the time of their publication, more than six years separated the *Razumovsky* Quartets from the composer's first essay in the medium, namely, the String Quartets Op. 18. In that time, Beethoven's compositional outlook had transformed immeasurably — elevated to a new zenith. The three Op. 59 Quartets are, in the words of the American musicologist Arthur Shepherd, 'a manifestation of conscious power ... inevitable in the [composer's] mature chamber music'.[iii] Inevitable for the reason that, by the time Beethoven returned to writing for the medium of the string quartet, he had already accomplished such large-scale works as: the *Kreutzer* Sonata in A, Op. 47 (first performed 24 May

1803); the *Waldstein* Piano Sonata in C, Op.53; the *Eroica* Symphony No. 3 in E flat, Op.55 (first performed 7 April 1805); and the *Appassionata* Piano sonata in F minor, Op.57.

When Beethoven commenced work on his first set of string quartets, the six of Op. 18, Vienna's claim to be Europe's musical capital of the world was in no small part associated with the status held at this period by the symphony and the string quartet; in the words of Barry Cooper 'the two noblest and most elevated forms of instrumental music'.[iv] The symphony afforded the composer an opportunity for the public display of his compositional craft, whilst the string quartet held sway in the more intimate environment of the salon — where the interplay between the four instruments had the authority and interest of informed conversation. Thereby, the first quartets of Haydn, published in 1764, were described as *quators dialogues*. He would elevate this aspect of his art in 1781 with his set of six Quartets, Op. 33.

The contemporary mystical poet and musician Christian Schubart considered the string quartet expressed no less than 'the music-universe condensed into one work'.[v] Haydn and Mozart enriched this universe by enhancing the quartet with ever more elaborate and novel strategies of musical realization. With his Op. 59 String Quartets Beethoven enriched and elaborated the genre even further with his own blend of intellect, wit and humour that would challenge both listeners and performers, 'deflating [their] expectations of easy comprehension with respect to the parallels between music and the assignment of meaning in the imagination'.[vi] With the Op. 59 Quartets, Beethoven expanded the boundaries of the genre as he had done in the domain of the symphony with the *Eroica,* Op. 55. As far as Beethoven was concerned, things would never be the same again for string-quartet players. In the words of Joseph Kerman: 'It is probably not too much to say that the Op. 59 doomed the amateur string quartet. Gone is the pretence of intelligent discourse. Due to their length and range of content, these quartets suggest epic poetry more than polite conversation.'[vii] We recall Beethoven's irate response to performers who complained of the finger-challenging difficulties posed by his new works: 'Do you suppose I consider your wretched fiddle when the spirit moves me.'[viii]

We consider for a moment the impulses on Beethoven that disposed him to explore new avenues in his music — new depths, scale, passion and intensity — that were to find expression in the *Razumovsky* String Quartets.

It was as a virtuoso pianist that Beethoven had first conquered Vienna's music salons and his keyboard works of the period — sonatas and sets of variations — bear testimony to his powers of invention and technical skills. Notwithstanding, about 1803 he felt a conscious desire to expand his musical horizons. According to his close friend at the time, the violinist and mandolinist Wenzel Krumpholz, Beethoven apparently exclaimed: 'God knows why my piano music still makes the worst impression on me.' With characteristic resolution, he confided to his sketchbook how he intended 'to make a fresh start'.[ix] His Op. 31 set of piano sonatas are considered to embody many features of the composer's desire to make this fresh start and thereby to embark upon a new path regarding his compositional style. Donald Tovey describes the three sonatas of Op. 31 as embodying the struggle of the transition to this new style and characterizes it for being 'as manifest as its accomplishment is triumphant.'[x] In his endorsement of these works, Philip Radcliffe makes special mention of the 'sombre rhetorical splendour' of the Sonata in D minor, Op. 31 and the Sonata for Violin and Piano in C minor, from Op. 30, as exhibiting 'perhaps the most obviously new and powerful side of his personality'.[xi] Other commentators cite the Quintet in C, Op. 29 with its two violas — Beethoven's own instrument in his youthful days as a string player — as being a worthy successor to the String Quartets Op. 18 and in effect being 'a bridge between two worlds', that is exemplifying characteristics that point to a new and expanding dimension in the composer's music.[xii]

In Beethoven's turning to a new style of expression in music, William Kinderman detects 'a shift to a fundamentally new aesthetic perspective'. In his evolution to what Kinderman describes as the composer's 'transition to Romantic ideals', he cites the distinguished philosopher Isaiah Berlin: 'There is no copying, there is no adaptation, there is no learning of the rules, there is no external check, there is no structure you must understand and adapt yourself to before you can proceed. The heart of the entire process is invention, creation, making, out of literally nothing, or out of any materials that may be to hand.'[xiii] In his interpretation of these words, Kinderman remarks how Beethoven's works, of the period under consideration, 'embody a new concept of music as *process*, whereby the potential for development of basic musical elements is probed on a broad scale'. As part of this new exploration of musical potential, he further asserts: 'Beethoven could begin with what seem to be mere fragments and enact a process of creative development within the work itself.' In the *Razumovsky* Quartets, Kinderman cites the manner in which 'texture becomes unified by the use of thematic material as its source'. Here, with others (for example Harold Truscott), Kinderman believes Beethoven may have been influenced by the innovations of the Czech composer and pianist Jan Dussek. In particular his set of three string quartets op. 60, composed at about the same time as the *Razumovskys*, show 'a strikingly new type of string-quartet writing' in line with much of what Beethoven developed in his Op. 59.[xiv]

In the estimation of the French musicologist Joseph de Marliave: 'The quartets of Op. 59 should more properly be called quartet-symphonies. In them all, and especially in the third in C major, one has the sense that the composer is striving after the symphonic idiom, with orchestral affects that sometimes seem to burst the slender framework of the quartet genre; the instruments too frail, the bows too slight to bear the burden of sound laid upon them.'[xv] We refer to Kinderman once more. He expresses similar thoughts: 'An orchestral ambition surfaces in the imaginative sonorities and enhanced scale of some of the movements of the *Razumovsky* quartets, from the broad opening *Allegro* of the F major Quartet to the nervously emphatic finale of the C major.'[xvi] The German historian-musicologist Frank Kämpfer also characterises the Op. 59 Quartets in the same manner: 'In certain sections the intensity of sound is reminiscent of a symphony, and the formal language has been expanded to include new and unfamiliar forms — a freedom that also had to be absorbed by the public.'[xvii]

Authorities are remarkably united in their estimation of Beethoven's *Razumovsky* String Quartets. They are acknowledging for being among the most representative works of his middle period and rank among 'the most perfect examples of his instrumental music as regards perfect harmony of substance with form, expression and inspiration'.[xviii] 'In effect, the *Razumovsky* String Quartets stand alone with no other contemporary composer seeking to emulate them or having the ability to do so.'[xix]

On 5 July 1806, Beethoven wrote to the music publisher Breitkopf and Härtell to inform him of the progress he was making with 'new violin quartets' — the Op. 59. The composer already had experience of working with the Leipzig-based firm of publishers. As early as November

1802, the head of the firm, Gottfried Christoph Härtel, had written to Beethoven in fulsome terms: 'It would be a true joy for us, in our esteem for your art, to request you to send our publishing house all of your new works and always to be able to remuncrate you to you greatest satisfaction.' Given the lack of secure copyright Härtel felt obliged to add: 'Unfortunately, however, it has come to pass that in Germany, with [the appearance of] every interesting new work, the pirate printers now often follow suit, so that the legitimate printers, who cannot set such low prices on them, often cannot sell a tenth as many copies as the pirate can.'[ix] In writing in this way, Härtel was doubtless mindful that Beethoven always demanded the highest prices for his works.

In his letter of July 1806, Beethoven remarks: 'I am thinking of devoting myself almost entirely to this type of composition' — string quartets.[xxi] It is implicit in this statement that Beethoven perceived the genre of the string quartet as being the preferred medium in which to give expression to his innermost thoughts. He did not, of course, carry out this intention. As Phillip Downs observes: 'In the event, however, it is not the introspective possibilities of the world of private music that was to speak most strongly to Beethoven. His urge to preach to the world of his newly discovered message of *per aspera ad astra* — conquering through suffering [more literally, 'through hardship to the stars'] — led him to public music such as the symphony and the concerto, and ultimately to the theatre.'[xxii] In this context, the philosopher and theorist Theodor Adorno finds in works such as the Fourth Piano Concerto, the Violin Concerto and to some extent the *Pastoral* Sonata, Op. 28, 'the idea of expressing tranquillity through motion'. He defines this as 'the innermost dynamic law of Beethoven's work' that was to find ultimate expression in the composer's late style. Regarding the *Razumovsky* String Quartets he observes: 'As far as I can see, after Op. 59, No. 1 and No. 2 Beethoven wrote only two more slow movements of [their] weight and, especially, of their sonata-like density: the *Largo* of the *Geister* ['Ghost'] Trio and the *Adagio* of the *Hammerklavier* Sonata.'[xxiii]

As remarked, in his Op. 18 Quartets, Beethoven, like Haydn and Mozart before him, had been content to regard the string quartet as a salon-style conversation piece — with noteworthy passages in the works of each of these composers that press against the boundaries of such formal constraints. In Beethoven's second-period music, however, there is no such ambiguity. With regard to the string quartet, the scale becomes 'symphonic' and the medium acquires 'a new ambition to project'.[xxiv] In their commentary to the *Razumovsky* Quartets, Donald Grout and Claude Palisca compare the structure of the Op. 59 with that of the *Eroica* Symphony. In particular, they comment on the manner in which both works expand the sonata form to new proportions within long and complex developments and extended codas. They add: 'Beethoven intentionally concealed the formerly clear dividing lines between the various parts of a movement: recapitulations are disguised and varied, new themes grow imperceptibly out of previous material, and the progress of the musical thought has a dynamic, propulsive character that toys with, if not actually scorns, the neat, symmetrical patterns of the Classic era.'[xxv] In his discussion of what he describes as 'peak experience', musicologist Malcolm Miller expounds: 'In the *Razumovsky* Quartets the expansion of structure characteristic of Beethoven's heroic period extends into the domain of extreme registers ... The recognition of the highest register as a distinctive sonorous domain harbouring its own possibilities of connectedness, has far-reaching structural implications.' He refers to the 'the linking up of *high events'* in the Op. 59

that reveals 'significant linear patterns' that he describes as 'rising lines'; the American musicologist Robert Fink dubs these 'arrows of desire'. Miller concludes: 'All three quartets may be seen to project large-scale linear patters that maintain tension between movements ... In each work, individual exploration and expansion of the Classic-Romantic sonata principle [adds] its own layer of narrative coherence.'[xxvi]

Before proceeding with our discussion of the creation origins of the Op. 59 Quartets, we pause here and consider other aspects the composer's life and work, thereby to round out our picture of Beethoven 'the man'.

At the close of the eighteenth century, Beethoven achieved popular recognition for the music he composed for the annual *Masked Ball* convened by Vienna's *Society of Plastic and Graphic Artists* (painters and sculptors). Their laudable aim was to raise money for the pension fund of fellow members who had fallen on straitened circumstances. This event presented Beethoven with the opportunity to showcase his skill at writing popular dance music. An advertisement of the period proclaimed: 'The beloved Minuets and German Dances of Herr Ludwig von [sic] Beethoven will be performed.' (Beethoven's Dutch 'van' was not infrequently confused with the German 'von' — sometimes to his advantage.) Typical of the pieces he composed for this, and similar occasions, are the 12 Minuets, WoO 7 and the 12 German Dances, WoO 8. Later, in 1801, he similarly contributed the 12 Contradances, WoO 14 that incorporate the celebrated theme he had recently used in the finale of his ballet *The Creatures of Prometheus* that he would use again in the Piano Variations, Op. 35 and the finale of the *Eroica* Symphony.

With his hearing still intact, Beethoven was in demand as a piano teacher — more correctly instructor in the art of pianoforte. Perhaps his most accomplished pupil was the composer-pianist Ferdinand Ries — we leave aside the child prodigy Carl Czerny who was a mere ten-year old when he was introduced to Beethoven for lessons. (At his audition he performed the solo part of a Mozart piano concerto and the *Pathétique* Piano Sonata!) Ries recollects: 'Beethoven takes more trouble with me than I could ever have believed. Each week I receive three lessons, usually from 1 o'clock to 2. 30 ... The precision he demands is hard to imagine ... To hear him improvise, however, may not be imagined at all — I have already had this pleasure five times.'[xxvii]

As Beethoven's fame grew, music publishers, amongst others, requested his portrait. Such images, in engraved form, served to adorn the frontispieces to printed copies of the master's latest productions. We have previously seen that the Leipzig music publisher Gottfried Christoph Härtel had written to Beethoven in encouraging terms. He was particularly anxious for his publishing house to receive 'piano sonatas without accompaniment, or with accompaniment of violin, or of violin and violincello'. Härtel added a touch of flattery, doubtless to secure the composer's commissions: 'The fame of your talents is established firmly enough.' Härtel concluded by requesting where Beethoven's portrait may be seen so that a likeness could be taken for its publication alongside his series of 'the most prominent composers'.[xxviii] An engraving of Beethoven duly appeared in Volume 6 of the *Allgemeine musikalische Zeitung* (October 1803 — September 1804). Johann Neidl created this from a drawing by the artist Gandolph Stainhauser — made sometime in 1800.

A further measure of Beethoven's growing fame at this period is indicated by the circumstance of him being persuaded to have his portrait painted by Joseph Mähler. He was a personal friend of the composer and it is assumed Beethoven actually sat for the portrait — an ordeal he disliked. He is portrayed in an Arcadian setting striking a lyre, in the background is a temple of Apollo. The painting remained in Beethoven's possession until his death.[xxix]

From 1803 is a miniature portrait of the composer created by the Danish artist Christian Horneman. This depicts Beethoven with stylish sideburns and elegantly dressed. Beethoven gave the miniature as a keepsake to his friend Stephan von Breuning with whose descendants it remained for a hundred years before it eventually found a home in the Beethoven House in Bonn, via the famous collector of Beethoven memorabilia Dr H. C. Bodmer.[xxx]

The composer and writer on music Johann Friedrich Reichardt visited Beethoven in late November 1808 and wrote to his wife about the experience: 'I have at last been to see the excellent Beethoven ... At length I discovered him in a large, lonely house: he looked at first as dark as his dwelling, but soon brightened up, and seemed pleased to see me ... and talked very freely on many subjects ... His nature is a strong one, with a cyclopean exterior, but truly affectionate, agreeable and good within.'[xxxi]

It is not surprising that Reichardt should describe Beethoven's appearance in 1808, metaphorically speaking, as 'dark'. By then deafness had made him reclusive and, in addition, he had to endure many tribulations and vicissitudes imposed by uncertain health. His correspondence makes reference to illnesses of various kinds often accompanied by 'fever' — a somewhat catchall medical expression — and lingering intestinal problems — usually referred to as 'colic'. In May 1804, Beethoven shared an apartment with his friend Stephan von Breuning who records: '[Beethoven] had a severe, almost critical illness followed by intermittent fever that smouldered on long after his recovery.' Indeed, throughout 1805 in his correspondence Beethoven makes frequent mention of poor health. In November he was obliged to write to the singer Friedrich Meyer (the first Pizarro in *Fidelio*): 'I cannot come for since yesterday I have been suffering from *colic pains — my usual complaint*' [Beethoven's italics]. He also remarks how 'the present *distressing crises*' had been affecting his work — a reference to the French occupation of Vienna by Napoleon's army.[xxxii] On 4 May 1806, he made a similar complaint to Baron von Braun, the impresario who staged *Fidelio*: 'It so happens that I am not very well'.[xxxiii] From 1807 on, Beethoven writes of 'terrible headaches', as, for example in a letter to Baron von Gleichenstein (see later) written on 13 June 1807: 'Yesterday and today I have been very ill, and I still have a terrible headache — Heaven help me to get rid of it.'[xxxiv] Later that month he complained to Prince Nikolaus Esterhazy of 'head troubles': 'I was afflicted ... by an illness that affected my head ... This prevented my at first from working at all and later, even now, has allowed me to do very little work.'[xxxv] From the poet Heinrich von Collin, author of the tragedy *Coriolan* — for which Beethoven wrote his Overture *Coriolanus* — we learn of the composer having 'a severe finger operation. This was probably the result of an infection to the tissues and could have been a permanent impediment had the operation not been successful.

Reflecting on Beethoven's many illnesses, the physician-musicologist Anton Neumayr comments: 'With such a general state of poor health, it is no wonder Beethoven often felt depressed.'[xxxvi] We reflect that when his illnesses are taken into consideration, Beethoven's compositional output is all the more astonishing. In addition to the works we have already mentioned, in 1806 he finished the Fourth Symphony, Op. 60 as well as the *Razumovsky* Quartets, Op. 59, the Fourth Piano Concerto in G major, Op. 58 and the Violin Concerto in D major Op. 61. In 1807 and 1808 he completed the Fifth Symphony in C minor, Op. 67 and the

Sixth Symphony in F major, Op. 67, the *Pastoral*. Beethoven had reached a new zenith in his composing.

Intimations of Beethoven's renewed interest in writing for the string quartet is discernable from correspondence between the composer's younger brother Kaspar Karl (Caspar Carl) and the publishers Breitkopf and Härtel. Karl (as we shall refer to him) was musically inclined — he is on record as saying he could play several instruments — and did a little composing. He moved to Vienna in 1794 where he worked as a clerk in the Finance Department. Over time he helped his brother with his business dealings with publishers.[xxxvii] Such was Beethoven's trust in Karl's negotiations that he wrote to Breitkopf and Härtel on 22 April 1802: 'You can rely entirely on my *brother* — who, in general, attends to all my affairs.'[xxxviii] It was in this spirit that Karl wrote to Breitkopf and Härtel on 10 October 1804 to negotiate the publication of several of Beethoven's compositions including the Symphony, No. 3, Op. 55, *Eroica*, and the Piano Sonatas Op. 53, *Waldstein* and Op. 57 *Appassionata*. At the close of the letter he adds: 'Then could [you] also tell me your opinion about string quartets and how much you would pay for two or three of them. To be sure, I cannot give you these immediately, but I would reserve them for you.' This is taken to be a direct reference to the origins of the three *Razumovsky* String Quartets. From Karl's wording they were still, however, only envisioned or at an early stage of composition.[xxxix] Gottfried Christoph Härtel, the principal partner in the publishing form, replied to Beethoven on 3 November. He offered the composer 1,100 florins for the various compositions suggested for publication by his firm. As to the string quartets, Härtel requested further details of the proposals.[xl] Karl responded on 24 November: 'Concerning the quartets, I cannot yet tell you anything specifically: as soon as they are ready, I shall write to you immediately.'[xli]

In the event, the disruption caused by the Napoleonic war and other factors thwarted the publication of the Op. 59 String Quartets by the Leipzig-based Breitkopf and Härtel. They eventually appeared in Vienna in January 1808, published at the *Kunst-und Industrie-Comptoir*, circumstances to which we refer in greater detail in due course.

The String Quartets Op, 59 derive their cognomen *Razumovsky* from their dedicatee the diplomat, art collector and music lover Count Andrey Razumovsky. In 1792 he was appointed Russian ambassador to the Austrian Court in Vienna. He was one of the most influential figures in the social and musical life of the capitol and one of its most generous patrons. Razumovsky was a subscriber to Beethoven's Trios Op. 1 published in 1795 and in 1808 Beethoven dedicated his Fifth and Sixth Symphonies jointly to Razumovsky and his patron Prince Lobkowitz. From 1808 Razumovsky maintained his own String Quartet whose members were: Ignaz Schuppanzigh, first violin — we say more about him shortly; Ludwig Sina, second violin and a member of the orchestra of the Theater an der Wien; Franz Weiss, viola and a regular performer at Prince Lichnowsky's recitals; and Joseph Linke who was also first cellist at the Theater an der Wien. Beethoven had a high opinion of Linke and it was with him in mind that he wrote his two Cello Sonatas, Op. 102. Count Razumovsky was an accomplished violinist himself and, when he chose not to listen to his quartet, took on the role of second fiddle.[xiii] Also worthy of mention as a regular second violinist in Schuppanzigh's String Quartet was Karl Holz. Like Beethoven's brother Karl, he was a civil servant but was much admired by Beethoven for his performing skills. The two became friends and for a period Holz helped Beethoven as his unpaid assistant. He is remembered today in Beethoven musicology for the two humorous canons WoO 197 and WoO 198 that were dedicated to him in 1826. Beethoven's death the following year is said to have affected Holz deeply.[xliii]

According to Beethoven's biographer Anton Schindler, Razumovsky's Quartet virtually became Beethoven's Quartet 'as the musicians were put at his disposal just as if they had been hired expressly for his use'. He continues: 'It is well known that Beethoven was ... much at home in the Razumovsky establishment ... every note [of his works] was played precisely as he wanted it played, with such devotion, such love, such obedience, such piety as could be inspired only by passionate admiration of his great genius ... One voice alone, Beethoven's, spoke through the music and through its interpretations.'[xliv] These experiences doubtless contributed to Beethoven's deepening understanding of writing for the medium of the string quartet.

As for Razumovsky, the artist Josef Lanzedelly created a likeness of the Count seated in all his finery that is today preserved in the Beethoven Archives in Bonn.[xlv] Some years later a second portrait of Razumovsky was painted by Ferdinand Georg Waldmüller. By then the Count was living a more secluded life of semi-retirement. He is depicted seated at his desk looking aged.[xlvi] Misfortune had befallen him when a disastrous fire consumed his palace, his treasures and much of his fortune. As a consequence he was obliged to disbanded his beloved Quartet, but not before honourably settling a pension on its members. Baroness du Montet had occasion to visit Razumovsky at this time and records: 'I found the Prince aged and depressed. His extravagant magnificence has ruined him [she appears not to have taken account of the fire and its consequences] ... He is a gentleman who commands respect and is generally amiable. His presence and appearance are imperious; he radiates pride in all things; pride in his rank and his honour.'[xlvii] Count Razumovsky's title of Prince, to which the baroness makes reference, derives from the period of the Congress of Vienna (1814) when it was conferred upon him by the Tsar.

Ignaz Schuppanzigh is a significant figure in the context of Beethoven's writing for the string quartet and also in connection with his role in the first performances of a number of his chamber and orchestral compositions. From 1794, when just eighteen years old, he led a quartet in the salon of Beethoven's patron Prince Lichnowsky. It was there, in April 1797, that he took part in a performance of the composer's Piano Quintet, Op. 16. At about this time he also gave Beethoven lessons in violin, an interesting experience for the composer given that Schuppanzigh was twenty-six years younger than himself. In 1804 he formed his own quartet that had the distinction of being the first to give subscription concerts to the wider public in Vienna. In 1805 he directed the first performance of Beethoven's Sextet, Op. 71. As we have already noted, in 1808 Razumovsky asked Schuppanzigh 'to assemble a fine string quartet for him'; this was at the prompting of Prince Lichnowsky who, through marriage, was Count Razumovsky's brother-in-law.

Schuppanzigh rendered service to Beethoven in the capacities of both orchestral leader and orchestral conductor. On 16 April 1812 he directed performances of the Overture *Egmont* and the Sixth Symphony and later in May the Overture *Coriolan*. The following year he similarly conducted performances of the Overture *Prometheus* and the Fifth Symphony (1 May). On 11 April he took part with Beethoven in the first performance of the Archduke Trio, Op. 97; as a consequence of the composers failing hearing this was to be one of his last public appearances at the keyboard. In May 1814 his Quartet gave the first performance of the String Quartet Op. 95 and later that year, on 8

December, he played first violin in a memorable performance of the Seventh Symphony that saw Beethoven enjoy his greatest public acclaim. Following the fire at Razumovsky's palace, Schuppanzigh made plans to leave Vienna. On 11 February 1816 he gave a farewell concert at which the String Quartet Op. 59, No. 3 was performed. On his eventual return to Vienna, in 1823, Schuppanzigh soon became absorbed in the capitol's musical life and, more significantly for our narrative, was reunited with Beethoven. He directed the first performances of the Ninth Symphony on 7 and 23 May 1824 and later gave the first renditions of the Quartets Op. 127 (6 March 1825), Op. 132 (6 November 1825), and Op. 130 (with fugue) on 21 March 1826.[xlviii]

Beethoven valued Schuppanzigh both as a fellow musician and to some extent as a friend — although not an intimate one. On account of the his considerable girth Beethoven, ever the punster, made reference to Schuppanzigh — with a nod to Shakespeare — as 'My Lord Falstaff'. The pencil-charcoal study of the violinist by Josef Danhauser[xlix] portrays a florid, somewhat handsome young man but a profile view, taken a few years later, does indeed convey something of Schuppanzigh's corpulence.[l] We recall that Friedrich Reichardt was in Vienna in 1808 when he met Beethoven. He also heard Schuppanzigh perform. On 10 December he wrote to his wife: 'I must tell you about a splendid quartet party which Schuppanzigh, a first rate violinist, has started for the winter subscription under the auspices of the Russian ambassador Razumovsky. It is to meet at a private house every Thursday ... It is a kind of [music-making] best of all adapted to produce sympathetic enjoyment among refined music lovers.' He continues: 'Herr Schuppanzigh himself has a peculiarly piquant style, most suited for the humorous quartets of Haydn, Mozart and Beethoven ... He plays the most difficult passages clearly.' Reichardt makes special mention of Schuppanzigh's facility for accentuating 'very accurately and expressively' and how his cantabile was 'very singing and full of feeling'. Reichardt considered Schuppanzigh to be a good leader but could not refrain from commenting 'he frequently disturbs me by his execrable habit — which is universal here — of beating time with his foot.'[li]

More seriously, and significantly, Schuppanzigh's dedication to quartet performance is acknowledged for playing a pivotal role in the elevation of quartet performance and indeed of the genre of quartet composition. In our opening remarks we have noted that in the era of Haydn and Mozart — and Beethoven up to the Op. 18 Quartets — the quartet repertoire could be performed by proficient amateurs. With the emergence of the three *Razumovsky* Quartets, the medium was transformed. It required the dedication of such pioneers as Schuppanzigh and his colleagues to overcome the many new technical difficulties that required serious application and rehearsal. In his study *The String Quartet*, Paul Griffiths writes it was with the attainments of the Schuppanzigh Quartet in mind — and Schuppanzigh in particular — that Beethoven composed the *Razumovsky* Quartets. He states: '[In] so doing he was writing for a violinist who, unlike those for whom Haydn had composed, was primarily a quartet player. Thus Op. 59 presumes not merely brilliance, though on occasion the three works do require that for first violin, but also dedication and understanding.'[lii]

An early pioneer of Beethoven's string quartets outside of Vienna was the violinist-composer Karl Möser. In 1812 he became concertmaster of the Court Opera in Berlin where the following year he established a regular series of quartet recitals — to rival those of their kind organised in Vienna by Schuppanzigh. His chamber series lasted until

1843. Under Möser's sponsorship, Beethoven's quartets became familiar repertory pieces. Furthermore, he was adventurous – if not audacious – in his programming. For example, in 1828 he realised a performance of the composer's challenging String Quartet in A minor, Op. 132 and in subsequent concerts performed, Op. 59, Nos. 2 and 3 from the *Razumovsky* set, Op. 74 (*The Harp*) and Op. 95 (*Quartetto Serioso*).[liii]

We turn now to a consideration of the origins of the three *Razumovsky* String Quartets.

From the exchange of letters in October-November 1804 between Beethoven's brother Karl and the music publisher Breitkopf and Härtel, it is evident Beethoven was actively turning his mind to the composition of a set of string quartets; we recall Karl explaining: 'I cannot yet tell you anything specifically; as soon as they [the quartets] are ready, I shall write to you immediately.' Concerning Razumovsky, the warmth of feeling and respect that existed between himself and Beethoven has been illustrated; we have seen the freedom the composer enjoyed in having his works rehearsed and performed in the Count's salon. Razumovsky clearly held Beethoven in high regard. From the time when the young compose arrived in Vienna it is recorded that his secretary, von Klüpfeld (Klüpfell), told him about 'the new star, Beethoven, in the firmament'.[liv]

No formal contract between the Count and Beethoven requesting a set of string quartets survives – if such ever existed. It seems more probable the Count commissioned the compositions informally at one of his musical gatherings. According to Beethoven's indefatigable biographer Alexander Thayer: 'At any rate, at the end of 1805 Beethoven received a commission for three quartets from the Count.'

We may ask, why three quartets and not six? The creative process of publishing six collected works as a single opus was a legacy from the late eighteenth century. Both Haydn and Mozart composed string quartets in groups of six and Beethoven had followed their example with his Op. 18. Moreover, at this period publication practice decreed that a single quartet or sonata did not carry sufficient 'authority' to be regarded as a single work worthy of its own opus number. That said, Beethoven had issued his six String Quartets Op. 18 in two series – 'books' – as had Haydn with his Op. 76. David Wyn Jones comments: 'Commissioning three works rather than six is part of a broader trend at the turn of the century.'[lv] We have also seen that Beethoven's compositions were expanding in scale and proportion. It would not be long before his string quartets would be conferred the status of an *individual* opus number. With regard to the *Razumovsky* Quartets, they constitute a musically satisfying whole – an *opus* – a *triptych*; they stand together and, in their contrasted nature, can form the basis of a recital programme. In the words of Paul Bekker: 'The F major and E minor Quartets are founded on conflict and contrast, acute and violent in the first, subtle and subjective in the second, but the C major has another basis. It is entirely free form problems and forms, a reconciling close to the group of which it is the final number.'[lvi]

Central to the character of the *Razumovsky* String Quartets is the incorporation of Russian folk melodies. These occur in the final movement of the Quartet F major, Op 59, No. 1 and the third movement of the Quartet in E major, Op. 59, No. 2. The second movement of the Quartet in C major, Op. 59, No. 3 also has an elegiac character suggestive of the plaintive feeling found in Russian folk melody. Beethoven does not make direct reference in the score to his adoption of a *théme russe*. Some authorities consider, however, he absorbed the Russian idiom, made it his own and then freely adapted it into his music.'[lvii]

The reason for the adoption of these melodies into the Op. 59 set has been the subject of speculation. Some authorities are of the view that Beethoven, mindful of Count Razumovsky's noble Russian connection — and his deep love of music, sought to compliment his patron by absorbing themes from his homeland into his compositions. Others believe Razumovsky himself may have suggested them.

We know from other of Beethoven's compositions that he was not averse to setting the themes of other composers — as a trigger to his powers of invention. For example, in 1796 he composed twelve variations on the theme *See the conquering hero comes*, WoO, 45, from Handel's Oratorio *Judas Maccabaeus* and in 1799 he composed ten variations on *La stessa, la stessissima*, WoO 73, from Salieri's Opera *Falstaff*. More distantly, Beethoven would establish an entire genre of Scottish folksong setting in collaboration with the Edinburgh-based music publisher George Thomson. We call to mind also the rustic enchantment that infiltrates the *Pastoral* Symphony, Op. 68 of 1808.[lviii]

There are contemporaneous precedents by other composer's for incorporating idiomatic melodies into their chamber works. Perhaps the most notable — and popular — of these is Haydn's Piano Trio No. 39 in G major from 1795 that incorporates in its finale the celebrated *Gypsy Rondo* in the Hungarian style.

Beethoven's motivation to incorporate Russian themes into his music may have been influenced by extra-musical factors. In 1802 the journal *Allgemeine musikalische Zeitung* carried an article promoting Russian music that, in the words of Alexander Thayer, promoted 'a constant intercourse between Vienna, Moscow and St. Petersburg'.[lix] In common parlance amongst the musically inclined, Russian airs were 'the talk of the town'. Their influence appears to have percolated down to Beethoven's piano pupil

Carl Czerny. The present writer recalls, from one of Czerny's piano tutors, a study titled *A tune from Russia* that was undoubtedly derived from a poignant Russian folk song. Although more tenuous, there was the influence of things Russian in the form of the physical presence of wounded Russian soldiers who occupyied Vienna following the confrontation between the French and Russians at the Battle of Austerlitz; many found refuge in Vienna's hospitals and charitable institutions such as convents.[lx]

The Russian melodies in question have their origins in a collection compiled by the Czech-Silesian composer Ivan Pratsch. He lived and worked in St. Petersburg and is said to have adopted a manner in his music suggestive of Mozart. He published his Russian collection originally in 1790 with a second edition following in Vienna in 1806. This found an immediate response and doubtless augmented the feeling towards Russian folk melodies that had been stirred a few years previously by the article in the *AmZ*.[lxi]

By whatever promptings, Beethoven noted the melodies that had taken his fancy in his sketchbook — see later and our separate discussion of the individual quartets. Suffice it to say here that Beethoven was not content to merely reproduce the themes he had noted down, any more than he was twenty years later when he transformed Anton Diabelli's waltz theme into his majestic set of thirty-two variations, Op. 120; he had initially dismissed Diabelli's theme for being banal and a *schusterfleck* or 'cobbler's patch'. In the *Razumovsky* Quartets, to quote Alfred Einstein, 'the classical and Russian dissolve in the personal'.[lxii] Pratsch's themes are not quoted but are adopted and integrated into the ensuing music.[lxiii] The French musicologist Joseph de Marliave says much the same thing in an expanded form: '[The] use of Russian themes gives no specifically Russian cast to these quartets, in the sense that one finds it in [Anton] Rubinstein's Quartet in C minor [Op. 66], for example, or in the quartets of Borodin; they are pure Beethoven. The artist took two melodic ideas, and his genius developed them into original works of a character unmistakably his own.'[lxiv] In so doing Beethoven drew on the influences gestating in his mind in such works as the concertos and symphonies — to which we have made earlier reference — and then transferred them to the genre of the chamber medium, 'subjecting them to rhythmic and tempo modification'.[lxv] When Artur Schnabel was invited to discuss the music of various countries, he responded: 'The good pieces from one country are very much like the good pieces of other countries ... Even the use of folklore elements does not change that.' With the Razumovsky Quartets in mind he concluded: 'When Beethoven uses a Russian them in a quartet, it sounds like Beethoven, not like Russia.'[lxvi]

Unlike the composer's String Quartets Op. 18, for which the composition had been both protected and at times tentative, the composition of the three *Razumovsky* Quartets was completed within a short period of time. This was from late spring (about April) through the summer and autumn (until about November) of 1806. Moreover, their creation came about with Beethoven in a mood of creative self-confidence — notwithstanding the several illnesses to which we have made reference. For much of the two preceding years he had been occupied with his Opera *Leonora* that was performed in March and April of 1806, following its substantial revision after its unsuccessful premier the previous November. We have already mentioned, but worthy of reiteration, that alongside the Op. 59 Quartets, Beethoven turned his mind to the completion of the Triple Concerto, Op. 56; work on the two Piano Sonatas, Op. 54 and 57; work on the Fourth Piano Concerto, Op. 58; the Fourth Symphony (summer-autumn of 1806, autograph dated

1806); and the Violin Concerto, performed on 23 December 1806. Kinderman refers to the Op. 59 as 'This trilogy that stands at the centre of a splendid series of masterpieces.'[lxvii]

Beethoven's progress with the composition of the *Razumovsky* Quartets can be traced through his, and his brother Karl's, correspondence with the composer's intended publisher and other of Beethoven's close associates. In his previously mentioned letter of 5 July 1806, to the music publisher Breitkopf and Härtell, Beethoven states that his brother Karl was travelling to Leipzig and remarks: '[You] may discuss with him the question of the violin quartets, one of which I have already finished.' Of interest is that the main reason for Karl's visit was to deliver piano reductions of the Overture to *Fidelio* as well as the music to his Oratorio *Christus am Ölberge* (Christ on the Mount of Olives) composed in 1803.[lxviii] On 3 September Beethoven once more corresponded with Breitkopf and Härtel. He first discussed business matters in which he assured his Leipzig publisher he was definitely interested in an exclusive contract with them for the sale of his works in Germany. However, he explains he reserved the right to sell single works abroad if the offers were sufficiently lucrative — testimony to Beethoven's business acumen. Regarding the Op. 59 he adds: 'I can then send you immediately *three violin quartets, a new pianoforte concerto* [Fourth Piano Concerto, Op. 58], a new symphony [Fourth Symphony, Op. 60], the score of my Opera [*Leonora*, Op. 72] and my Oratorio [*Christus am Ölberge*, Op. 85]. As so frequently in his negotiations with publishers, Beethoven overstated the case; the Op. 59 Quartets may have been well in hand but were not yet available for publication.[lxix] When the *Razumovsky* Quartets were nearing completion, Beethoven wrote to Breitkopf and Härtel again to discuss business terms: 'I am offering you three quartets and a pianoforte concerto [Op. 58] ... from you I ask 600 gulden for the three quartets and 300 gulden for the concerto.'[lx] In the event the arrangement was not acceptable to the publisher and Beethoven's negotiations with Breitkopf and Härtel were terminated (see later).

Confirmation of Beethoven's progress with the Op. 59 Quartets comes from another source. In the autumn of 1806 Beethoven wrote to Count Razumovsky in the following terms: 'J'ai l'honneur de vous envoyer le second Quatuor [Op. 59, No. 2], en vous avertissant, que le 3emm [Op. 59, No. 3] sera achevé dans peu.' He takes leave of the Count: J'ai été bien charmé de ce que le premier Quatuor [Op. 59, No. 1] a eu le Bonheur do vous plaire; j'espère que ce sera le meme avec le second.'[lxi] This letter, styled in the French diplomatic language with which Razumovsky was conversant, was written by another hand and signed by Beethoven — a procedure he adopted on such occasions (Beethoven's own French not being equal to the task). As can be inferred from the text, it was clearly written during the composition of the third *Razumovsky* Quartet, Op. 59, No. 3. Beethoven authority Barry Cooper considers this letter to be clear evidence that Count Razumovsky had indeed commissioned the String Quartets Op. 59 from Beethoven.[lxii]

For evidence of further progress with the Op. 59s we consider the relevant events of the following year. From a letter of 11 May 1807 we learn that Beethoven had sent copies of the quartets, in parts, to Count Franz Brunsvik, a member of an aristocratic Hungarian family, a close friend of the composer and an admirer of his music. Schindler describes the Count as 'one of the most perceptive connoisseurs of Beethoven's music'.[lxiii] Beethoven reciprocated the Count's feelings towards him by conferring on him the dedications to his Piano Sonata Op. 57 and the Fantasia Op.

77. The letter in question was sent to Countess Josephine Deym, Franz's sister and one of the great loves of Beethoven's life. He requested the return of the quartet parts since he could not find his own score — an indication of the domestic disorder that could sometimes overwhelm him. He explains the parts were required so they could be copied for sending to Muzio Clementi.

Clementi first met Beethoven when on a business trip to Vienna. On 22 April 1807 he wrote to his partner William Frederick Collard in London: 'By a little management and without committing myself, I have at last made a complete conquest of that *haughty beauty* [Clementi's italics] Beethoven'. Clementi explains how had persuaded the composer to have his works published in England (London) and how his publishing house would take care of him. Beethoven obligingly gave an undertaking to prepare a list of his available publications. Clementi tells Collard he had agreed with Beethoven to take in manuscript: the three String Quartets Op. 59; Symphony No. 4, Op. 60; the Overture *Coriolan*, Op. 62; the Concerto for Pianoforte No. 4. Op. 58; and the Violin Concerto, Op. 61 that Clementi describes as being 'very beautiful' and which, at his request, Beethoven had offered to adapt for the pianoforte (Op. 61a). For all these works, Beethoven was to receive two hundred pounds sterling. Regarding the Op. 59 Quartets he adds: 'You may get Cramer or some other very clever person to adapt the Quartets — that is prepare them for publication.[lxxiv] Clementi is referring here to Johann Baptist Cramer, the celebrated the German born pianist and composer then resident in London.

In writing directly to Count Franz Brunsvik, Beethoven was anxious to ensure the return of the quartet parts to fulfil his obligations to Clementi. He could not resist enthusing over his contract with Clementi: 'I am to get 200 pounds sterling — and, what is more, I shall be able to sell the same works [including the *Razumovsky* Quartets] in Germany and France — so that means I may hope even in my early years to achieve the dignity of a true artist.'[lxxv]

A letter of 23 June to Baron Ignaz von Gleichenstein is relevant to our discussion.[lxxvi] He rendered various services to Beethoven, particularly with his correspondence, and was a witness to the composer's contract with Clementi. Beethoven urged Gleichenstein to ensure the copyist would complete work on the remaining String Quartet Op. 59, No. 3. If delays were to be anticipated then Gleichenstein was instructed to have the work undertaken by the copyist at the Bureau des Arts et d'Industrie that was also known by the name Kunst und Industrie Comptoir. This firm of music publishers also dealt in maps and art prints and was Beethoven's principal publisher between the years 1802–08. They brought out his Fourth Symphony, Fourth Piano Concerto, the Violin Concerto, the Overture *Coriolan* as well as the three *Razumovsky* String Quartets.

We have seen that in the spirit of Beethoven's newfound confidence, the Op. 59 String Quartets were composed in the relatively short period between April and November 1808. Moreover, whereas the Op. 18 Quartets show evidence of methodical, extensive and painstaking sketching, the Op. 59s proceeded under different circumstances and with the composer in a quite different frame of mind. They did not, to re-quote Lenz's phrase, descend like 'three miracles dropped from Heaven' but do appear to have been created without recourse to extensive sketching. The sketches that do survive give witness, in Richard Kramer's phrase, 'to a marvellous disarray of compositional options taken, rejected and reconsidered'. The sketches are scattered today and consequently are preserved in various archives. The following is an overview — we provide further details in our commentaries to the three individual string quartets.

The Gesellschaft der Musikfreunde, Vienna has an unbound folder, designated 'A 36' that contains 32 leaves of which 25 have been found to relate directly to the Op. 59 Quartets.[lxxvii] Authorities consider Beethoven's work for the first movement shows the influence of Mozart's C major Quartet, K. 465 and the D major Quartet K. 575. The slow movement is not well represented but sketches for the minuet and trio of the third movement are located at leaves 1, 14, 20–4, 26, 47 and 50. Ideas for the fourth movement show a preoccupation with the work's fugal beginning. The Beethoven House, Bonn has two leaves relating to the first movement of the C major Quartet,[lxxviii] and the Royal College of Music, London has a sketch fragment for the second movement of the C major Quartet. The Staatsbibliothek Preussischer Kulturbesitz, Berlin holds two miscellanies that include sketches for the E minor Quartet. Authorities have shown, however, these are not continuous and therefore do not reveal insights into the composer's sequential compositional process. The third movement and finale of the E minor Quartet are represented in the so-called Landsberg 10 sketchbook.[lxxix]

The Staatsbibliothek also possess the *Leonore* Sketchbook that once belonged to Ernst Mendelssohn Bartholdy containing sketches for the third and fourth movements of the F major Quartet. The designation *Leonora* is the colloquial terminology for the so-called Mendelssohn 15 Sketchbook. This derives from the time it was owned by the collector Heinrich Beer of Berlin who designated it: 'L.v. BEETHOVEN SKIZZENBUCH zu FIDELIO' – Beer adopting the later name of *Fidelio* for Beethoven's opera. It was subsequently donated in 1908 to the Royal Library in Berlin. Sketches for the last three movements occupy pages

183—6 and page 346 of the sketchbook, 'although these may be extraneous leaves not occupying their original locations having been interpolated at a later date'. In addition the Staatsbibliothek holds the so-called Grasnick 20b sketchbook also containing two leaves bearing material destined for the *Razumovsky* String Quartets.[lxxx]

Beethoven's autographs have been described as 'the final link in the chain of his process'. Concerning the autographs to the Op. 59 Quartets: 'In addition to the evidence to be found in the surviving sketches, the autograph scores also reveal Beethoven's editorial revisions, variously identifiable in pencil, ink and red crayon.'[lxxxi] Today, the autographs of the Quartets No. 59, Op. 1 and 2 are preserved in the archives of the Staatsbibliothek Preussischer Kulturbesitz, Berlin. These are catalogued as Mendelssohn 10 and Autograph 21.[lxxxii] [lxxxiii] Facsimile reproductions of these autographs have been published with an introduction by Alan Tyson (Alan Tyson, London, Scolar Press). The autograph of Quartet No. 59, Op. 3 is preserved at the Beethoven Archive, Bonn.[lxxxiv]

We return to further consideration of Beethoven's expanding stylistic tendencies — typical of his *heroic* period — and their bearing on the format and construction of the *Razumovsky* Quartets. In this context worthy of mention once more is the *Eroica* Symphony that authorities consider marks the end of the first phase in the composer's artistic life and inaugurates his second. In his survey of the emergence and evolution of Beethoven's heroic style, musicologist Michael Broyles comments: 'What we notice ... is the emergence of a new set of musical values of great historical significance.' He elaborates: 'Most of the values may be found individually in Beethoven's earlier music, and virtually none represents sudden or radical shift of Beethoven's compositional orientation. Collectively, however, they initiate a stylistic crucible in Beethoven's compositional orientation.' Broyles cites the manner in which the scale of Beethoven's compositions, through the Op. 50s and Op. 60s, results in a new sense of spaciousness and breadth 'as the pacing broadens to allow larger and more relaxed gestures'. He also draws attention to the Violin Concerto Op. 61, the first movement of which encompasses no fewer than 535 measures. Alongside this majestic work stand the two Romances for Violin and Orchestra Op. 40 and Op. 50 and the Triple Concerto for Piano, Violin and Cello, Op. 56 — all distinguished for having passages of sustained eloquence and lyricism. To this genre of compositions, Broyles includes the first *Razumovsky* Quartet, notably with regard to the sense of spaciousness in its first movement.[lxxxv]

The increased scale of the first movement of Op. 59, No. 1 embodies the character of the set: all three works have a performing time of the order of thirty to forty minutes compared with the twenty to thirty minutes typical of the string quartets of Haydn and Mozart. In the context of performance practice, Paul Griffiths makes the following related observations: 'A Haydn or Mozart quartet need something else to complete half a recital programme or the whole of a disc, whereas one of Beethoven's *Razumovsky* quartets can legitimately stand alone. The works have attained a size where they become independent, self-sufficient entities.' He qualifies his remarks: 'But of course this is not just a matter of duration. The singleness of each of these quartets is guaranteed ... by a sustained psychological impetus throughout the four movements.'[lxxxvi] Marion Scott's insights are relevant here: 'Formerly Beethoven [in his Op. 18 Quartets], like Haydn and his contemporaries, had sought no more when arranging a set of quartets that they should contrast well and follow each other agreeably. Now his instinct had advanced; he felt the need for unity in diversity.'[lxxxvii]

In the spirit of the foregoing, Downs draws attention to the manner in which 'each of the *Razumovsky* Quartets is strongly differentiated from each other'.[lxxxviii] Maynard Solomon makes similar observations: 'Although they were conceived as a set, the *Razumovsky* Quartets resemble each other far less than do the six quartets of Op. 18, or even the last five quartets.' He maintains they constitute 'a trio of sharply characterised, consciously differentiated individuals' — quoting Joseph Kerman (*Beethoven Quartets*, p. 118). That said, Solomon suggests unity can be found in the *Razumovskys* in what he describes as their 'common pre-occupation with triumphal finales' and the manner in which Beethoven 'strives for diversity of mood and structure' as well as 'experimentation with many new (and even bizarre) effects and procedures'. With regard to the latter, he identifies: the use of *pizzicato* for expressive purposes, brilliant string writing and voicing, rich harmonic patterns, rhythmic drive, and flowing and continuous melodies. He concludes: 'If there are excesses and wayward moments, they are the excesses of sudden discovery and the wayward- ness of the explorer's vision upon reaching a prospect that stretches in all directions.'[lxxxix] This collective newness in Beethoven disposed Heinz Becker to exclaim: 'How far away the tonal world of Haydn — who was still alive — seems here! No wonder that a new audience had to be brought to maturity before the forward-looking ideas and forms of this music could be understood.'[xc]

In the medium of the string quartet, the Op. 59 Quartets demand more from both players and listeners than other works of the time — particularly in the case of the F major Quartet: 'Beethoven does not pamper the players as he realizes the quartet's sonorous potential in precisely the same way he had done with the piano sonatas: for that instrument he had separated the hands and set them at the extreme limits of the keyboard; with the opening measures of Op. 59, No. 1 he expands a three-note texture contained within an octave through a crescendo to an eight-note texture covering over four octaves.'[xci] When David Blum discussed the art of quartet playing with members of the Guarneri String Quartet, second violinist John Dalley remarked on the extent to which Beethoven, in the *Razumovsky* Quartets, had changed the sonority of the quartet sound since his pioneering Op. 18: 'The four parts are more nearly equal in prominence; the lower voices have more resonance. The melodies have a more sustained cantilena quality. There is more concentrated sound ... fuller, richer than before.'[xcii]

It is necessary to the progress of our narrative to return once more to Beethoven's negotiations with publishers. We have seen his dealings with Breitkopf and Härtel, concerning the Op. 59 Quartets, were not fruitful. However, on 20 April 1807 Beethoven entered into his contract with Muzio Clement (see above) to sell the Quartets for two-hundred pounds together with the Piano Concerto No. 4, Op, 58; the Symphony No. 4, Op. 60; the Violin Concerto, Op. 61 including a version with solo part arranged for piano; and the Overture *Coriolan*, Op. 62.[xciii] Thayer comments: 'If an English publisher could afford to pay so high a price for the manuscripts of a German composer, why not a French one?'[xciv] Such indeed was Beethoven's intention and he duly put in hand negotiations to sell the six mentioned compositions in France (Paris), Germany (Vienna) and England (London) more or less simultaneously. On 26 April 1807 he wrote to the publisher Nikolaus Simrock who was then based in his native town of Bonn. He offered the set of six compositions explaining that to protect himself, and his publishers, from the problem of piracy, it was his intention to have these works published simultaneously, as remarked, in Paris, Vienna and London, provided the release dates of the works concerned could by arranged so that no one particular publisher would be disadvantaged. Since Bonn was then occupied by the French, it was through the agency of Nicklaus Simrock that Beethoven sought to achieve publication in Paris. The rights for publication in England were to go to Muzio Clementi. Beethoven requested 1200 gulden from Simrock for the set of works that he considered to be 'a very low price'.[xcv]

At the same time that Beethoven had written to Simrock in Bonn, he wrote in similar terms to Camille Pleyel in Paris. He offered the Op. 59 Quartets together with the other works mentioned for 1200 florins (interchangeable with the gulden) and explained how everything could be organised respecting the dates of publication to the satisfaction of all parties without financial loss.[xcvi] Pleyel's response to Beethoven's proposal is not known but on 31 May Simrock felt obliged to reply to Beethoven in terms of caution. He complains that, as a consequence of the war, 'the music business has been very slow and it keeps getting slower'. Concerning Beethoven's publication proposals, he regrets: 'All that I can do in my lean situation is to scrape together 1,600 livres' (the French currency being then in use). He trusts Beethoven will understand 'and find his offer reasonable'.[xcvii] In the event Breitkopf and Härtel were unable to publish Beethoven's latest works, perhaps through a combination of his financial circumstances and as a consequence of the disruption caused by the Napoleonic conflict.[xcviii]

The Op. 59 Quartets were eventually published in Vienna by the Kunst und Industrie-Comptoir — Bureau des Arts et d'Industrie — in January 1808. Rare copies of the draft wording have survived that Beethoven initially intended to be the dedication to the Op. 59s; normally, after use by the publisher's engraver, they would be discarded. These drafts were once in the possession of Anton Schindler and are contained in a set that includes references to the Fourth Piano Concerto, Fourth Symphony, Violin Concerto (including the transcription for piano) and the Overture *Coriolan*. Of particular interest is that Beethoven changed the dedicatee of the Quartets Op. 59 from 'son Excellence Monseigneur le Comte de Rasoumoffsky' to 'son Altesse Monseigneur le Prince Charles Lichnowsky'. When the Quartets were subsequently published by the Bureau des Arts et d'Industrie, Beethoven had a further change of mind and reverted to the dedications by which they are known today. Alan Tyson conjectures, Beethoven may have briefly contemplated conferring the dedication to Prince Lichnowsky – the former patron to whom he was so indebted – as a means of restoring the friendship between them that had been severed following a severe quarrel in October 1806; Beethoven had taken offence at the provocative behaviour, as he construed it, of some French officers when he was in their company one evening during a stay with the Prince.[xcix]

The Op. 59 Quartets were duly announced with the Title Page styled as follows: 'TROIS QUATUORS / pour deux Violons, / Alto / et / Violoncello. / Composés par / Louis van Beethoven / Oeuvre 59me / Livraison 580. 584. 585. / à Vienne au Magazin de J. Riedel. 582. Hohenmarkt. / [Dedication Page:] TROIS QUATUORS / Très humblement Dédiés à / son Excellence Monsieur Le / COMTE DE RASOUMOFFSKY / Conseiller privé actuel de / SA MAJESTE L'EMPEREUR DE TOUTES LES RUSSIES / Sénateur, Chevalier des ordres / de Saint André, de Saint Alexandre-Newsky et Grand-Croix / de celui de Saint Wladimir de la prémière Classe. &c. &c. / par / Louis van Beethoven.'[c]

A review of the three Op. 59 Quartets was published in

the *Allgemeine musikalische Zeitung* on 18 March 1807, based probably on a private performance when the compositions were still in manuscript.[ci] The reviewer informs his readers: 'Three new, very long and difficult violin quartets by Beethoven, dedicated to the Russian ambassador, Count Razumovsky, also attract attention of all connoisseurs. They are deep in conception and marvellously worked out, but are not universally comprehensible, with the possible exception of the third one, in C major, which by virtue of its individuality, melody, and harmonic power must win over every educated friend of music.'[cii] It is on record that when Count Razumovsky's players first read through the music they were convinced the composer was playing a sophisticated musical joke on them; some present even protested: 'Surely you do not consider these works to be music?'[ciii] Recalling these events years later Carl Czerny told the Beethoven musicologist Otto Jahn: 'When Schuppanzigh first played the Razumovsky Quartet in F, they laughed and were convinced that Beethoven was playing a joke and that it was not the quartet that had been promised.'[civ]

The *Razumovsky* String Quartets were performed in Russia for the first time at the house of the music lover Marshall Count Soltykow; Razumovsky himself had sent him copies of the works to further their appreciation. However, it is on record: 'At the first performance of the *Allegretto* [Quartet in F major, Op. 59, No. 1] at St. Petersburg, where Rasumovsky has sent it, general amusement and surprise were caused by the entry on the cello, and it was thought to be a mistake on the part of the performer.'[cv]

In considering the initial bleak response to the Op. 59 Quartets, Thayer remarks: 'Perhaps no work of Beethoven's met with a more discouraging reception from musicians than these now famous quartets.'[cvi] With the exception of the C major Quartet, the first reactions were a combination of mistrust and open opposition: 'As to society? Its members laughed and spoke of "verrückter musik" — "insane music" or quite openly called the composition the "fickwerk eines wahnsinnigen" — "botched work of a lunatic".'[cvii] While Beethoven's contemporaries were now used to being surprised by his new ideas, those who heard these quartets were utterly perplexed: 'For the first time they were unable to follow Beethoven.'[cviii] In his recognition of Beethoven's departure from the orthodoxy of the period, Joseph Kerman writes: 'The richness of detail, the originality and fertility of musical idea, the commanding coherence, the sheer density and complexity of it all, are fairly breath-taking.' He concludes: 'Little wonder that in the 1800's quartet players who liked Op. 18 found Op. 59 a closed book.'[cix]

The Czech composer and conductor Adalbert Gyrowetz was resident in Vienna at the time the Op. 59 Quartets were in circulation. His own inspirational model was Haydn and he found Beethoven's music difficult to digest. Also at this time in Vienna was one of the composer's ardent admirers Jan Doležalek. He was a composer, instrumentalist and a teacher based in Vienna, having received instruction from Georg Albrechtsberger; Doležalek was renowned for being both an excellent pianist and cellist. Following his inclinations, Doležalek bought a copy of the *Razumovsky* Quartets and later confided this to Gyrowetz — who promptly remonstrated that his friend had wasted his money! Undeterred, Doležalek remained an admirer of Beethoven. He was among his visitors during his final illness and was a pallbearer at his funeral. Years later, in 1852, he spoke to Beethoven's biographer Otto Jahn about the unsympathetic and even hostile attitude of certain Viennese composers towards the composer at the period in question.[cx]

Reflecting on the opinions expressed in the *AmZ* review

of March 1807, William Kinderman writes: 'Time has reversed [hostile contemporary judgements] and the F major and E minor Quartets are now placed among Beethoven's surpassing essays in this genre, overshadowing Op. 59, No.3.'[cxi] As familiarity with Beethoven's new style of string quartet writing became better understood and assimilated into the repertoire, even such differently gifted composer's as Rossini were won over by them. He declared the Op. 59s to be 'the most remarkable productions of the age' and on becoming acquainted with them made it his intention to meet Beethoven — a resolution he eventually fulfilled when he visited Vienna in 1822 to promote some of his own compositions.[cxii] We give the last words here, concerning these circumstances, to Harold Truscott: 'Beethoven had not contemplated cutting off his music from all contact with human understanding, although he may have made the mistake, made by many great artists, of crediting future generations with an advanced degree of intelligent understanding they have not always shown.'[cxiii]

We recall Clementi's Contract to publish several of Beethoven's compositions in England. The *Razumovsky* Quartets duly appeared in London in 1809–10 announced as follows: 'THREE QUARTETS/FOR/Two Violins, Tenor/and VIOLINCELLO/COMPOSED/and Dedicated to His Excellency/COUNT RASOUMOFFSKY/Privy Councillor ... / BY LOUIS VAN BEETHOVEN/Op. 59 – Price 12s [shillings] / ... PRINTED BY CLEMENTI ... / Where may be had by the above author /A Trio Op. 3 / Three Quartets Op. 18, Book first ... A Quintet, Op. 20 ... Op. 18, Book second ... Op. 20, Book second.'[cxiv] It can be seen that in addition to selling the Op. 59 Quartets, Clementi was also offering for sale the String Quartets from the earlier Op. 18 set.

Something of the challenge the Op. 59 Quartets posed

to English players, at the period of their first appearance, derives from an anecdote concerning Thomas Appleby. He was a prominent figure in the musical life of Manchester and a principal director of concerts there. After receiving the Op. 59s in London, Clementi sent a copy of them to Appleby as a friendly gesture to a fellow musician. It so chanced, shortly afterwards, that Appleby received a call from the Italian violin virtuoso Felix Radicati — a pupil of Paganini — who was then on concert tour in England. Radicati noted the string quartet's parts that were on display and exclaimed: 'Ha! Beethoven, as the world says, and as I believe, is a musical madman — for these are not music!' He told Appleby how, when he was in Vienna, Beethoven had showed him the quartets that were still in manuscript. Not being an accomplished string player himself, Beethoven invited Radicati to suggest suitable fingering. On studying the compositions Radicati told Appleby how he had remarked to Beethoven 'he surely could not consider these compositions to be music?' To which Beethoven's response was: 'Oh, they are not for you, but for a later age!'

Appleby's younger son Samuel, an admirer of Beethoven, considered the quartets to be worthy of greater respect. From Thayer we learn: 'Young Appleby believed in them, in spite of Radicati, and after he had studied his part thoroughly, his father invited players of the other instruments to his house and the first [Quartet] in F [the most challenging] was tried. The first movement was declared by all except Appleby to be "crazy music." At the end of the violincello solo on one note, they all burst out laughing; the next four bars all agreed were beautiful. Sudlow, an organist, who played the bass, found much to admire and so much to condemn in the half of the second movement which they succeeded in playing, as to call it "patchwork by a madman".' The group gave up any further attempt to play the work, and it was not until 1813, in London, that Samuel Appleby succeeded in hearing the three Op. 59 Quartets performed in their entirety, finding them, as he believed, 'worthy of their author'.[cxvi]

Beethoven's dealings with the Edinburgh-based George Thomson offer additional insights into the nature of the early reception of the Op. 59 Quartets in Great Britain. In September 1813 he wrote to the composer primarily to inquire regarding his progress with the setting of various Scottish airs. He also found time to remark: 'I am extremely desirous of seeing some more of your charming quartets and sonatas. I spent some days recently in the country with a small select coterie of amateur friends, where, among other things, we played your first *Razumovsky* Quartet in F. We repeated them everyday [by which he means the Quartet and the Quintet in C, Op. 29] with growing pleasure, and we drank with enthusiasm to the health of the composer.' Thomson exclaims: 'What an immortal theme, that adagio'; in his letter the melody is written out. He continues: 'To hear it would give me solace even when dying!' Concerning the abilities of instrumentalists to perform the works, he adds: 'But alas, my friend, in Scotland we do not have a dozen persons (the professionals included) who could take part in these quartets, and not one who could play *correctly* the first violin part in all three! What would my happiness have been, if fate had placed me in Vienna, where I would have been able to hear your quartets, sonatas, symphonies well played everyday!'[cxvii]

Five years later Thomson was once more contractually engaged with Beethoven concerning further settings of Scottish airs. On 22 June 1818 he felt obliged to write to the composer: 'Alas my good sir! Everyone in this country finds that your works are much too difficult; there are only a very small number of masters of the greatest skill who will be able to play them.' Citing his experience of dealing with his agent in London, he states: 'I recently wrote to my correspondent, one of the foremost music dealers in London, to note how much this surprised and distressed me, and his response — "Although a great and sublime artist, *Beethoven is not understood* and his arrangement of your songs is *much too difficult* for the public".' Thomson expressed the hope that Beethoven would publish a volume of quartets 'with all the richness of your genius, but easy to play, particularly first violin'. He asked him if he had published any trios or quartets of late? He considered this would be a great gift to amateurs 'and for that matter our connoisseurs themselves'. Regarding the String Quartets, Op. 59, he complains: 'I have only twice had the extreme pleasure of hearing the Quartets dedicated to Count Razumovsky played well, although I have had them for several years. Our professors do not play them because of the intense study and great work that they demand. I infinitely regret this, because I admire them with enthusiasm.' Thomson's final plea to Beethoven would have fallen on deaf ears (unfortunate pun unintended): 'Could your genius not lower itself to compose music equally superb, but less difficult of execution, so amateurs could partake of the feast?'[cxviii]

For an understanding of the early reception of the *Razumovsky* Quartets in France, we turn to the writings of the musicologist Joseph de Marliave. He opens his account: 'The success of Op. 59 in France was no more propitious [than it had been in Vienna].' He cites the enterprising endeavours of The Bohrer String Quartet, established by the brothers Tilman and Urham who included them in their programme for 1831, but with little public interest. De Marliave next mentions the Beethoven enthusiast François Antoine Habeneck. He is remembered today in Beethoven musicology primarily for drawing Beethoven's symphonies to the attention of French concertgoers. However, an ardent admirer of Beethoven's chamber music, and anxious to create wider popularity of these works, he conceived the idea of having separate movements of the string quartets performed by a string orchestra, selecting those likely to make the most general appeal. In 1832, at the fourth concert on 18 March, the programme included two movements from the Op. 59 set – the *Adagio* from the F major Quartet and the Fugue from the C major Quartet. A measure of the standing of these concerts is that Mendelssohn played the composer's Fourth Piano Concerto. A critic in the *Review musicale* of 24 March 1832 found the *Adagio* in the third Quartet 'far from satisfying' on the grounds that 'it failed to hold attention and sustain flagging interest ... One felt it to be no more than an orchestral piece, lacking the variety of colour and phrasing that wind instruments afford'. The critic in question was, however, more impressed by the Fuge, the performance of which he considered to be 'technically perfect and artistically flawless'. He commended the piece provided it was well played: 'The vigorous movement of this fugue demands only perfect ensemble, accuracy, and finish ... exact precision and fine balance of bowing that blend all these technical difficulties into a perfect whole, finally, incomparable zest.'[cxix]

According to de Marliave, with the passing of time the Op. 59 Quartets enjoyed greater success – but only slowly. He records how between 1830 and 1850 the Op. 59 Quartets appeared several times in the programmes of chamber concerts, but not with any regularity. In 1839 two more brothers founded the Franco-Mendès Quartet and performed the C major Quartet to some acclaim. De Marliave also identifies the instrumentalists Aumont and Armaingaud as pioneering the F major Quartet in January 1840 at the house of the music-lover M. Petzold. This rendering of the work disposed the critic of the *Revue et Gazette musicale* to comment fulsomely: 'The finest virtuoso in the world, playing one of the loveliest of melodies, could never equal the effect produced by the four instruments in this beautiful quartet, especially in the slow movement, where each successive entry of the exquisitely moving theme in F minor stirred the audience to applause and admiration.'

Beethoven *Razumovsky* String Quartets may be said to have found a secure place in the French chamber music repertoire from about 1850. It was then that the distinguished cellist Pierre-François-Alexandre Chevillard founded the *Société des Quatuors de Beethoven*. De Marliave states: '[From] that time forward a sustained effort was made to arouse public appreciation of these magnificent works by means of regular performances both in France and in Germany, and it is to the honour of Chevillard that the attempt met with unqualified success.'[cx]

We draw our account of Beethoven's String Quartets Op. 59 to a conclusion with a section of modern-day estimations of their merits.

Joseph Kerman: 'To think back over the dozen separate movements of Op. 59 is to be struck by the boldness of the expressive imagination at work. The exaggerated lament of the F minor *Adagio molto e mesto*, the stellar quiet of the E major Hymn, the wonderfully brilliant *Allegretto vivace e sempre scherzando* of the F major Quartet, the parody minuet of the C major – Beethoven is manipulating unheard-of extremes with an enthusiasm that is infectious or awesome or both ... Pre-eminently the *Razumovsky* Quartets are explorers, experimenters.' Kinderman considers 'Beethoven's vision sometimes outstrips his achievement' – with its overtones of Robert Browning's: 'Ah, but a man's reach should exceed his grasp, Or what's a heaven for?' But, he concludes: The *Rasumovsky* Quartets 'may be flawed by a hectic infusion of Beethoven's characteristic vital energy ... we could hardly expect it to have been otherwise ... We would hardly want it otherwise.'[cxxi]

Paul Bekker: '[The] central idea of triumph gives rise to the monumental style of the *Razumovsky* Quartets and impels to a mighty display of force ... It is an idea which strains the form of the string quartet to the uttermost, and the result is a series of works of a majesty and expressive power such as no one before Beethoven had dreamed of obtaining from four string instruments. This was the victory won in the *Razumovsky* Quartets.'[cxxii]

Maynard Solomon: 'If the heroic symphonies are "speeches to the nation" [Paul Bekker, *Beethoven*, 1925] then the quartets are interior monologues addressed to a private self whose emotional states comprise a variegated tapestry of probing moods and feelings ... Here in these Quartets, he will reveal his deepest feelings, his sense of loss, his pain his strivings.'[cxxiii]

Igor Stravinsky: 'Razumovsky deserves a twenty-one gun salute for commissioning the set of three quartets and praise for having the nimbleness of fingers to be able to participate in their performance as second violin.'[cxxiv]

[i] Wilhelm von Lenz, *Beethoven et ses trois styles*, 1855, pp. 144–5, quoted in: Joseph de Marliave, 1925, (reprint 1961), pp. 141–2.
[ii] Rebecca Clarke, *The [Beethoven] quartets as a player sees them*, in: *Music & Letters, Beethoven*, Special Issue: Vol. VIII, No. 2, 1927, pp. 180–1.
[iii] Arthur Shepherd, 1935, p. 28.
[iv] Barry Cooper, 2000.
[v] Cited in: Robert Winter and Robert Martin, editors, 1994, p. 150. Christian Schubart outlined his views in: *Ideen zu einer Aesthetik der Tonkunst* (1806). Beethoven was interested in Schubart's writings, particularly his theory in which he characterised the musical keys with feelings and ascribed to them a certain 'psyche'. For example, he considered A-flat minor implied 'difficult struggle' and 'wailing lament' and B minor suggested 'patience' and 'calm awaiting one's fate'. In comparison, C major was the key with the connotation 'completely pure'. For an account of Schubart's theories and

Beethoven's attachment to them, see: Anton Schindler, 1860, English edition: Donald MacArdle, 1966, pp. 366-7.

vi As expressed by Leon Botstei, *Music, culture and society in Beethoven's Vienna*, in: Robert Winter and Robert Martin, editors, 1994, pp. 91–2.

vii Joseph Kerman, 1967, p. 151.

viii The words quoted appear in several Beethoven sources, sometimes in a modified form. We cite them here from Paul Yarbrough, Liner notes to The Alexander String Quartet, *Ludwig van Beethoven, The String Quartets*, Arte Nova Classics (undated, c. 1980).

ix Derived, in part, from: Ludwig Nohl, 1880, p. 48. See also, Peter Clive, 2001, p. 197; and Denis Matthews, 1997, p. 2.

x Donald Francis Tovey in: Michael Tilmouth, editor, *The Classics of Music: Talks, Essays, and Other Writings Previously Uncollected*, 2001, p. 336.

xi Philip Radcliffe, 1978, p. 48.

xii This is the opinion of Robert Simpson; see: *The chamber music for strings*, in: Denis Arnold, and Nigel Fortune editors, *The Beethoven companion*, 1973, p. 251. Simpson considers the Quintet in C 'to be shamefully neglected'.

xiii William Kinderman, editor, 2005, p. 5.

xiv Harold Truscott, 1968, p. 28.

xv Joseph de Marliave, *Beethoven's quartets*, 1925, (reprint 1961), p. 56.

xvi William Kinderman, 1997, p. 108.

xvii Frank Kämpfer, Liner notes to The Alexander String Quartet, *Beethoven: String Quartets*, Arte Nova Classics.

xviii Anonymous, Introduction to Philharmonia Score, *Ludwig van Beethoven, String Quartets, Op. 59*, Nos. 1–3, Wiener Philharmonischer Verlag, No. 318. (undated).

xix Paul Griffiths, 1983, pp. 86–7.

xx Theodore Albrecht, 1996, Vol. 1, Letter No, 47, pp. 80–1.

xxi Emily Anderson, editor and translator, 1961, Vol. 1, Letter No. 132, pp. 150–1.

xxii Philip G. Downs, 1992, p. 596.

xxiii Theodor W. Adorno, 1998, pp. 88–9.

xxiv Joseph Kerman, *Beethoven quartet audiences: actual, potential, ideal*, in: Robert Winter, and Robert Martin editors, *The Beethoven quartet companion*, 1994, p. 15.

xxv Donald Jay Grout and Claude V. Palisca editors, 1988, p. 640.

xxvi Malcolm Miler, *Peak Experience* in: William Kinderman, editor, *The string quartets of Beethoven*, Urbana, 2005, p. 85.

xxvii Theodore Albrecht, 1996, Vol. 1, Letter No. 58, pp. 100–1.

xxviii *Ibid*, Letter No. 34, pp. 63–4.

xxix See: Beethoven House Digital Archives, *Beethoven Gallery* and Library Document B 2388. Although this portrait situates Beethoven in a somewhat idealised pastoral setting, the artist is not considered to have sacrificed his appearance in striving for Romantic effect.

xxx A facsimile reproduction of a later portrait of the composer can be seen in the Beethoven House Digital Archives, Library Documents B 7 and HCB Bi 1. A copy of this portrait is in the New York Public Library. For his portrait, Beethoven wore a blue tailcoat and white neckerchief, then both very fashionable. See also: H. C. Robbins Landon, 1970, p. 7.

xxxi Quoted in: Ludwig Nohl, *Beethoven depicted by his contemporaries*, 1880, p. 58.

xxxii Emily Anderson, editor and translator, 1961, Vol. 1, Letter No. 124, p. 142.
xxxiii *Ibid*, Letter No. 131, pp. 149—50.
xxxiv *Ibid*, Letter No. 144, pp. 169—70.
xxxv *Ibid*, Letter No. 150, p. 174.
xxxvi For a comprehensive account of Beethoven's many illnesses, see: Anton Neumayr, Medi-Ed Press, 1994—1997, pp. 252—3.
xxxvii For a detailed account of Kaspar Karl and his dealings with Beethoven's publishers see Peter Clive, 2001, pp. 20—1. Kaspar Karl had a reputation for driving hard bargains, was known as a 'skinflint' and did not always act circumspectly in his relationships with Beethoven's publishers.
xxxviii Emily Anderson, editor and translator, 1961, Vol. 1, Letter No. 58, p. 74.
xxxix Theodore Albrecht, 1996, Vol. 1, Letter No. 86, pp. 144—6 and footnote 10.
xl *Ibid*, Letter No. 87, pp. 146—7.
xli *Ibid*, Letter No. 91, pp. 149—50.
xlii For biographical details of the members of Count Razumovsky's Quartet, see Peter Clive, 2001.
xliii A portrait of Karl Holz is reproduced in facsimile in the Beethoven House, Digital Archives, Document B 837. Another of Schuppanzigh's second violinists was Joseph Mayseder. He joined the Quartet around 1800 and later performed in several of Beethoven's orchestral concerts A portrait of Joseph Mayseder is reproduced in facsimile in the Beethoven House, Digital Archives, Document B 618.
xliv Anton Felix Schindler, *Beethoven as I knew him*, edited by Donald W. MacArdle and translated by Constance S. Jolly from the German edition of 1860, 1966, p. 60.
xlv Beethoven House, Digital Archives Document B 858/a.
xlvi Beethoven House, Digital Archives Document B 168.
xlvii H. C. Robbins Landon, 1970, p. 112.
xlviii With acknowledgement to Peter Clive 2001, pp. 329—31.
xlix Beethoven House, Digital Archives, Document B 930.
l Beethoven House, Digital Archives, Document B 1333.
li Ludwig Nohl, *Beethoven depicted by his contemporaries*, 1880, pp. 61—3. A More accessible account is given by Robert Winter in, *Performing Beethoven quartets in their first century* in: Robert Winter and Robert Martin, editors, 1994, p. 37.
lii Paul Griffiths, 1983, p. 86.
liii Derived from: Robert Winter, *Performing Beethoven quartets in their first century*, in, Robert Winter, and Robert Martin, editors, *The Beethoven quartet companion*, 1994, pp. 43—4. See also Joseph de Marliave, 1925 (reprint 1961), pp. 48—9.
liv Elliot Forbes editor, *Thayer's life of Beethoven*, 1967, p. 401.
lv David Wyn Jones: *Beethoven and the Viennese legacy* in: Robin Stowell, editor *The Cambridge companion to the string quartet*, 2003, pp. 214—6.
lvi Paul Bekker, 1925, p. 316.
lvii See, for example, Nicholas Mathew, Internet article, *The three Razumovsky quartets*, Op. 59, 2014.
lviii Mentioned in the context of the *Razumovsky* Quartets by Phillip Radcliffe, 1973, p. 49.
lix Elliot Forbes editor, *Thayer's life of Beethoven*, 1967, p. 401.
lx As remarked by Maynard Solomon, 1977, p. 145.

[lxi] Nicolas Slonimsky, *Writings on music*, in: Electra Slonimsky Yourke, editor, 2003–5, p. 4.
[lxii] Catherine Dower, *Alfred Einstein on music: selected music criticisms*, 1991, p. 125.
[lxiii] Denis Matthews, 1985, p. 133.
[lxiv] Joseph de Marliave, 1925 (reprint 1961), p. 60.
[lxv] John Daverio, *Manner, tone and tendency in Beethoven's chamber music for strings*, in: Glenn Stanley editor, *The Cambridge companion to Beethoven*, 2000, pp. 154–5.
[lxvi] Artur Schnabel, 1961, pp. 187–8.
[lxvii] William Kinderman, 1997, p. 108.
[lxviii] Emily Anderson, editor and translator, 1961, Letter No. 132, pp. 150–1. For an audio version of this letter, together with the German text, see: Beethoven House, Digital Archives, Document Sammlung H. C. Bodmer, HCB Br 67. In his letter, Beethoven indicates he was prepared to have the whole of *Fidelio* transcribed for piano – a task he later entrusted to his pupil Carl Czerny.
[lxix] Emily Anderson, editor and translator, 1961, Letter No. 134, p. 150 and note 8. For an audio version of this letter, together with the German text see: Beethoven House, Digital Archives, Document Sammlung, H. C. Bodmer, Br 68.
[lxx] Emily Anderson, editor and translator, 1961, Letter No. 137, pp. 156–8.
[lxxi] *Ibid*, Letter No. 135, p. 153.
[lxxii] Barry Cooper, 1990, p. 36.
[lxxiii] For an account of Beethoven's relationship with Franz Brunsvik and his family, see Peter Clive, 2001, pp. 61– 4.
[lxxiv] Emily Anderson, editor and translator, 1961, Letter No. 142, p. 167. For an audio version of this letter, together with the German text, see: Beethoven House, Digital Archives, Document Sammlung H. C. Bodmer, HCB BBr 84.
[lxxv] *Ibid*, Anderson, Letter No. 143, pp. 168–9. In this letter Beethoven asked Brunswick if he will arrange for the Hungarians to invite him to give a series of concerts for which he requests payment of 200 gold ducats. Nothing, however, came of this suggestion.
[lxxvi] *Ibid*, Anderson, Letter No. 148, pp. 172–3. For an audio version of this letter, together with the German text, see: Beethoven House, Digital Archives, Document Sammlung H. C. Bodmer, HCB Br 125.
[lxxvii] When Alexander Thayer undertook his researches, 'A36' may have contained 34 leaves. See: Elliot Forbes editor, *Thayer's life of Beethoven*, 1967, p. 408.
[lxxviii] See: Beethoven House, Digital Archives Documents BH 100 (SBH 616) and Mh 72 (SBH 617).
[lxxix] Alan Tyson, *Sketches for the String Quartets, Op. 59 (1806)*, in: Douglas Porter Johnson, editor, *The Beethoven sketchbooks: history, reconstruction, inventory, 1985*, pp. 524–6 and Alan Tyson, *The Razumovsky Quartets: Some aspects of the sources*, in: *Beethoven studies 3*, 1982, pp. 107–140. The sketch-origins of the Op. 59 Quartets are also discussed by Joseph de Marliave, *Beethoven's quartets*, 1925 (reprint 1961), p. 56; Michael Broyles, *Beethoven: the emergence and evolution of Beethoven's heroic style*, 1987,

lxix p. 102; and William Kinderman editor, *The string quartets of Beethoven*, 2005, p. 325.
lxx Douglas Porter Johnson, editor, *The Beethoven sketchbooks: history, reconstruction, inventory*, 1985, pp. 147–8.
lxxi Richard Kramer, see above, p. 230. See also Beethoven House Digital Archives, Document BH 62, SBH 544.
lxxii For additional commentary, see Beethoven House Digital Archives, Document BH 62, SBH 544. See also Richard Kinderman, 2005, p. 325.
lxxiii Ernest and Paul Mendelssohn, the latter brother of the composer, possessed one of the finest nineteenth-century collections of Beethoven manuscripts in private ownership. It was donated to the Berlin Royal Library in 1908 and included autographs of the Fourth, Fifth and Seventh Symphonies, the String Quartets Op. 59, No.1, Op. 74 and Op. 132, the Septet and the *Archduke* Trio. See Douglas Porter Johnson, editor, *The Beethoven sketchbooks: history, reconstruction, inventory*, 1985, p. 37.
lxxiv See Beethoven House Digital Archives, Document BH 62.
lxxv Michael Broyles, 1987, pp. 97–98.
lxxvi Paul Griffiths, 1983, pp. 86–7.
lxxvii Marion M. Scott, 1940, p. 255.
lxxviii Philip G. Downs, 1992, p. 596.
lxxix Maynard Solomon, 1977, p. 201.
xc Heinz Becker, Liner notes to The Amadeus Quartet, *Beethoven: The string quartets*, 1974. He adds: 'It was in the *Razumovsky* Quartets that Beethoven succeeded for the first time in creating a perfect synthesis between homophonic and polyphonic styles of writing.'
xci Philip G. Downs, 1992, p. 596.
xcii David Blum, *The art of quartet playing: the Guarneri Quartet in conversation with David Blum*, 1986, pp. 15–8.
xciii Beethoven's negotiations with Clementi are discussed by Anton Felix Schindler, *Beethoven as I knew him*, edited by Donald W. MacArdle and translated by Constance S. Jolly from the German edition of 1860, 1966, p. 137. For the text of Beethoven's Contract with Clementi, set out in French – as was the composer's custom in his dealings with foreign publishers – see Emily Anderson, editor and translator, 1961, Vol. 3, pp. 1419–20.
xciv Elliot Forbes editor, *Thayer's life of Beethoven*, 1967, p. 420.
xcv Emily Anderson, editor and translator, 1961, Letter No. 141, pp. 166–7. For an audio version of this letter see: Beethoven House, Digital Archives, Document H.C. Bodmer, HCB Br 222.
xcvi Beethoven House, Digital Archives, Documents HCB Br 222m BGA 278 and NE 161.
xcvii Theodore Albrecht, 1996, Vol. 1, Letter No. 121, pp. 189–90.
xcviii *Ibid*, Vol. 1, commentary to Letter No. 118, p. 185.
xcix Alan Tyson, *The Razumovsky Quartets: Some aspects of the sources*, in *Beethoven studies 3*, 1982, pp. 134–5 and Plates III and IV – the plates illustrate Beethoven's draft texts for the dedications that he originally had in mind.
c Beethoven House, Digital Archives, Document Sammlung Jean van der Spek, C Op. 59. Another edition is illustrated by the publisher Tobias Haslinger as Digital Archives, Document C 59/2.

[ci] Joseph de Marliave, 1925, (reprint 1961), p. 138.
[cii] Wayne M. Senner, Robin Wallace and William Meredith, editors, *The critical reception of Beethoven's compositions by his German contemporaries*, 1999, Vol. 1, pp. 52–3.
[ciii] Donald Jay Grout and Claude V. Palisca editors, A history of Western music, 1988, p. 640.
[civ] Elliot Forbes editor, *Thayer's life of Beethoven*, 1967, p. 409.
[cv] Joseph de Marliave, 1925 (reprint 1961), pp. 139–40.
[cvi] Elliot Forbes editor, *Thayer's life of Beethoven*, 1967, p. 409. Thayer cites a later article in the May issue of the *AmZ* anticipating the Quartet's publication: 'In Vienna Beethoven's most recent, difficult but fine quartets have become more and more popular. Music-lovers hope to see them printed soon.'
[cvii] Heinz Becker, Liner notes to The Amadeus Quartet, *Beethoven: The string quartets*, 1974.
[cviii] *Ibid*.
[cix] Joseph Kerman, *The Beethoven quartets*, 1967, p. 100.
[cx] Elliot Forbes editor, *Thayer's life of Beethoven*, 1967, p. 409. See also Peter Clive, 2001, p. 93.
[cxi] William. Kinderman, 1997, p. 108.
[cxii] Joseph de Marliave, 1925, (reprint 1961), p. 139
[cxiii] Harold Truscott, 1968, p. 5.
[cxiv] Alan Tyson, 1963, p. 53.
[cxv] Elliot Forbes editor, *Thayer's life of Beethoven*, 1967, p. 409.
[cxvi] *Ibid*, p. 410.
[cxvii] Theodore Albrecht, 1996, Vol. 2, Letter No. 176, pp. 14–19.
[cxviii] *Ibid*, Vol. 2, Letter No. 249, pp. 142–7.
[cxix] Quoted and adapted from, Joseph de Marliave, 1925, (reprint 1961), pp. 139–40.
[cxx] *Ibid*, p. 141.
[cxxi] Joseph Kerman, 1967, pp. 151–2.
[cxxii] Paul Bekker, 1925, p. 317.
[cxxiii] Maynard Solomon, 1977, p. 201.
[cxxiv] Igor Stravinsky, 1972, p. 256.

STRING QUARTET IN F MAJOR, OP. 59, NO. 1

'The first of these quartets, that in F major, moves, emotionally, from a quiet consciousness of power to a fantastic and excited display of activity, thence to sorrowful plaints and, finally, to a sense of vigorous well-being.'

Paul Bekker, *Beethoven*, 1925, p. 316.

'With an assurance and felicity never equalled before or since, Beethoven extracts here from the four instruments every conceivable effect within their capacity. With them he seems literally to tread new paths of sound, and when the full expression of his thought demands a richer colouring he manages to create the effect pro-

> duced by other instruments, the oboe, the clarinet, even the organ or harp, or, especially in the *Scherzo*, the horn.'

Joseph de Marliave, *Beethoven's Quartets,* 1925 (reprint 1961), p. 62.

> 'The Quartet in F touches heights immeasurably above anything that had ever before been attempted in this form. Both in content and in treatment of the instruments it must have seemed astonishing beyond words at the time it was written ... But the varied yet intensely logical moods of the first movement, the Olympian humour of the *scherzo* and the poignant sensibility of the *adagio* ... make it now one of the most entrancing works to the player in the whole repertoire of chamber music.'

Rebecca Clarke, *The Quartets as a Player sees them*, in *Beethoven: Musical Times*, Special Issue: Vol. VIII, No. 2, 1927, p. 181.

> 'The composer's unparalleled power of enriching and expanding his forms, and adapting his media thereto, is revealed just as vividly in the first of this great set as in any other work of the *middle* period. Here, once and for all, the salon and the peruke [periwig] are left far behind, and the four instruments of the ensemble assume a measurably higher degree of artistic power and dignity than ever before,'

Arthur Shepherd, *The String Quartets of Ludwig van Beethoven*, 1935, p. 28.

'The F major *Razumovsky* Quartet — the greatest of the three in Op. 59, I should say, in spite of something unsettled in the sequence of the movements, certainly the greatest in its superb opening *Allegro* — can serve, almost as well as the [*Eroica*] Symphony to introduce Beethoven's second period and whatever critical equipment may be brought to bear upon it ... [Coming] upon the first *Razumovsky* Quartet after the six of Op. 18 is like coming into a new artistic universe.'

Joseph Kerman, *The Beethoven Quartets*, 1967, pp. 92–3 and p. 100.

'Of the three *Razumovsky* Quartets [Op. 59, No.1] is the longest and gives perhaps the fullest and most comprehensive picture of Beethoven's personality at this stage of his career. Of the contemporary orchestral works, it comes nearest, in its massive power and range of mood, to the Third Symphony [*Eroica*]; the broadly melodious flow of the first movement also has kinship with that of the Violin Concerto.'

Philip Radcliffe, *Beethoven's String Quartets*, 1978, p. 60.

'Modern critical judgement has largely reversed the opinion of the *Razumovsky's* first audiences, who found only the third quartet acceptable. Today it is the first of the two quartets, with their use of sonata form in so many of the movements, their vast expressive range, and above all their

> symphonic strivings and scale, that come in for admiration.'

Alan Tyson, editor, *The Razumovsky Quartets: Some aspects of the sources, Beethoven studies 3*, 1982, p. 131.

> 'The Op. 59 are a world apart from the Op. 18, they are post-*Eroica* works and exhibit many aspects of that great deepening of Beethoven's musical style which the composition of the *Eroica* Symphony seems to have affected. Most obviously, in the enormous size of the individual movements, the straining of the medium and the generally symphonic, orchestral character of the work, which have led some writers to dub Op. 59, No. 1 an *Eroica* for string quartet.'

Barry Cooper, *The Beethoven Compendium: a guide to Beethoven's life and music*, 1991, p. 234.

On the Autograph to the String Quartet in F major, Beethoven wrote: '*Quartetto 1mo. La prima parte solamente una volta – Quartetto angefangen am 26 May. 1806.*' By then work on the composition was well advanced and his words may be taken to indicate not so much a beginning but rather the date of his final working out of the text.[i] A sense of scale is evident from the outset. Despite being designated *Allegro*, the work has a performing time approaching, and occasionally surpassing, forty minutes. The proportions of the composition were not lost to the reviewer writing in the contemporary March issue of the *Allgemeine musikalische Zeitung*. Commenting on the Op. 59 set as a whole he observed: 'Three new, very long and difficult violin quartets by Beethoven, dedicated to the

Russian ambassador, Count Razumovsky ... attract attention of all connoisseurs.[ii]

A convincing interpretation demands the highest level of musicianship from the four performers and makes considerable demands upon them. By way of illustration we cite the recollections of the Edinburgh-based music critic Conrad Wilson. He recalls interviewing Norbert Brainin, the leader of the celebrated Amadeus String Quartet, who declared: 'Of all Beethoven's great quartets, it is the one that still places the greatest physical demands on its performers — more even than the big introvert works of his last years.' He admitted the piece was so exhausting, and likewise Schubert's G major Quartet, D 887, that he and his colleagues endeavoured never to take it on tour.[iii] String player and musicologist Alison Bullock, writing on the occasion of the BBC's celebration of Beethoven's music, remarked in similar vein: '[It] is a fiendishly complex piece of composition, with dramatic harmonic twists, among other features, and a double fugue in the middle of the movement.'[iv] Philip Downs concurs with the foregoing, asserting: '[The Op. 59s] demand more from players and listeners than other works of the time ... Beethoven does not pamper the players as he realizes the quartet's sonorous potential in precisely the same way he had done with the piano sonatas: for that instrument he had separated the hands and set them at the extreme limits of the keyboard; with the opening measures of Op. 59, No. 1 he expands a three-note texture, contained within an octave through a crescendo, to an eight-note texture covering over four octaves.'[v]

Many commentators find the opening *Allegro* bears comparison with the corresponding movement of the *Eroica* Symphony. Amongst these is William Kinderman who draws attention to the movement's 'immense scale', the development of which is much longer than the exposition and, moreover, is 'studded with a big double fugue'.[vi] But other considerations than mere largeness of scale are also at work: 'The broadness and spaciousness of the opening theme also defines the general tone and character of the movement. Its spaciousness is so apparent that some writers have, on those grounds, defined the entire quartet as symphonic ... The lyricism of Op. 59, No.1 is too predominant, the motion too relaxed, and the melodic emphasis too oriented towards ornamental variation to permit it to fall within the symphonic category.'[vii] In similar manner Beethoven authority David Wyn Jones elucidates: 'Although the scale of the three works [Op. 59] has always invited comparison with the *Eroica* Symphony, this is, in many ways, an inadequate juxtaposition, for Beethoven draws on a range of musical resources not evident in the symphony; in particular, non of the three quartets evokes the characteristic heroic quality evident in that work and others from the period such as the *Coriolan* Overture, the Fifth Symphony and *Leonore*.' Of the F major Quartet in particular, Jones believes the expansive nature of its opening movement owes more to the *Pastoral* Symphony than to the *Eroica* – 'with its leisurely paragraphs that prefer lyricism to forceful drama and its many pages of slow harmonic movement ... The first subject is remarkable [for its] nineteen bars of melody'.[viii] Alan Tyson refers to the work's 'dizzy sense of scale'. His study of the sketch sources reveals Beethoven originally planned a repeat of the second part of the development and recapitulation in the first movement. Only after the movement was completed in score, and he was able to contemplate the vastness of his creation, did he delete the repeat signs.[ix]

Dennis Matthews opens his commentary to the work with the remark: 'The new scale of Op. 59, No. 1 in F is apparent in the length and breadth of its opening subject ... [Its] theme is the source of much that follows: the transitional material, the cadence theme of the exposition, the fugato development, and the harmonised apotheosis in the coda.'[x] The development section alone, in what is one of Beethoven's longest first quartet movements, runs to a length of more than one hundred and fifty measures. With regard to Beethoven's craftsmanship, in the art of writing for the medium of the string quartet, the 'largeness of utterance is enhanced through the widened range of the string-registration'.[xi] In this context, Romain Rolland admired 'the remarkable unison passage for full strings ... high work for first violin ... [and] wonderful colour effects'.[xii] To quote Jones once more: 'The variety of sonority and texture that is suggested by the first subject and the fugato passage in the development section is a major advance on the more circumspect textures of Op. 18.'[xiii] In the words of Philip Radcliffe: 'The whole course of the development is wonderfully planned; it is resourceful, imaginative and full of carefully graded and controlled tension that is characteristic of the whole movement.'[xiv]

In his analysis of Beethoven's construction, Michael Broyles finds 'a note of uncertainty' permeates the opening movement deriving from the use of six-four harmony. He elaborates: 'As the theme progresses, tonal direction becomes clearer ... Rhythmically the first eighteen bars have an introductory quality ... The theme moves in a series of spacious motivic gestures.' In his estimation: 'The theme provides a wealth of motivic potential, and a great deal of the theme is an exploration.' He quotes Joseph Kerman who calls the main theme 'the *protean theme*' that comes back again and again transformed.[xv]

The American musicologist Arthur Shepherd draws attention to '[Beethoven's] matured and deepened powers of expression' that he considers are in evidence from the very outset of the work: 'The principal theme takes a longer curve ... The superb expansion of the theme as it reaches its apex in the high register of the first violin gives token of a splendid virility that is utterly devoid of strained rhetoric or bombast.'[xvi] The French musicologist Joseph de Marliave was moved to write of the composer's 'inspired spirituality' in response to the music's large-scale unfolding themes and flowing transitions between its various sections.[xvii] Beethoven gives the opening theme to the cello, heard above a pulsating accompaniment, which is taken up by the first violin that 'at once suggests vast space and breadth ... a sense of suspended motion'.[xviii] It is thought that when composing the cello part of the F major String Quartet, Beethoven had in mind Joseph Linke, then first cellist at the Theater an der Wien and a member of Ignaz Schuppanzigh's String Quartet. Beethoven had a high opinion of Linke and it was for him that he composed his two Cello Sonatas, Op. 102; Linke also took part in the first performances of the late quartets.

Expanding on his imagery of 'inspired spirituality', de Marliave offers his response to the F major's opening: 'The cello gives out its subject ... The phrase moves on its way serenely through the unchanging beat of the accompaniment, meditative and sweet, like the calm after a storm ... With unhesitating precision this wonderful fabric of sound is woven strand by strand before our eyes ... Each instrument is a voice singing in turn the poet's joy and strife.' He concludes in his characteristic fulsome manner: 'The whole passage is wonderfully effective. No composer ever realized quite as Beethoven did the latent expressive force in a series of long-held *mezzo piano* chords. Voices from an invisible choir seem to float up out of a mysterious gulf to the soul of the artist hovering above.'[xix] Philip Radcliffe expresses his response to Beethoven's creation in more strictly musicological terms: '[When] the music is on a larger scale the harmonies move with greater deliberation. This results in a spaciousness which is one of the most distinguishing features of Beethoven's style, sometimes giving a feeling of deep serenity and sometimes of prolonged suspense.' He cites the spaciousness of the first movement of Mozart's Quintet in C major, adding 'Beethoven's first *Razumovsky* Quartet begins in a rather similar way, with the same mixture of repeated chords and slowly moving harmonies ... [but] considerably more leisurely, with passages which could only make their effect in a movement planned on a very large scale.'[xx]

Regarding Beethoven's constructional procedures, Radcliffe finds him developing ideas he pioneered in the Piano Sonata in D, Op. 28 and the String Quintet in C, Op. 29 – both from 1801: '[He] builds, not upon short incisive figures, but on flowing and continuous melodies that are capable of being divided at a later stage into smaller units.'[xxi] Worthy of reiteration is that Beethoven does not make use of repeats in the first movement. We quote Paul Griffiths in support of our previous remarks: 'The first movement of the first *Razumovsky* Quartet in F major, is famously the first sonata movement to dispense with the customary repeat of the exposition, but this is no gratuitous innovation. On a simple level it is necessary because the movement is amply long enough without any repetition, extending for nearly four hundred bars in common time.' On a more deeply structural level he argues the absence of repeats makes the movement a single broad sweep, 'since the beginning is now only a beginning, never to be rediscovered'.[xxii] The sketches reveal Beethoven planned to have both the development and recapitulation repeated and contemplated a projected large internal repeat in the scherzo and in the coda of the finale, all of which were subsequently rejected. If he had retained these, the F major Quartet would have rivalled the *Eroica* Symphony in its duration. As it stands, the first movement alone has an expressive performing time of about twelve minutes.

Grand though it is in breadth of design, Basil Lam reminds us that Beethoven keeps within the tradition he had inherited, suggesting Mozart's C major Quintet, K 515 may have been his inspirational model.[xxiii] All four movements are cast in sonata form and the companion Quartets, Nos. 2 and 3 each have three movements also in sonata form. The conspicuous role of the cello at the outset of the movement has been mentioned. With this in mind, Robin Stowell contends: '[It] is surly the spacious opening melody, presented without preamble by the cello, that makes the F major *Razumovsky* Quartet, Op. 59, No.1 the most memorable of the set; nor is the cello prepared to relinquish its lead, supplying the second subject, initiating the *scherzando* with its monotonous rhythm and presenting the *thème russe* of the finale (see later). In none of his earlier quartets is the cello so consistently called upon to initiate.'[xxiv] Perhaps it is not surprising that the composition was once known to an earlier generation as the *Cello Quartet* on account of the prominence given to that instrument.[xxv]

Regarding the construction of the movement, the entire *Allegro* grows steadily but assuredly from the opening cello melody. In Harold Truscott's opinion: 'This is one of the greatest of all Beethoven's openings, held tonally in suspension from the beginning until it sounds the first decisive tonic chord in bar nineteen.' He likens the four-bar opening cello phrase to a seed from which are drawn, bit by bit, not only the structure of the first movement but also its texture and aspects of the other movements as well.[xxvi] In Truscott's invocation of growth from a seed, we are reminded of the philosopher Isaiah Berlin's views of the concept of creation-origins when under the impulse of a transition to Romantic ideals: 'There is no copying, there is no adaptation, there is no learning of the rules, there is no external check, there is no structure you must understand and adapt yourself to before you can proceed. The heart of the entire process is invention, creation, making, out of literally nothing, or out of any materials that may be to hand.'[xxvii]

Counterpoint comes to the fore as the music becomes evermore contrapuntal. In his study of Beethoven's writing for the string quartet, Joseph Kerman comments on the manner in which contrapuntal episodes 'had haunted the development sections of the Op. 18 Quartets'. With regard to the first movement of the F major Quartet, his recognition of the composer's new powers is unqualified: 'Beethoven had never before worked on a scale that allowed or demanded the massive formality achieved by counterpoint here.'[xxviii] An expansive double fugue unfolds and we are reminded of the youthful composer's years of study of thorough bass and counterpoint under the tutelage of Joseph Haydn and Johann Albrechtsberger. Writing about this aspect of the composer's achievement, de Marliave enthuses: 'The first Movement of Op. 59, No. 1, is a veritable revelation of Beethoven's perfect command over academic form, to which his genius gave new life.'[xxix]

An anecdote from the spring of 1940 connects the first movement of the Op. 59, No. 1 String Quartet with the American musician Dika Newlin who was then studying composition with Arnold Schoenberg at the University of California; Schoenberg was known affectionately as 'Uncle Arnold'. One day, as a requirement of his study in musical analysis, a student quartet played the first movement of the F major Quartet. Newlin recollects: 'They broke down in two or three spots, but on the whole did very well ... Uncle Arnold was really tickled with their performance and told them so.' The consequence was, Schoenberg set the class hard at work in analysing the movement. Four members of the class were each required to study a section of the music and to report their findings the following week. He offered a clue saying, in his opinion, some of the 'harmonic peculiarities in the first movement might be due to Russian folk-influences ... such as occur in the last movement'.[xxx]

Beethoven designates the second movement *Allegretto vivace e sempre scherzando* that may be taken to mean 'at a moderately quick tempo but always scherzo-like – lively and playful'. As a consequence of the expansive nature of the first movement, and its rather grave nature, it has been suggested Beethoven elected not to follow with a slow movement but instead to continue with music in a lighter vein.[xxi] Radcliffe remarks how it was unusual at this stage in the composer's development to give a second movement a scherzo-like character.[xxii] He would do so again with the Cello Sonata in A major, Op. 69 (1808) and the Piano Trio in B-flat major, Op. 97 (1811) both of which, like the F major Quartet, have first movements that are particularly broad and melodious in character. But at the period in question, as de Marliave points out, 'this is the first of the succession of great [*scherzo*] movements written in this form'. He quotes Robert Schumann who considered the movement to be 'one of the most wonderful utterances in the world'. De Marliave endorses this encomium with a characteristic expression of his own admiration for the music, describing it as 'built into a majestic structure of sound that only a full orchestra, with woodwind, brass, and percussion, could realize in all its massive significance'.[xxiii] Shepherd is equally responsive to this *Allegretto* movement but is more restrained: 'No single feature of Beethoven's tremendous tone-art becomes more truly a symbol of his transforming fantasy than his scherzos ... In one respect, the *scherzo* of the Quartet in F major, displays a kind of baroque extravagance.'[xxxiv]

Kinderman avows the *Allegretto — scherzando* to be 'an astonishingly original conception' that he likens to 'a piece ... conceived as a search for its own thematic material'.'[xxxv] Kerman remarks in similar fashion: 'What seems central to [the] *Allegretto vivace e sempre scherzando* is not counterpoint in the ordinary sense, but the very process of bodying out ... the effect is one of wonder and whimsy — Beethoven starts from something impossibly slight and carries it to implausible lengths, in bewildering variety.' In his estimation: 'This *Allegretto vivace e sempre scherzando* is one of the signal masterpieces of the second period, as much as the opening *Allegro*.'[xxxvi] The opening first motif is essentially a rhythmic variation tapped out on the cello on a single note. It calls to mind Robert Schumann's remark: 'Beethoven picked up his *motifs* in the street, but re-created them into the most beautiful utterances in the world.'[xxxvii] The manner in which the cello drums out its monotone rhythm has disposed modern-day authors to suggest, if Beethoven were writing this passage in the present era, 'he might have asked the cellist to tap it, un-pitched, on the back of his instrument'.[xxxviii]

At its first appearance, the opening cello passage was not understood. In the words of Alexander Thayer: 'The *Allegretto — vivace* of the first of these quartets was long a rock of offence.' By way of illustration, we recollect an incident in 1812 when the movement was played for the first time to a musical circle of Field Marshall Count Soltikoff (Soltykow) in Moscow. The cello part was played by the distinguished German cellist Bernhard Romberg, with whom Beethoven had been on friendly terms since their youthful days in Bonn; they had played in the same orchestra. Beethoven respected Romberg as a musician and even offered to write a cello concerto for him. To posterity's loss, Romberg declined on the grounds that he had difficulty in understanding some of Beethoven's ideas. This was evident on the evening when the F major Quartet was performed in Soltikoff's salon. It is recorded Romberg threw his part on the floor and trampled it under foot 'as a contemptible mystification [of] the bass part which he was to play'. Accordingly, the Quartet was set aside. A few years later the work did not fare any better when it was performed at the house of Privy Councillor Lwoffin, in St. Petersburg; the company broke out in laughter when the bass played his solo on one note and once again the Quartet was laid aside.[xxxix]

Beethoven's *Allegretto vivace e sempre scherzando* is not strictly a scherzo nor does it conform to an easily classifiable sonata form. In his interpretation of Beethoven's workmanship, Denis Matthews proposes: 'Instead of the usual scherzo or minuet-and-trio Beethoven wrote a highly original through-composed *scherzando* movement ... beginning with a one-note rhythmic idea on the cello that serves as a springboard for a host of miniature themes, lyrical, witty or pathetic.'[xl] De Marliave is content to surrender to the composer's enchantment: 'One can find no meaning in this dance, whose outward aspects are ever changing yet always akin; perhaps it is that this light-hearted fantasy finds in itself its own purpose. But it is the fantasy of an eager and sensitive spirit; joy and sorrow are reflected like sunlight and shadow flickering over a vast plain as the clouds move across the sun.'[xli]

In 1913 Artur Rubinstein was in London during the so-called Season. He was invited to a musical soirée in Kensington. Arriving somewhat late, he writes: 'I was about to enter the enchantment of this place, I heard the theme of the second movement of the F major Quartet of Beethoven, the Op. 59, No. 1. Nothing more beautiful has ever been written. Paul Draper [an American singer] showed me the way to the music room, and we sat down on one of the steps so as not to disturb the musicians ... I was happily surprised to see not more than six or seven persons listening intently to accents of proud imagination of this sublime work.'[xlii]

The character and expansive nature of the third movement — the Quartet's slow movement — is conveyed by the heading Beethoven gave to it: *Adagio moto e mesto — attacca,* 'slowly with movement and sadly'. It is set out on a more expansive scale than the opening movement with a performing time of around twelve minutes; string quartets seeking to emphasize the music's anguish and pathos adopt an even more expansive time-scale. A measure of the significance Beethoven attached to his wording may be inferred from the fact that this is only the second occasion that he had used the term *mesto* since the composition of the great Piano Sonata in D major, Op. 10, No. 3 (1798–99).s

Gerald Abraham's response to the elegiac music of the third movement embodies the feelings of many commentators: 'Beethoven certainly reached new heights in the beauty of the opening of the *Adagio* of [Op. 59] No. 1.'[xliii] 'The slow movement in F major is piercingly expressive and beautiful, one of the finest of Beethoven's slow movements'.[xliv] 'The Adagio is one of the most inscrutable that Beethoven ever composed — it is a document of lamentation and articulated tone.' [xlv] '[Covered] with subtly conveyed confusion, permeated by human pathos ... the only possible reaction [to the opening movement] ... a sonata form of great irregularity ... but organic ... founded upon productive tonal instability.'[xlvi] 'Sad introspection [is] enhanced in due course by the cello in its higher registers.'[xlvii] Donald Tovey's response to the feeling implicit in the third movement was: 'Nothing can be more quiet than the way in which such a melody will disengage itself from symmetry and broaden into something evidently part of a larger whole; and the process is as dramatic as it is quiet.'[xlviii] The atmosphere Beethoven creates disposed Tovey to quote from Shakespeare's *Twelfth Night*: 'If music be the food of love, play on'.

In this slow movement Beethoven changes the key to F minor and the ensuing lament has been compared with the funeral march in the *Eroica* Symphony: 'At any rate, the movement is grave, sombre and touching — a long sad song throbbingly sung, with radical use of pizzicato notes expressly for emotion.'[xlix] For his inspiration Beethoven may have drawn upon the expressiveness he imparted in the slow movement of Op. 18, No. 1 and the finale of Op. 18, No. 6.[l] Heinz Becker characterizes the mood of the *Adagio* as 'the expression of the most mature, manly grief'.[li] This observation corresponds with thoughts expressed by Basil Lam who considered the music may have a personal connotation: '[The] music is elegiac, with a brooding intensity far from common in Beethoven, though there is an obvious affinity suggested, partly by the F minor tonality, with Florestan's soliloquy. (We remember that early work on these three quartets was contemporary with the first version of *Fidelio*.) This music is, of course, above autobiography, but it is perhaps allowable to find something personal to Beethoven's lost hopes of happiness in the words sung by Florestan in the aria following the F minor Introduction: "In des Lebens Frühlingstagen ist das Glück von mir geflohn" — "Happiness has fled me in the springtime of my life".'[lii] Lam is making reference here to the anguish experienced by Beethoven through his unrequited love and the menacing impairment of his worsening hearing.

The song-like elegiac melody of the *Adagio* may have other personal associations with the composer that have been the subject of some speculation and conjecture.

Written against the sketches for the *Adagio*, Beethoven inscribed the words: 'Eine Trauer-weide oder Akazien-Baum aufs Grab meines Bruders' — 'A weeping willow or an acacia tree over my brother's grave'. Since the composer's brother's Karl and Johann were still alive, they can be discounted. The only other candidates are the other Ludwig, who died in infancy, or Franz Georg who died age two in Bonn when the composer was just twelve years old. Is the *Adagio* then 'a serene resignation, a lament over the death of a child'?[liii] Most modern-day commentators are wary of endorsing such a conjecture for the reason it seems unlikely that such profoundly felt music can have been prompted in Beethoven's mind by feelings towards siblings who had died so many years previously. Another suggestion offered to explain Beethoven's wording, is that it may have been added some years later following the death of Karl in 1815. Beethoven was then still in possession of the F major Quartet sketches at this time and could well have felt moved to inscribe them against the poignant music he had composed.[liv] Setting aside all such speculation, David Wyn Jones concludes: 'Whatever its particular stimulus or indebtedness ... the intense melancholy and lyricism of the movement are unpatrolled.'[lv]

Arthur Shepherd believed the movement's romantic lyricism, as expressed in its rising and drooping contours, anticipated the procedures of 'a later age': 'The decorative arabesques with which the composer adorns his lamenting strains are much more than figural accessories; they become ... integral to the poignancy and passion of this noble threnody.' In his enthusiasm he quotes de Marliave: "One of the most instructive and interesting movements that Beethoven ever wrote; it recalls and even surpasses the finale of the Fourth Symphony in originality and vigour, in ingenuity of device, and in perfect grasp of form".'[lvi]

In his designation of the movement Beethoven includes the term *attacca* – an indication to the performers at the close of the movement 'to continue to the next without a break'. Beethoven's brings this about by introducing the first notes of the *thème russe* that he had identified in Ivan Pratsch's collection of Russian folk melodies. The cello first introduces the borrowed melody *sotto voce* whilst above are heard paeans of persisting trills on the first violin, just one of the many technical challenges Beethoven imposes on the performer; we recall his rejoinder when instrumentalists complained of such impositions – 'Do you suppose I consider your wretched fiddle when the spirit moves me.'[lvii]

In response to Beethoven's directions, the final movement – marked *théme russe Allegro* – opens without a break, the first violin leading the way in an airy, ornate cadenza that immediately lightens the darker mood from what has gone before. Beethoven is in effect transforming – metamorphosing – the original Russian melody to his own requirements. The refrain of the Russian folksong, on which the greater part of the finale is based, tells of a mother's misfortune on greeting her wearied son on his return from distant realms and asks him: "What is it, my son, my dear one? What has aged thee?" He replies: "[The] cruel services of my sovereign in a far land."[lviii] Beethoven originally marked the passage in his sketches *molto andante* 'very slow' but changed this to *Allegro*, thereby imparting a light-hearted, almost dance-like manner to the 'stately character and moderate tempo' (Philip Radcliffe) of the original melody. Commenting on this transformation, Gerald Abraham wittily observes: 'We must not blame him for this ... his business was musical composition, not musical ethnology.'[lix] Perhaps there is a more innocent explanation as Nicolas Slonimsky explains: 'It is open to question how much Beethoven could have appreciated the meaning of the [folksong] text, since no German translation accompanied Ivan Pratsch's Russian edition.'[lx]

The Russian melody chosen for the theme of the final movement has been described as 'curiously suggestive' insofar as it reflects 'all the bitter-sweetness that flows out of the Russian temperament in joy and sadness alike, and moulds the natural idiom of Slav folk song'. This was not lost on Beethoven who builds the *Allegro* movement on these twofold characteristics in a manner 'that sparkles with life and gaiety, but [which] is a gaiety touched with underlying gloom'.[lxi] Lam makes the observation that folk tunes, in the hands of a lesser composer than Beethoven, typically resist development beyond mere repetition but here, he affirms, 'Beethoven treats his Russian theme as much as if it were his own invention'.[lxii] Beethoven superimposes upon it his own style of 'cheerful rough humour' (Paul Becker) and an air of 'good natured parody' (Joseph Kerman). 'Beethoven, remembering perhaps the elegiac character of the folk tune in its original form, presents it in slow tempo, over gently nostalgic harmonies, but, as so often, brushed aside with much vigour.'[lxiii] 'An air of good natured parody is present: for example, in the canons, which instantly start chiming away at the folksong ... At the end of the piece, Beethoven plays various tricks on the *théme russe*, combining two of its phrases to make double counterpoint'.[lxiv] Adopting his characteristic style, philosopher-musicologist Theodor Adorno comments: 'Here, the change of character, the way in which the folksong theme is made interchangeable, acts both as a means of creating tension and as a disguise which brings about ... resolution.'[lxv]

Beethoven's sketches reveal he originally contemplated introducing repeats in the last movement, just as he had considered in the first movement, but subsequently deleted them.[lxvi] As it stands some commenters, for example Romain Rolland, attest to the music's 'full effects ... almost orchestral style'.[lxvii] '[Just] before the end, the speed slackens and the violin, at the top of its register, sings nostalgically, for the last time, at the sort of speed a Russian folk singer might consider appropriate.' Music critic Conrad Wilson, whom we have just quoted, comments: 'Depending on how the players treat it, it is a beautiful effect and a reminder that, from the very beginning, singing lines have been a vital feature of this long quartet.'[lxviii] As the music and the work draw to a close: 'An eloquent farewell [is] uttered by each voice in turn, slipping away in the distance ... A little pianissimo rustling seems to silence it altogether.'[lxix] In fact Beethoven requests the players to adopt *ppp, pianississimo* – a rare marking in his scores. Nine bars of *presto* in *fortissimo* chords bring the music to a close: 'In the last few bars before the *Coda*, all the pent-up forces of the finale break out in an exultant *fanfare* on the chord of the seventh on C; it is the trumpet-call of the *Leonora* Overture.'[lxx]

When the American musician Robert Craft asked his close friend Igor Stravinsky if he would identify some of his favourite events in the quartets of Beethoven, Stravinsky made reference to the Op. 59 set in the following terms: 'The music of the Op. 59 Quartets is always so marvellously sustained and the substance to be sustained so good that I cannot cite out of context, yet what a stroke is the A flat in measure 266 of Op. 59, No. 1, or, in the second movement, what marvels are measures 65–6, 394–404 (on the strength of this last passage alone Beethoven must be considered first among rhythmic innovators).'[lxxi]

Joseph de Marliave quotes from the Italian musician and musicologist Giuseppe Ippolito Valetta who made a study of the Beethoven quartets (*I Quartetti di Beethoven, 1905*) and had experienced them performed in a series of quartet concerts in Rome under the direction of the great violinist Joseph Joachim. According to de Marliave, Valetta enthused: 'To realize the full force of this brilliant [F major Quartet] finale one should have actually seen one of these national festivals held in Asiatic Russia; when the first breath of spring melts the snow, and the Steppe casts off its icy cloak and reappears in its sweet-scented garment of flowers.'[lxxii] We conclude with the equally enthusiastic summation of Joseph Kerman: 'The image of what we take as our musical tradition is marked indelibly by the strengths and weaknesses of Beethoven's second period — or better, by its perfections and its excesses. The F major *Razumovsky* Quartet stands with the *Eroica* at dead centre of that image, a magnificent embodiment of both.'[lxxiii]

[i] Elliot Forbes, editor, *Thayer's life of Beethoven*, 1967, p. 408.
[ii] Wayne M. Senner, Robin Wallace and William Meredith, editors, 1999, Vol. 1, pp. 52–3.
[iii] Conrad Wilson, p. 52.
[iv] Alison Bullock, *Notes to the BBC Radio Three Beethoven experience*, Thursday 9 June 2005, www.bbc.co.uk/radio3/Beethoven
[v] Philip G. Downs, 1992, p. 596.
[vi] William Kinderman, 1997, p. 109.
[vii] Michael Broyles, 1987, p. 106.
[viii] David Wyn Jones: *Beethoven and the Viennese legacy* in: Robin Stowell, editor *The Cambridge companion to the string quartet*, 2003, pp. 214–6.
[ix] Alan Tyson, *The Razumovsky Quartets: Some aspects of the sources in: Beethoven studies 3*, 1982, pp. 132–3.
[x] Denis Matthews, 1985, pp. 133–4.
[xi] Arthur Shepherd, 1935, p. 29.
[xii] Romain Rolland, 1917, p. 183.
[xiii] David Wyn Jones: *Beethoven and the Viennese legacy* in: Robin Stowell, editor *The Cambridge companion to the string quartet*, 2003, pp. 214–6.
[xiv] Philip Radcliffe, 1978, p. 53.
[xv] Michael Broyles, 1987, pp. 102–4. The reference is to Joseph Kerman, *The Beethoven quartets*, 1967.
[xvi] Arthur Shepherd, 1935, p. 29.
[xvii] Joseph de Marliave, 1925 (reprint 1961), p. 89.
[xviii] Robert Winter and Robert Martin editors, 1994, p. 176.
[xix] Joseph de Marliave, 1925 (reprint 1961), p. 63 and p. 66.
[xx] Philip Radcliffe, 1978, p. 17.

[xxi] *Ibid*, p. 49.
[xxii] Paul Griffiths, 1983, pp. 86–7.
[xxiii] Basil Lam, 1975, p. 40.
[xxiv] Robin Stowell editor, 1999, pp. 169–70.
[xxv] Romain Rolland, is one such as he remarks in his *Beethoven and Handel*, 1917, p. 183. In an untypical oversight, Rolland describes Razumovsky as being a cellist.
[xxvi] Harold Truscott, 1968, p. 28.
[xxvii] Adapted from William Kinderman, editor, 2005, p. 5.
[xxviii] Joseph Kerman, 1967, p. 94.
[xxix] Joseph de Marliave, 1925, (reprint 1961), p. 70.
[xxx] Dika Newlin, 1980, pp. 192–3.
[xxxi] Paul Griffiths, 1983, p. 89.
[xxxii] Philip Radcliffe, 1978, p. 53.
[xxxiii] Joseph de Marliave, 1925 (reprint 1961), p. 70 and p. 75.
[xxxiv] Arthur Shepherd, 1935, p. 29.
[xxxv] William Kinderman, 1997, pp. 109–10.
[xxxvi] Joseph Kerman, 1967, p. 105 and p. 108.
[xxxvii] Quoted in Joseph de Marliave, 1925 (reprint 1961), pp. 71–2. De Marliave also quotes Wagner's view: 'Beethoven shows his originality by beginning with these fragmentary motifs and using them to build up a structure of increasing loftiness and power.' We recall in our own time that Alfred Brendel has likened Beethoven to 'a master builder'.
[xxxviii] Robert Winter and Robert Martin editors, 1994, p. 181.
[xxxix] Elliot Forbes, editor, *Thayer's life of Beethoven*, 1967, pp. 408–9.
[xl] Dennis Matthews, 1985, p. 134.
[xli] Joseph de Marliave, 1925, (reprint 1961), p. 70.
[xlii] Arthur Rubinstein, 1973, p. 404.
[xliii] Gerald Abraham, *Beethoven's chamber music*, in: *The Age of Beethoven, The New Oxford History of Music, Vol. VIII*, Gerald Abraham, editor, 1988, p. 289.
[xliv] Marion M. Scott, 1940, p. 257.
[xlv] Frank Kämpfer, Liner note to The Alexander String Quartet, *Beethoven: String Quartets*, Arte Nova Classics.
[xlvi] Robert Simpson, *The chamber music for strings*, in: Denis Arnold and Nigel Fortune, editors, *The Beethoven companion*, 1973, p. 253.
[xlvii] Denis Matthews, 1985, p. 134.
[xlviii] Donald Francis Tovey, 1944, p. 82.
[xlix] Conrad Wilson, 2003, p. 53.
[l] As suggested by David Wyn Jones: *Beethoven and the Viennese legacy* in: Robin Stowell, editor *The Cambridge companion to the string quartet*, 2003, pp. 214–6.
[li] Heinz Becker, Liner notes to The Amadeus Quartet, *Beethoven: The string quartets*, 1974.
[lii] Basil Lam, 1975, p. 42.
[liii] As invited for consideration by Joseph de Marliave, 1925, (reprint 1961), pp. 58–9.
[liv] See, for example, Gerald Abraham, 1944, p. 24.
[lv] David Wyn Jones: *Beethoven and the Viennese legacy* in: Robin Stowell, editor

[lvi] *The Cambridge companion to the string quartet*, 2003, pp. 214–6.
[lvi] Arthur Shepherd, 1935, pp. 30–1.
[lvii] The words quoted appear in several Beethoven sources, sometimes in a modified form. We cite them here from Paul Yarbrough, Liner notes to The Alexander String Quartet, *Ludwig van Beethoven, The String Quartets*, Arte Nova Classics (undated, c. 1980).
[lviii] Derived from Gerald Abraham, 1944, p. 27. Alternative wordings, to those quoted, are cited by other authorities according to their translation and interpretation of the original text. For example, Romain Rolland cites the words "Ah! is this my fate? And what fate!" See: Romain Rolland, 1917, p. 183.
[lix] *Ibid*.
[lx] Nicolas Slonimsky, *The great composers and their works*: edited by Electra Slonimsky Yourke, 2000, p. 160.
[lxi] Joseph de Marliave, 1925 (reprint1961), p. 85.
[lxii] Basil Lam, 1975, p. 46.
[lxiii] Philip Radcliffe, 1978, p. 59.
[lxiv] Joseph Kerman, 1967, p. 113.
[lxv] Theodor W. Adorno, 1998, p. 25.
[lxvi] Alan Tyson, *The Razumovsky Quartets: Some aspects of the sources in: Beethoven studies 3*, 1982, pp. 132–3.
[lxvii] Romain Rolland, 1917, p. 184.
[lxviii] Conrad Wilson, 2003, p. 54.
[lxix] Joseph de Marliave, 1925 (reprint1961), p. 89.
[lxx] Conrad Wilson, 2003, p. 54.
[lxxi] Igor Stravinsky and Robert Craft, 1968, p. 113.
[lxxii] Joseph de Marliave, 1925 (reprint1961), p 85.
[lxxiii] Joseph Kerman, 1967, p. 116.

STRING QUARTET IN E MINOR, OP. 59, NO. 2

> 'Let the amateur reflect that a single idea taken from among any of the movements of this Quartet, and analysed, will be found to be intrinsically not less *sublime*, as an emanation of profound thought and extraordinary genius, though heard with but one instrument to a part.'

John Ella, *Musical Sketches, Abroad and at Home: with original music by Mozart, Czerny, Graun, etc., vocal cadenzas and other musical illustrations*, Vol. 1., 1869, p. 165.

> '[The] Quartet in E minor struggles repeatedly with pathos all through its compressed, nervous

> fast movements, admitting in its middle an exaggerated contrast of grim serenity.'

Joseph Kerman, *The Beethoven Quartets*, 1967, p. 119.

> '[In] the E minor Quartet there is a furious driving force, and, as in the C minor Quartet of Op. 18, the taut minor mode is decisively reaffirmed.'

Paul Griffiths, *The String Quartet*, 1983, p. 90.

> 'While the F major Quartet that stands at the head of Op. 59 is richly expansive in the new manner defined most strikingly by the *Eroica* Symphony of 1803–4, this work reflects Beethoven's parallel interest in the taut and terse statement.'

Robert Winter and Robert Martin editors, *The Beethoven Quartet Companion*, 1994, p. 183.

> 'It is easy to see why such a work [as the E minor Quartet] was misunderstood in the early 1800s. The Quartet's lack of satisfying melody (the second movement excepted) and obsession with short motifs and shifting harmonies does not make for easy listening. But here we have Beethoven the true radical, and this work, perhaps more than any other, moved the string quartet genre on from the Classical, salon-music mastery of Haydn and Mozart, and towards its final destination of symphonic depth and expression.'

Alison Bullock, *Notes to the BBC Radio Three Beethoven Experience*, Thursday 9 June 2005, www.bbc.co.uk/radio3/Beethoven

The String Quartet in E minor, Op. 59, No. 2, following on from its immediate predecessor the Quartet in F major, exemplifies Beethoven's disposition, and capacity, to work on two or three compositions of the same genre simultaneously, turning from one to the other. In this manner he was able to explore and contrast such aspects of his art as key relationships, textures, moods and the scale of a particular movement or work as a whole. Much of this is evident in the E minor Quartet. '[Op. 59, No. 2] is, apart from its slow movement, tenser, darker in colour, more highly strung, and less spacious in material [than Op. 59, No. 1].'[i] Whereas the F major disposes of repeats, the E minor makes extensive use of them and contrapuntal writing 'of a more general character informs every important section'.[ii] The E minor Quartet is a monotonic composition: 'All the movements are in E minor: in the first movement, third movement and finale, major; in the slow movement, and in the trio section of the scherzo, a balance of opposites rather than a dramatic move from minor to major.'[iii] Although the E minor has a shorter performing time than the F major, it is nevertheless an expansive work laid out with a performing time of more the half an hour.

Gerald Abraham's response to the *Allegro* of the E minor Quartet provides a fitting opening to our commentary to the first movement: 'The nature of the intense feeling of this movement, like that of the first movement of the F major Quartet, is quite indefinable in words. The music is as far from being an expression of any specific emotion or emotions as it is from being a mere abstract pattern of sounds. Profound questions are put and answered; challenges are issued; the argument is as impassioned as it is logical. But the questions and answers are purely musical questions and answers; the challenges and the argument are conceivable in no terms but those of music.'[iv] Other commentators have been moved to remark in similar fashion: 'The *Allegro* of the E minor Quartet, calm and unfaltering, lays bare the depths of the dark mystery of music ... a bitter and unavailing struggle with a hostile fate is pictured ... A mighty wrath, stubborn, impotent, seems to break out at the beginning of this work, presented in the symmetrical form of tradition ... As a wonderful portrayal of a troubled, suffering spirit, beset by hostile influences, this first movement of the quartet in E minor is perhaps more self-revealing than any.'[v] 'This is indeed music of sublime contemplation, foreshadowing later works, such as the *Benedictus* of the *Missa Solemnis* and the celestial central variation in E major in the slow movement of the first of the late quartets, [commencing] Op. 127.'[vi] David Soyer, cellist member of the Guarneri String Quartet, likened the music to 'a stream constantly running over rocks and rushing down in little torrents and cascades'.[vii]

The contrast between Op. 59, No.1 and Op. 59, No. 2 is nowhere more striking than at the very outset when two sonorous staccato chords set the music in motion. These 'hammer strokes' have been compared with the manner in which the *Eroica* Symphony starts its long journey, notwithstanding that the two openings 'are worlds apart'.[viii] 'As an alert, compressed, peremptory gesture, the first two bars beat even the Fifth Symphony.'[ix] Whereas Op, 59, No. 1 opens melodically and spaciously, Op. 59, No.2 'plunges at once into a world of high drama'. Denis Matthews, whom we have just quoted, finds, in the atmosphere that subsequently develops, a parallel with the *Appassionata* Sonata, Op. 57 and an anticipation of the more vehement harmonies at the start of the String Quartet in F minor, Op. 95. He asserts: 'The first two chords are more than introductory, playing a vital role in the first movement's development.'[x] Philip Radcliffe also finds 'an obvious kinship' with the opening of the *Appassionata* Sonata.[xi] '[From] the start of the first movement: its nervous, sporadic phrases create a feeling of tension that is heightened by irregular rhythms and terse exchanges between the instruments.'[xii] Basil Lam also considered the first movement to be 'tense rather than tragic'.[xiii]

Arthur Shepherd further emphasizes the differences between the opening movements of Op. 59 No. 1 and Op. 59, No. 2: 'Placed side by side, the first movements of the F major and the E minor *Razumovsky* Quartets afford a vivid study in contrasts. In the first, there is an Olympian deliberateness and expansiveness of design; in the second there is terseness of form and epigrammatic forcefulness of syntax. The firm lyrical contours of the first are offset by the ejaculatory motifs of the second.[xiv] William Kinderman comments in similar manner: 'Whereas the F major Quartet is spacious and grand in its overall character, the E minor Quartet is more concentrated, at least in its first movement ... The introductory gestures of chords and silences is terse and arresting.'[xv] Silence takes on special significance in the first movement of the E minor quartet as Lam elucidates: 'Beethoven had discovered in the slow movement of the E flat [Piano] Sonata, Op. 7, the power of silence, and in the [E minor] Quartet the empty bars are even weightier than those of the similar opening in the *Appassionata*.'[xvi]

Abraham draws attention to Beethoven's construction in the first movement: 'The musical logic of this movement is so perfect, and so characteristic of Beethoven.' He singles out the manner in which the first fourteen bars are wholly derived from the two opening chords — a typical manifestation of the composer's gift for 'making something out of nothing'.[xvii] Restraint is also one of the hallmarks here of Beethoven's constructional workings-out. Joseph de Marliave considers Beethoven to be 'still a respecter of forms'[xviii] and Joseph Kerman believes '[the] first movement of the Quartet in E minor, stands almost alone in Beethoven's output for the wispiness of its thematic material'.[xix] The music may have an airy Mendelssohnian lightness about it — at least in certain passages (notably at the close) — but at the same time it is art that conceals art in the manner in which it poses challenges for the performers. 'The first movement ... is in fact one of the hardest things ever written from the point of view of the ensemble, and a great deal of rehearsal is made necessary by the frequent silent bars, the awkwardness with which certain passages lie under the fingers, the syncopations, and the way the different instruments have to step without apparent effort into long sliding phrases.'[xx]

Beethoven's heads the second movement *Molto Adagio. Si tratta questo pezzo con molto di sentiment* — 'This piece to be played expressively *Adagio* with a lot of feeling'. It is one of the composer's most expansive quartet movements having a performing time approaching twelve minutes. Its construction has been described as 'a textbook exercise in counterpoint' in which sonata form predominates with 'contrasted themes and tonalities ... woven into a continuous texture'.[xxi] Writing of the second movement, philosopher-musicologist Theodor Adorno states: 'The Beethovenian form is an integral whole, in which each individual moment is determined by its function within the whole only to the extent that these individual moments contradict and cancel each other, yet are preserved on a higher level within the whole. Only the whole proves their identity'.[xxii]

Given the choral-like opening of the *Molto Adagio*, Beethoven required a large-scale musical format upon which to project his thoughts. According to the composer's assistant and biographer Anton Schindler, the impulse to set the music in this manner was influenced by his contemplation of the starry night sky.[xxiii] Years later, Beethoven's piano pupil Carl Czerny corroborated this story when in conversation with the musicologist Otto Jahn and the violinist Karl Holz. Of related interest is that the piano maker Johann Andreas Stumpff visited Beethoven in 1824 and later wrote an account of his several meetings with the composer. Beethoven's biographer Alexander Thayer later drew on Stumph's accounts for his own study of the composer's life and work.[xxiv] In one of his recollections, Stumpff relates: 'Beethoven said, "When I contemplate ... the host of ... suns or earths my soul rises to the source of all creation".' Beethoven's disposition to think in this way may have been influenced by Immanuel Kant's writings on natural philosophy. In particular it is known Beethoven was familiar with Kant's *Theory of Heavens* (1755) and was inclined to invoke the philosopher's maxim about 'the starry heavens above and the moral law below'.[xxv] In his *Beethoven's empire of the mind*, John Crabbe writes eloquently of how such reflections were central to the composer's outlook: 'The breathtaking infinity of a star-strew sky and the feelings of awe and veneration which such a scene may inspire, of such things was Beethoven's inner empire made. Somehow he had to capture and convey at least a part of this exalted realm by means of his particular genius; but the work-day-world was a stubbornly difficult place in which to do it.'[xxvi] Philip Radcliffe reminds us: '[It] is important to remember that a mood of profound and serene contemplation was, all through Beethoven's life, at least as characteristic of him as were his more stormy periods.'[xxvii]

Marion Scott, in support of the anecdote of Beethoven gazing at the stars — and of its appositeness, as she saw it, to the nature of his music — quotes the following words of Walt Whitman's *A clear midnight*: 'This is thy hour, O soul, thy free flight into worldless ... Thee fully forth emerging, silent, gazing, pondering the themes thou lovest best/Night, sleep, death and the star.' She adds: 'After Beethoven became emancipated from the conventions of the suite form (where all the movements were in the same key) it was unusual for him to maintain one keynote — in this case E (minor and major) — throughout a large work. When he did so, he obviously had some special purpose ... In this *Razumovsky* Quartet, while yet standing in the shadows of the first movement, he suddenly directs our gaze upward by the change into E major, to behold the starry heavens above.'[xxviii]

The character of the *Molto Adagio* has moved commentators to reflect upon it with eloquence and feeling. De Marliave writes of 'a slow movement breathing an inspired idealism, profoundly spiritual yet deeply human'. He quotes Wilhelm von Lenz: "A vision of Paradise where mortal love finds eternal happiness" (*Beethoven et ses trois styles*, 1855, p. 65)[xxix] — words that call to mind Florestan's moving aria in *Fidelio* when he sings of his 'angel Leonora'. Kerman considers 'the *Adagio* transcends the tensions of the opening movement by a hushed, timeless ecstasy of contemplation — of the Pythagorean mysteries'.[xxx] Cooper, with others, believes the slow movement anticipates the feeling Beethoven was to instil, nearly twenty years later, in the *Heiliger Dankgesang* — 'Hymn to the Divine' — in the String Quartet Op. 132.[xxxi] In his tribute to Beethoven's achievement, Radcliffe postulates: '[It] may be doubted whether the posthumous [late] quartets contain anything more deeply thoughtful and serene than the *Adagio* of Op. 59, No. 2 ... one of the most profoundly serene that Beethoven ever wrote.'[xxxii] For Rebecca Clarke the *Molto Adagio* 'breaths with a deep rhythm the wonder and repose that [Beethoven] always found in nature'.[xxxiii] In his enthusiasm, Romain Rolland was more direct: 'Here again [Beethoven] is in new territory. It is a though he said to the players: "Wake up!

This is an entirely new kind of music".[xxxiv] Several authorities comment on the influence this music had on Franz Schubert. Could it be that he had this movement in mind when he composed his own serenely moving *Adagio* in the great Quintet in C major, D. 956?

The third movement — *Allegretto* — functions as the quartet's scherzo and is the movement in which Beethoven introduces the *thème russe*. Lam describes the opening as 'troubled restless brooding' with its 'alternating outbursts of energy'. He considers this forceful expression as being typical of Beethoven himself and disposed him to recall a passage in a letter Goethe wrote on 2 September 1812 to the musician Carl Friedrich Zelter. Goethe had made Beethoven's acquaintance at the Bohemian spa resort of Teplitz and wrote to his friend: 'His talent amazed me, but unhappily his is a character utterly lacking in self-control.'[xxxv]

'[The] *Allegretto* has a character all its own. It is not merely one of the those *jeux d'esprit* scintillating with the Master's wit and humour; it is no longer the expressive dance form of Haydn, or the graceful measure of Mozart. This *Allegretto*, with its emotional nature and romantic bearing, seems to foreshadow the Mazurkas of Chopin.'[xxxvi] Radcilffe endorses these observations, derived from Joseph de Marliave, but contends 'the dance rhythm', that he finds in the movement, to be 'of a far more sombre and agitated kind'. Regarding the movement's construction as a whole he maintains: 'Like everything in the E minor Quartet, this *Allegretto* is very unlike the equivalent in the first *Razumovsky* Quartet; it is simpler in form and, for the most part, more direct in its emotional expression.'[xxxvii] Kerman concurs: Here we have 'an E minor *Allegretto* of studied simplicity'.[xxxviii]

The *thème russe* makes its appearance in the Trio section of the movement. Rimsky-Korsakov used the same theme in his opera *The Tsar's Bride*, where it is invoked to symbolise the majesty of the Tsar. Modest Mussorgsky also employed the melody, to striking effect, in the Coronation Scene in his opera *Boris Godunov*. Despite these lofty associations, the melody has humble origins in the Russian folk song *Slava Bogu na nebe*. It is, notwithstanding, a hymn of glory to the Tsar and contains such lines as "Glory be to you, our Lord in Heaven! Glory be to our Tsar on this earth. His beautiful robes will not be worn out! His faithful servants will not grow old! His valiant steeds will not tire out! We sing this song to our Lord! We render him glory!"[xxxix] It is doubtless the melody that caught Beethoven's attention, and not the words, since no German translation accompanied Ivan Pratsch's collection of Russian folk melodies — their original source.

Although Beethoven may have been attracted to the potential the *thème russe* offered for melodic development, he was not prepared to be constrained by its limitations. As Rebecca Clarke muses: '[He] could succeed only in making the tune sound like Beethoven.'[xl] Kinderman elucidates: 'The theme is stripped of its solemn, ecclesiastical associations and treated in a parodistic fugal medley that is repeated in full after the return of the *Allegro*.'[xli] Beethoven also quickens the tempo until it becomes 'a jaunty tune' passed from one instrument to another. Such is the extent of Beethoven's liberties with the original theme that Kerman was disposed to respond: 'This does not sound as though the composer inserted the Russian tune as an urbane compliment to his Russian patron ... It sounds as though Count Razumovsky had been tactless enough to hand Beethoven the tune, and Beethoven is pile-driving it into the ground by way of revenge!'[xlii]

David Wyn Jones, mindful of Razumovsky's skills as an accomplished violinist, believes the Count 'would no doubt have taken delight in the unison of folksong and learned fugue that constitutes [the] movement'.[xliii] Beethoven certainly gave the Count, and succeeding generations of string players, much to find delight in. The Russian theme is heard first on the viola and is in turn apportioned to the other instruments in canonical imitation and in 'increasingly manic counterpoint'.[xliv] Long repeats convey 'an illusion of perpetual motion'.[xlv] To some authorities Beethoven's musical language is a precursor to what was to follow: 'Its bare textures look forward to late Beethoven.'[xlvi] 'The Russian theme is given a relentless, almost parodistic quasi-fugal treatment that gives rise to some particularly gritty counterpoint — a foretaste, if not of parts of the *Grosse Fuge*, then certainly of the concluding fugue in the Cello Sonata Op. 102, No. 2.'[xlvii]

In October 1836 the English composer William Sterndale Bennett was on tour in Leipzig and shared the company of Felix Mendelssohn and Robert Schumann. He attended one of the string quartet concerts promoted by the violinist and concertmaster Ferdinand David — a close friend of Mendelssohn. The programme included a performance of the E minor Quartet, prompting Bennett to record in his diary how the Quartet had 'laid hold of his ears' and 'I should think that the *Scherzo* was one of the most beautiful things ever written.'[xlviii]

The fourth movement — *Presto* — 'represents Beethoven's very happiest mood ... seldom do we find Beethoven so happy as here'.[xlix] '[The] boisterous finale has something about it of country manners ... This is music of roistering good humour ... [suggestive of] Haydnesque manner.'[l] 'In the principal theme, Haydn himself was never more carefree than here.'[li] Heinz Becker likens the spirited opening to music 'as though from a region of expression worlds away' with the movement skipping along under the guidance of the first violin, but with 'underlying tensions

[that] give it no chance to turn the piece into a carefree rondo'.[lii] The music switches alternately between the keys of C major and E minor with, in Radcliffe's words, 'hilarious gusto'. Could this passage, as he suggests, have influenced Schubert, in the finale of his Piano Sonata in B-flat major, D. 960, where he does much the same thing — though in a darker and more restrained manner?[liii] With its incessant emphasis on C major, the final movement seems to be tuning our ears to the key of the final quartet in the set, just as the first movement, with its invocation of F major, looked back to the key of the first.[liv]

When the American musician Robert Craft asked his close friend Igor Stravinsky if he would identify some of his favourite events in the quartets of Beethoven, he made reference to the Op. 59 set in the following terms. 'For me the most astonishing passages in Op. 59, No. 2, are measures 210–26 in the first movement, and measures 64, 79, 84 (the A natural!) in the second movement; one could write a book *Beethoven and the Octave* on this second movement ... The long B flat bass in the last movement is a wonderful surprise, and so is the passage in measures 344–50.'[lv]

Some commentators have detected an orchestral, even symphonic, conception in the final movement. We close our account of the String Quartet in E minor, Op. 59, No. 2 with a selection of their remarks. '[Sometimes] one can almost hear the triangle, bass drum, and piccolo of the Turkish Band assisting at some more ferocious *Entführung* or *Ruins of Athens*.'[lvi] 'This great boisterous finale [foreshadows] in some respects the finale of the Seventh Symphony.'[lvii] 'Beethoven's finale is one of his most remarkable, and it rivals that of the Eighth Symphony in its blend of high spirits and profundity.'[lviii] 'The last page, *più presto*, expresses mock fury in its clenched-fist.'[lix] 'In these twenty-seven bars the distinctive rhythm of the principal theme soars up in a magnificent flight ... six massive chords bring the movement to an end with a blare of trumpets. Never had the string quartet revealed such an intensity of emotion.'[ix]

[i] Philip Radcliffe, 1978, p. 61.
[ii] Bernhard Jacobson Liner notes to: *Ludwig van Beethoven; The early string quartets*, Op. 18, Alban Berg Quartet, EMI, 1981.
[iii] David Wyn Jones: *Beethoven and the Viennese legacy* in: Robin Stowell, editor *The Cambridge companion to the string quartet*, 2003, pp. 214–6.
[iv] Gerald Abraham, 1944, p. 33.
[v] Joseph de Marliave, 1925 (reprint 1961), pp. 89–90.
[vi] William Kinderman, 1997, p. 111.
[vii] David Soyer in conversation with David Blum, *The art of quartet playing: the Guarneri Quartet in conversation with David Blum*, 1986, pp. 92–3.
[viii] John Daverio, *Manner, tone and tendency in Beethoven's chamber music for strings*, in: Glenn Stanley editor, *The Cambridge companion to Beethoven*, 2000, p. 155 and Robert Winter and Robert Martin editors, *The Beethoven quartet companion*, 1994, p. 183.
[ix] Joseph Kerman, 1967, p. 120.
[x] Denis Matthews, 1985, p. 134.
[xi] Philip Radcliffe, 1978, p. 61. He illustrates the similarity by making reference to the composer's sketches.
[xii] Alison Bullock, *Notes to the BBC Radio Three Beethoven experience*, Thursday 9 June 2005, www.bbc.co.uk/radio3/Beethoven
[xiii] Basil Lam. 1975, p. 51.
[xiv] Arthur Shepherd, 1935, p. 32.
[xv] William Kinderman, 1997, p. 111.
[xvi] Basil Lam, 1975, p. 51.
[xvii] Gerald Abraham, 1944, p. 32.
[xviii] Joseph de Marliave, 1925 (reprint1961), p. 98.
[xix] Joseph Kerman, 1967, p. 120.
[xx] Rebecca Clarke, *The [Beethoven] quartets as a player sees them*, in: *Music & Letters, Beethoven*, Special Issue: Vol. VIII, No. 2, 1927, pp. 181.
[xxi] Basil Lam, 1975, p. 55.
[xxii] Theodor W. Adorno, 1998, p. 29.
[xxiii] Anton Schindler, 1860, English edition: Donald MacArdle, 1966, pp. 405–6.
[xxiv] Elliot Forbes, editor, *Thayer's life of Beethoven*, 1967.
[xxv] As discussed by Basil Lam, 1975, pp. 54–5.
[xxvi] John Crabbe, 1982, p. 102.
[xxvii] Philip Radcliffe, 1978, p. 67.
[xxviii] Marion M. Scott, 1940, p. 258–9.
[xxix] Joseph de Marliave, 1925 (reprint1961), p. 99.
[xxx] Joseph Kerman, 1967, p. 128.
[xxxi] Barry Cooper, 1991, p. 234 and Robert Winter and Robert Martin editors, 1994, p. 187.
[xxxii] Philip Radcliffe, 1978, pp. 64–5 and p. 178.
[xxxiii] Rebecca Clarke, *The [Beethoven] quartets as a player sees them*, in: *Music & Letters, Beethoven*, Special Issue: Vol. VIII, No. 2, 1927, pp. 181.
[xxxiv] Romain Rolland, 1917, p. 184.
[xxxv] Basil Lam, 1975, pp. 56–7.

[xxxvi] Joseph de Marliave, 1925, (reprint 1961), p. 105.
[xxxvii] Philip Radcliffe, 1978, p. 68.
[xxxviii] Joseph Kerman, 1967, p. 129.
[xxxix] For a translation and commentary to the Russian text see Slonimsky Yourke, 2000, pp. 160–1 and Gerald Abraham, 1944, p. 37 and 1985, p. 98.
[xl] Rebecca Clarke, *The [Beethoven] quartets as a player sees them*, in: *Music & Letters, Beethoven*, Special Issue: Vol. VIII, No. 2, 1927, pp. 182.
[xli] William Kinderman, 1997, p. 111.
[xlii] Joseph Kerman, 1967, p. 130.
[xliii] David Wyn Jones: *Beethoven and the Viennese legacy* in: Robin Stowell, editor *The Cambridge companion to the string quartet*, 2003, pp. 214–6.
[xliv] Alison Bullock, *Notes to the BBC Radio Three Beethoven experience*, Thursday 9 June 2005, www.bbc.co.uk/radio3/Beethoven
[xlv] Denis Matthews, 1985, p. 135.
[xlvi] Basil Lam, 1975, p. 56.
[xlvii] Barry Cooper, 1991, p. 234.
[xlviii] James R. Sterndale Bennett, *The life of William Sterndale Bennett*, 1907, p. 51. This anecdote is also recorded in Frederick Niecks, *Robert Schumann*, 1925, pp. 164–5.
[xlix] Roman Rolland, 1917, p. 185.
[l] Robert Winter and Robert Martin editors, 1994, p. 187.
[li] Arthur Shepherd, 1935, p. 33.
[lii] Heinz Becker, Liner notes to The Amadeus Quartet, *Beethoven: The string quartets*, 1974.
[liii] Philip Radcliffe, 1978, pp. 68–9.
[liv] With acknowledgment to Paul Griffiths, 1983, p. 90.
[lv] Igor Stravinsky and Robert Craft, 1968, p. 113.
[lvi] Joseph Kerman, 1967, p. 130.
[lvii] Gerald Abraham, 1944, p. 39.
[lviii] Philip Radcliffe, 1978, pp. 68–9.
[lix] Basil Lam, 1975, p. 57.
[lx] Joseph de Marliave, 1925 (reprint 1961), p. 115.

STRING QUARTET IN C MAJOR, OP. 59, NO. 3

'The composer of the C major Quartet has not yet learned the last secrets of laughter; he is still the victor not the philosopher.'

Paul Bekker, *Beethoven*, 1925, p. 317.

'Above all, the interest of the [C major Quartet] lies in showing how between the first and the third of the Op. 59 compositions their quality of psychological objectivity developed. The finale of Op. 59, No. 3, assumes symphonic proportions in pure brilliance of objective conception and expressive power.'

Joseph de Marliave, *Beethoven's Quartets*, 1925 (reprint 1961), p. 116.

'While the first quartet of Op. 59 expends its major energies on the first two movements, and the second achieves a viable balance, if a rather stiff one, the third quartet tilts sharply in the opposite direction.'

Joseph Kerman, *The Beethoven Quartets*, 1967, p. 134.

'If the *Razumovskys* had been at the end of the line, we would be exhibiting them as the *ne plus ultra* of the [quartet] literature, and no doubt putting a futuristic interpretation on such passages as the beginning of the Quartet in C Major, discovering in its breathbating, left-field harmonic movement the very fever of the future.'

Igor Stravinsky, *Themes and Conclusions*, 1972, p. 255.

'Would it be far-fetched to deduce a connection between the extraordinary plan of this work and the composer's now severe affliction? Could the introduction be deafness itself, and the ensuing *Allegro vivace* relief perhaps that the inner ear is unimpaired? Is the obsessive pain of the *Allegretto* perhaps what Beethoven felt about the outward effects of deafness? Might the Minuet be a memory of the kind of music he once heard most clearly? In my view it would be neither romantic nor sentimental to suppose what I have tentatively suggested; the inner life of the music seems to support the idea.'

Robert Simpson, *The Chamber Music for Strings*, in: Denis

Arnold and Nigel Fortune editors, *The Beethoven Companion*, 1973, p. 259.

> 'The third *Razumovsky* Quartet is as different from the other two as they are from each other. It has not quite the sweeping breadth and power of the others and is on the whole less memorable thematically. On the other had it made the most immediate appeal of the three when first heard, and this, as Abraham has pointed out [Gerald Abraham, *Beethoven's Second-Period Quartets*, 1944], may well be due to the fact that it contains features that have roots in the eighteenth century.'

Philip Radcliffe, *Beethoven's String Quartets*, 1978, p. 72.

> '[The] C major Quartet is viewed not merely as being smaller in scale ... but more conventional, in certain passages perfunctory, less convincing as a whole, perhaps even a little dissociated. It is only the slow movement that regularly comes in for commendation, even if the integration into the Quartet is not clear to everyone.'

Alan Tyson, *The Razumovsky Quartets: Some aspects of the sources*, in: Alan Tyson, editor, *Beethoven Studies 3*, 1982, pp. 131–2.

> 'If the A major Quartet, Op. 18, No. 5, is a bow toward Mozart's quartet in the same key, K. 464, so does Op. 59, No.3 owe something to Mozart's C major Quartet, K. 465. It attests equally to Beethoven's apprenticeship with Haydn.'

Robert Winter and Robert Martin editors, *The Beethoven Quartet Companion*, 1994, p. 189.

> 'Early listeners to the [C major Quartet] may well have detected Mozartian undertones in its outer movements, and in particular its finale, whose fusion of sonata form and brilliant fugal writing echoes the concluding *Allegro* of the first of Mozart's series of "Haydn" Quartets, K. 387 ... Beethoven's finale is perfectly judged: it crowns a work that had begun hesitantly, and as though in a void, with a triumphant affirmation of faith.'

Misha Donat, *Notes to the BBC Radio Three Beethoven Experience*, Tuesday 7 June 2005, www.bbc.co.uk/radio3/Beethoven

> 'The C-major Quartet displays a mixture of retrospective and futuristic qualities, with certain bold features, such as chromatic slow introduction, showing an affinity to earlier models — in this case, especially to Mozart's *Dissonant* Quartet, K. 465, in the same key. Another break with the past in this last *Razumovsky* Quartet is its perpetuum finale, whose muscular virtuosity and blending of fugal procedure with dramatic sonata rhetoric leave behind all traces of graceful conversation. The genre seems transformed here from music for the private salon to music for the concert hall.'

William Kinderman editor, *The String Quartets of Beethoven*, 2005, p. 5.

The musician and writer Adolph Bernhard Marx — co-founder of the influential *Berliner Allgemeine musikalische Zeitung* — waxed eloquent over the spirit he found enshrined within the String Quartet in C major, Op. 59, No. 2. He compared it, no less, with the Fifth Symphony in C minor, pronouncing it to be one of those works of the composer 'that most perfectly reveal the indomitable spirit of the Master, the courage of the man who did not shrink from probing the very depths of his being, and finding there only darkness and lonely despair, could yet greet his destiny with a cry of defiance'.[i] Perhaps it was the composer's adoption of the key of C major — a key associated with Beethovenian indomitability of spirit and earnestness — that disposed Marx to respond to the Quartet in such a manner. In this context, the observations of Philip Radcliffe have relevance: 'When Beethoven uses [C major] for slow movements it often expresses the deepest serenity as in the Piano Sonata, Op. 111. But in quick movements it is usually the key of brilliance, sometimes broad and triumphant, as in the finale of the Fifth Symphony, sometimes tempered by mysterious shadows, as in the first movement of the *Waldstein* Sonata. The first and last movements of Op. 59, No. 3 are also characterised by brilliance, in the latter more dynamic and powerful, in the former more subtle and whimsical.'[ii] Joseph Kerman proclaimed the Op. 59, No. 3 to be 'the most decidedly overall dynamic' of the three *Razumovsky* Quartets and, indeed, 'a herald for the Fifth Symphony'.[iii]

Some authorities have suggested Beethoven's working of the raw material of the C major Quartet owes a debt to Mozart's earlier style and is reminiscent of both his instrumentation and the distribution of the parts.[iv] Barry Cooper, however, cautions that Beethoven's reliance on Mozart, for example regarding his frequently cited String Quartet K.

465, should not be overstated. Cooper maintains that after the experience of composing the *Eroica* Symphony, Beethoven was not as reliant on Mozart as he had been when adopting his K. 464 as a model when composing his Op. 18 No. 5. He suggests Mozart's K. 465 should be regarded as more of an inspirational model than one from which he needed to learn and imitate.[v]

Op. 59, No. 3 is the only one of the Razumovsky set that does not incorporate a Russian folk melody — *thème russe*. Mindful that the C major Quartet was composed quickly, perhaps even hastily, Alan Tyson suggests this may have imposed on the composer a measure of expediency; we recall Beethoven had entered into specific undertakings, in writing, to Count Razumovsky regarding the timeous delivery of the Op. 59s.[vi] This may go some way to explain Beethoven's failure to incorporate a *thème russe* for the reason he could not spare the time to search through Ivan Pratsch's collection of Russian folk melodies to find a suitable theme.[vii] Moreover, in the minuet Beethoven made use of material he had sketched years earlier — perhaps a further indication of his pragmatism and the need to make haste in the compositional process.[viii] The C major Quartet also has the shortest performing time of the three Op. 59s.

From our previous discussion of the creation origins of the *Razumovsky* String Quartets, we recall the C major was regarded as being the most accessible of the set by the composer's contemporaries. Writing in the *Allgemeine musikalische Zeitung* on 18 March 1807, the reviewer informs: 'Three new, very long and difficult violin quartets by Beethoven, dedicated to the Russian ambassador, Count Razumovsky ... attract attention of all connoisseurs. They are deep in conception and marvellously worked out, but are not universally comprehensible, with the possible exception of the third one, in C major, which by virtue of its individuality, melody, and harmonic power must win over every educated friend of music.'[ix]

As the C major String Quartet became better known, it gradually entered into the repertoire of the more accomplished string players. For example from sometime in 1815 we learn the following. The destruction of Count Razumovsky's palace — and with it the loss of many treasures — together with his approaching old age and failing sight, obliged him to disband his celebrated string quartet (see our commentary to the origins of the Op. 59s). Before their departure, the Count's Quartet gave a series of farewell concerts. One such, led by Ignaz Schuppanzigh, took place in the house of Count Deym, one of the composer's closest associates. The programme was made up entirely of Beethoven's works and included the String Quartet in C major, Op. 59, No. 3. According to a contemporary account in the *AmZ*, 'Beethoven entered at the beginning of the Quartet and 'shared in the deafening applause of the crowded audience'.[x] Further testimony to its popularity is that in 1819 the composition appeared in an arrangement for piano and 1820 for the unusual combination of two guitars.

The first movement is designated *Andante con motto — Allegro vivace*, 'slowly but with motion — very fast'. This was the first time Beethoven had begun a string quartet with a slow introduction. As Gerald Abraham has observed, composers in the eighteenth century seem to have been reluctant to open a string quartet with a slow movement.[xi] Haydn did so in his Op. 71, No. 2 and also Mozart, first in his early K. 171 and then, more memorably twelve years later, in his great C major Quartet, K. 465. None of Beethoven's Op. 18 Quartets have a slow introduction. Perhaps the prejudice against slow-movement openings may be explained on the grounds that even polite, musically inclined audiences take time to settle down and a muted opening is less effective in calling an audience to attention that a declamatory one.

Beethoven's opening of the first movement of the C major Quartet, has been described as a 'piece of sustained mood-painting'.[xii] Perhaps, when composing his introductory bars, Beethoven's mind subconsciously recalled the manner in which Haydn opens his Oratorio *The Creation* with a *Representation of Chaos* expressed in shifting, ambiguous harmonies on muted strings.[xiii] Composed between 1797–98, and performed just a few years before Beethoven set to work on the *Razumovsky* Quartets, it was very much perceived as being progressive, contemporary music. More certain is that Beethoven took as his compositional model Mozart's so-called *Dissonance* Quartet, K. 465. This too was contemporary music having been composed (completed) in 1785.

In the third *Razumovsky* Quartet the introduction is concerned with solely creating 'an atmosphere of mystery and suspense, through slowly shifting chromatic harmonies with no suggestion of either theme or tonality ... It would be hard to find anywhere else in Beethoven's music a passage that relies so predominantly on colour for its own sake.'[xiv] Writing from the viewpoint of the string player, violist Rebecca Clarke remarks: 'The introduction to the third *Razumovsky*, in C, is one of those things in which the tension is so great, both technically and musically, that one hardly dares breathe and can almost see the internal counting of one's companions floating like an astral shape above them.'[xv] Abraham likens the sound-atmosphere that Beethoven creates to 'an atonal fog from which not a single thematic idea emerges'.[xvi] The only discernable feature is a descending scale heard on the cello that is sustained for all of twelve bars – a further nod by the composer in the direction of

Mozart's K. 465.

Beethoven exerts the maximum tension from his opening statement. The introduction expands to fill no fewer than twenty-nine bars, 'spaced chords in tonalities far removed from the principal key of the work'. These are heard only to disappear, allowing the harmony to wander at will 'as the voices die away into the distance'.[xvii] The mood Beethoven engenders disposed Marion Scott to invoke lines from Shakespeare for reasons she explains: 'Beethoven deliberately leads in from silence, by harmonies so shifting that they seem "like the baseless fabric of [this] vision".' [*The Tempest*][xviii]

In contrast to the somewhat dark and forbidding introduction, the ensuing *Allegro vivace* 'breathes the air of the eighteenth century'.[xix] Perhaps it was this part of the C major Quartet that won over the critic of the *Allgemeine musikalische Zeitung*, disposing him to write, as remarked, 'the third [Quartet] in C major, which by virtue of its individuality, melody, and harmonic power, must win over every educated friend of music'. When Abraham's 'fog' is dispelled the music emerges into the sunlit atmosphere of the *Allegro vivace*. 'Beethoven is in one of his happiest moods.'[xx] Robert Simpson contributes to the metaphorical (meteorological) imagery: '[The] first *Allegro* is as sunny as that of the Fourth Symphony.'[xxi] Beethoven's manner here may be more Mozartian and eighteenth century but the music is no mere backward glance to the age of the rococo: 'It is mature Beethoven deliberately imitating Mozart.'[xxii] 'In some ways the music is curiously capricious; here and there are phrases that look back to the eighteenth century, while sometimes ... it looks ahead.' Perhaps Haydn is more evident in spirit here than Mozart in the music's 'brittle texture and semi-jocular manner'.[xxiii] 'In this *Allegro* Beethoven shows ... how he can breathe life into what in other hands would be mere instrumental passage work. It is full of runs and arpeggios, meaningless out of context, but here full of sap and purpose ... A fine cellist can ... make a most impressive effect ... with the low drum-like pizzicato notes of which practically two-thirds of his part is composed.'[xxiv] 'It is the all-pervading use of the tiniest possible motive that gives this movement its real life, its real unity, and finally stamps it as the work of the mature Beethoven.'[xxv] Lam comments on Beethoven's capacity to develop ideas from small motives, what he describes as 'unconsidered trifles' that Beethoven was to demonstrate so memorably years later in the *Diabelli* Variations. He suggests: 'Perhaps he was conscious of the supreme demonstration of this possibility in the finale of Mozart's last symphony; his own example can bear the comparison ... Here is the music for Dante's image of being lost in a dark wood, unable to find the right way.'[xxvi]

A single sketchleaf containing thoughts for the first movement is preserved today in the Beethoven House Archives; it once formed half of a bifolium. In a miscellany in the archives of the Gesellschaft der Musikfreunde, Vienna is a further (corresponding) bifolium that also contains sketches for the first movement.[xxvii] The Autograph Score of the C major String Quartet also forms part of the Beethoven House Collections.[xxviii] Musicological detective work has identified that water-staining on the surviving manuscript sketches indicates Beethoven had sketched the first movement of Op. 59, No. 3 before writing out the score of the last two movements of Op. 59, No. 2.[xxix]

'A moment of uncertainty ... A sense of mystery-making ... The first movement here ends inconclusively, as though to anticipate the contrast of the *Andante* [that follows].' Beethoven is once more following Mozart's precedent in his K. 465. The Austrian music critic Theodor Helm, author of the pioneering *Beethovens Streichquartette* (1885), identified the passage in question as a near quotation from Mozart, describing it as an '*oeuvre d' hommage*'.[xxx]

The second movement is the slow movement and is headed *Andante con moto quasi allegretto* – 'moderately slow with movement, almost quickly'. We have remarked, the C major String Quartet is the only one of the *Razumovsky* Quartets not to incorporate an authenticated *thème russe*. However, such is the intensity of feeling Beethoven bestows upon the *Andante*, that it disposed Marion Scott to remark: 'I firmly believe ... that the theme of the slow movement (*Andante con moto quasi allegretto*) is a Russian folksong. Or shall I say *was* a folksong, since Beethoven handled it so freely? Yet at the back of his version there is still a character recognisably Slavonic if one is acquainted with the folk tunes of Russia and their melodic and rhythmic peculiarities.' In support of her contention Scott cites words of J.W.N. Sullivan, author of *Beethoven* (1927). Writing of the second movement he states: 'There is here a remote and frozen anguish, wailing over some implacable destiny. This is hardly human suffering; it is more like a memory from some ancient and starless night of the soul.' Scott asks: 'Could any words better describe immemorial Russia?'[xxxi] 'Perhaps the second movement, with its melancholy main theme and its highly original use of cello pizzicato, represents Beethoven's attempt to evoke a Slavic character?'[xxxii]

Evidence from the surviving sketches suggests Beethoven's first thoughts for the slow movement were discarded, only to be used later for the *Allegretto* of the Seventh Symphony.'[xxxiii] Basil Lam's observations here are of particular interest: 'The presence among the sketches of the theme that became the *Allegretto* of the Seventh Symphony suggests it was intended for this quartet, but its nature, realisable in cumulative repetition, needed the orchestra and Beethoven seems to have left it as an isolated *Einfall* [idea – thought] and to have turned to the present movement.' He adds, with one of his characteristic literary invocations: 'His strange though wonderful invention eludes all classification – "Errantes silve in magna sub luce maligna".' ['They wander in deep woods, in mournful light.']xxiv For his part, Simpson considered the slow movement to be 'as uniquely hypnotic as the *Allegretto* of the Seventh Symphony.xxv The depth of feeling in the slow movement disposed Joseph de Marliave to respond in his typically effusive style: 'Above heavy, muffled *pizzicati* on the cello a long drawn melancholy phrase is unfolded, expressing, not keen suffering of a recent grief, but some old remembered heartache, coming back out of the past to lie heavy upon the spirit with the dreary weight of despair ... [The] melody is divided among the three upper voices and floats forlornly above them in drifting mists of sadness.'xxxvi Perhaps Beethoven was projecting his own inner sorrow into this music? Amongst the sketches for the movement he wrote: 'Even as you are today being drawn into the stream of society, so it is possible, in spite of social hindrances, to continue your work. Let your deafness be no longer a secret – not even in art.'

Other commentators in addition to those already cited have been moved by the depth of emotion that prevails throughout the *Andante*. Heinz Becker writes: 'In the second movement [Beethoven] creates an image of the endless wastes of the Russian landscape.'xxxvii Although not authenticated as a Russian theme, Robert Winter and Robert Martin perceive it as 'strangely melancholic ... the most touching representation of the exotic ... [as] the first violin sings its distinctly east-of Vienna A-minor song'.xxxviii And likewise, David Wyn Jones: 'As many commentators have noted ... the rather bleak slow movement, a sonata form in A minor ... was probably intended as an evocation of Russian folk music, even if it des not actually quote a folk theme.'[xxix] William Kinderman suggests the melancholy slow movement 'may harbour a more elusive relationship with Russian style'.[xl] For Joseph Kerman: 'What Beethoven plumbs in his slow movement is exactly the mystery of the primitive, the *urmenschlich* [primitive], as [Theodor] Helm put it. This is the well in which each menacing, half-articulate cello stroke seems to find deeper resonance.' Kerman further suggests Beethoven's *Andante* may have served as a model for the instrumental work behind Schubert's A minor String Quartet of 1822.[xli] For Arthur Shepherd, the movements 'sombre wistfulness' foreshadows the intermezzo-like movements in the symphonies and quartets of Brahms. He maintains: 'The movement has an ineffable charm by reason of its reticence and the graceful yet insistent rhythmic patterns not unsuggestive of a gravely executed dance bearing echoes of some dream-like apparition of the past.'[xlii]

With performance practice in mind we quote de Marliave once more: 'The *Andante* is profoundly moving and impressive when given a lyrical interpretation, free from any trace of emotional insincerity, and in which much is made of delicate grace – a rare quality in Beethoven's work.'[xliii] The temptation to overlay the music with an excess of feeling was all too prominent in the nineteenth century when the *portamento* style of playing found favour – in effect, sliding from one note to another.[xliv] The intense feeling implicit in the *Adagio* can tempt even restrained modern-day performers. When in conversation with musicologist David Blum, David Soyer, the cellist member of the celebrated Guarneri Quartet, admitted they did once sentimentalize the movement. Violist Michael Tree accepted this was wrong adding: 'It has a lilt – It's a dance.' That said, second violin John Dalley reminded the group: The atmosphere is hushed to the point of being sinister ... The *sfp* [sudden accent] should be no more than a muted shudder; the bow just touches the string.'[xlv]

The third movement is a minuet that Beethoven requests to be played gracefully (*grazioso*) and to lead straight on to the closing movement (*attacca*). In so doing, and forsaking a scherzo-style of expression, 'it suggests a more conscious awareness of eighteenth-century inheritance than is evident in the two other quartets.'[xlvi] This is music that is easy on the ear: 'a stately dance'[xlvii] played out in music that is 'smooth and lovely'.[xlviii]

We recall the C major Quartet was the only one of the three *Razumovsky's* to find immediate favour with the composer's contemporaries. Doubtless this owed much to the manner in which the music 'glances back to the past' and shares many of its 'classical propensities'.[xlix] Perhaps for these very reasons, this movement has been the object of some opprobrium on the part of certain critics. Vincent d'Indy dismissed the movement as 'a return to the style of 1796'.[l] Musicologist Alan Tyson expresses similar thoughts but in his more restrained, scholarly fashion: 'The use of an old melody in the Minuet ... can also be taken as a further hint of a greater-than-usual infirmity of purpose and readiness with quick solutions.'[li] De Marliave adopts a placatory tone in his assessment of the Minuet: 'Beethoven perhaps felt the incongruity of placing side by side with the profound pessimism of the slow movement a purely light-hearted *jeu d'esprit*. Deliberately, perhaps, he set against the emotional intensity of the *Andante* this unimpassioned movement, in which gradually it was to find relief.'[lii] Gerald Abraham offers a balanced summation: 'This rather square-built movement emphasises the general inferiority of the third *Razumovsky* to its two companions ... But the music of the mature Beethoven must be judged by its own very high standard, and by that standard the movement is a little disappointing.

Yet we must guard against criticising it as if it were a separate composition; it gains considerably from its context.'[liii]

In the fourth and final movement, Beethoven challenges would-be performers of the C major Quartet, Op. 59, No. 3 to the utmost. His marking of *Allegro molto* — 'very fast' — sets the tempo for what one commentator has described as the music's 'barnstorming fury' and its 'commanding ebullient power' with an anticipation even of the drama of the Fifth Symphony — another composition in the key of C.[liv] '[A] glance at the last movement shows that this third quartet is intended to form the grand finale to its sister works, thereby raising the group of three quartets to the stature of a monumental, cyclic *superwork*.'[lv] 'As for the finale, its tumult comes from within, blotting out the despair and the nostalgia of the two previous movements, drowning a sense of failure where ordinary means of communication were concerned. Fugato and sonata are fused together with a heat that Mozart could never have conceived, generating defiant realistic energy — with these means Beethoven hammers out his greatest quartet finale so far, fiercely stretching the medium, yet never breaking it.'[lvi] Other commentators proclaim this movement to be 'the most vertiginously virtuosic of all Beethoven's quartet finales ... one that he would not equal in fierce energy for twenty years.'[lvii]

Radcliffe suggests Beethoven may have drawn inspiration for his creation from the last movement of Haydn's String Quartet, Op. 64, No. 5. With this in mind, he cites the composer's attraction to the idea of a *moto perpetuo* finale to which he had previously given expression in the *presto* to his String Trio in G major, Op. 9, No. 1. Here in the C major Quartet, however, he had to confront the challenge of combining sonata form with fugal texture. Radcliffe finds parallels with Beethoven's solution — the marriage between the contrapuntal and non-contrapuntal — and Mozart's manner in the finale of his String Quartet in G major, K. 387. He admits, Beethoven is more concerned 'mainly with over-all effects' and the result must be judged on its own merits — that he finds 'is irresistible'.[lviii] With this movement Beethoven was initiating a series of more-or-less fugal finales that he would continue in the Piano Sonatas, Opp. 101, 106 and 110, the Cello Sonata, Op. 102, No. 2, and the original finale of the Quartet in B flat, Op. 130, known and performed as a separate work as the *Grosse Fuge*, Op. 133.[lix]

The final movement is written in *fugal style* and to call it a fugue would be, in the punning words of Arthur shepherd, 'stretching several points (as well as counterpoint)'. He continues: 'Despite the fugal presentation of subject matter ... and the free utilization of various fugal devices throughout, the procedures, harmonically and structurally, are those of the sonata rather than the fugue.'[lx] Lam defends Beethoven's procedures in the following terms: 'Both the theme and its exposition have been criticised on the false assumption that Beethoven was attempting a fugue. There are indeed successive entries in tonic, dominant and tonic positions, but the formal argument of fugue would destroy the essential quality of this opening, with its immediate release of a stream of energy.'[lxi] In the previous century, Hans von Bülow had written in similar terms: 'For Beethoven the fugue is not an end in itself, but the most perfectly expressive means of obtaining effect ... Consequently, the emotional nature of the fugue of Beethoven has nothing in common with the purely formal, objective and classical beauty of the fugue of Bach, which is an end in itself.' In the same spirit de Marliave, writing of the composer's fugal style in the final movement of the C major Quartet, remarks: 'All Beethoven wished to borrow from the fugue form was the dynamic impulsion, gained by the strengthening of one part with another, the impetus that each successive entry of the subject gives to the musical idea, as each part adds its own to swell the voice of the others ... It was his breath that gave life to these empty forms; it is of no account whether, in so doing, he disorganised any part of their conventional mechanism ... Beethoven may have written music more profound, but never more triumphant.'[lxii]

Becker is another commentator who accepts that the fugato of the last movement is not constructed 'with baroque strictness'. Rather, he perceives Beethoven's construction as a manifestation of his 'dormant genius' in which he allows the instrumental lines to converge from time to time in 'harmonic oases' from which they 'strike out, refreshed, to plunge once more into the contrapuntal struggle.'[lxiii] For Daniel Brandenburg: '[The] *fugato* of the last movement ... provides the listener with some indication of those strokes of genius that this master composer from Bonn would employ in later works.'[lxiv] Casting her eye over the movement as a whole, Marion Scott singles out for remark the manner in which the instruments 'take it in turn to mount in fiery sequence' events she describes as 'incredibly exciting'; she adds 'the whole movement is so exciting that one forgets the enormous intellectual power controlling it'.[lxv] It was the final movement that captivated the music critic writing in the *Review musicale* of 24 March 1832: 'The vigorous movement of this fugue demands only perfect ensemble, accuracy, and finish ... exact precision and fine balance of bowing that blend all these technical difficulties into a perfect whole, finally, incomparable zest.'[lxvi] The movement must also have captivated Johannes Brahms when he played a challenging piano reduction of the piece, from memory, as an encore at a concert he gave in Vienna in 1867.[lxvii]

The origins of Beethoven's progress in the art of contrapuntal writing may be traced back to his studies with Haydn and, notably, those with the music theorist Johann Georg Albrechtsberger. He was also familiar with the fugal writing of such other pedagogues as Johann Joseph Fux. Moreover, he made a close study of the sonata-fugue passage in Mozart's String Quartet, K. 387, writing out the text in full. It has been suggested Beethoven, ever eager to learn from the innovations of other composers, would have been familiar with the string quartets of the pioneering French composer Antoine Reicha.[lxviii] In particular, his so-called String Quartet *Quatuor scientifique*, that makes prominent use of fugal writing — from which its name derives — is almost contemporaneous (1806) with Beethoven's *Razumovsky* Quartets. In our preceding studies, we have seen that Beethoven used fugal constructions in Op. 59, No. 1 (*Allegro*, first movement) and in Op. 59, No. 2 (*Allegretto*, third movement) but in Op. 59, No. 3 fugue features 'in a climatic position' in combination with sonata form in the finale.[lxix] Thereby, and in other ways too, Beethoven unifies each of the three quartets 'and asks us to accept Op. 59, as itself, a totality — a triptych'.[lxx]

The fugue subject is first heard on the viola in a manner that Denis Matthews describes as 'amusingly garrulous'. This opens up into a movement which, although 'only intermittently contrapuntal', develops into 'a near tour de force for the players' possessed as it is of 'extrovert energy and high spirits' — 'further testimony of the composer's newly relaxed mastery'.[lxxi] In his study of performance practice in Beethoven's chamber music for strings, John Daverio instances the capacity of Haydn and Mozart 'to conflate sonata-form rhetoric and fugal techniques' and thereby to present them as 'a venue for high comedy'. In the finale of Op. 59, No. 3 he considers Beethoven 'intensified the dialectic between learned and comic styles'. He cites '[the] breathless almost frantic quality' of the movement and, in similar fashion to Matthews, describes the fugue subject as 'chatty'. 'This high-spirited spoof on the learned style reaches a highpoint in the development section, where the comic derivative of the subject — hurled from the top to the bottom of the textures — knows no better than to march up an octave and back down again.'[lxxii]

'This fugue, one of the greatest movements in the whole of quartet literature, is a most intoxicating thing to play from beginning to end ... In the unanimous crescendo towards the end of the movement the volume of tone becomes so incredibly full one feels oneself part of an orchestra.'[lxxiii] The movement culminates in a breathless crescendo 'which threatens the limits of the Classical quartet'.[lxxiv] Sacheverell Sitwell, discussing Mozart's *Jupiter* Symphony, describes it as 'a masterpiece on the purest lines of classical architecture', the fugal treatment of the final allegro being in his estimation 'without any parallel in music'. Turning to considerations of the C major Quartet, Op. 59, No. 1, he remarks: 'If the wonderful fugue with which Beethoven ends the Third *Razumovsky* Quartet is, perhaps, a little the same in spirit and in intention as this finale to the *Jupiter*, it is hardly necessary to stress the difference between a piece laid out for a quartet of strings and a movement employing the full orchestra.'[lxxv] Basil Lam, alongside Sitwell, believed Beethoven drew inspiration for his sonata-polyphony from the closing pages of the *Jupiter* Symphony.[lxxvi] In the same spirit, David Wyn Jones contends the final movement of the C major Quartet 'is an obvious statement of pedagogical mastery to be placed alongside the finales of Mozart's *Jupiter* Symphony, his Quartet in G major (K. 387) and Haydn's Symphony No. 95'.[lxxvii]

When the American musician Robert Craft asked his

close friend Igor Stravinsky if he would identify some of his favourite events in the quartets of Beethoven, he made reference to the Op. 59 set in the following terms. 'In Op. 59, No, 3, the *Andante* movement anticipates Schuman and Mendelssohn, neither of whom were capable of anything as original as the *pizzicato* idea itself or as mighty as the upbeat to measure 66 and the great arc from measure 127 to measure 135.[lxxviii]

In conclusion we draw on the enthusiasm and eloquence of Joseph de Marliave: 'Nothing has ever been written for the quartet to equal this climax of monumental power; the *sforzando* chord on the three instruments bursts like a wild cry in response to each dazzling flash; it brings to mind the song of Orpheus in Gluck's opera, and the relentless interruption of the furies. (Compare also the trumpet-call of the second *Leonora* Overture, closely akin to this movement.)'[lxxix] 'It is inconceivable that modern criticism should undervalue this magnificent finale.'[lxxx]

[i] Quoted in Arthur Shepherd, 1935, p. 35.
[ii] Philip Radcliffe, 1978, p. 74.
[iii] Joseph Kerman, 1967, p. 119.
[iv] Quoted in Arthur Shepherd, 1935, p. 35.
[v] Barry Cooper, 1991, p. 234.
[vi] Emily Anderson, editor and translator, 1961, Letter No. 135, p. 153.
[vii] Alan Tyson, *The Razumovsky Quartets, Some aspects of the sources*, in: Alan Tyson editor, *Beethoven studies 3*, 1982, pp. 131–2.
[viii] William Kinderman, 1997, pp. 108–9.
[ix] Wayne M. Senner, Robin Wallace and William Meredith, editors, *The critical reception of Beethoven's compositions by his German contemporaries*, 1999, Vol. 1, pp. 52–3.
[x] Elliot Forbes, editor, *Thayer's life of Beethoven*, 1967, p. 640.
[xi] Gerald Abraham, *Beethoven's Chamber Music*, In: *The Age of Beethoven, The New Oxford History of Music, Vol. VIII*, Gerald Abraham, editor, 1988, p. 44 and p. 340.
[xii] Philip Radcliffe, 1978, p. 78.
[xiii] See Robert Winter and Robert Martin, editors, 1994, p. 189.
[xiv] Philip Radcliffe, 1978, p. 73.
[xv] Rebecca Clarke, *The [Beethoven] quartets as a player sees them*, in: *Music & Letters, Beethoven*, Special Issue: Vol. VIII, No. 2, 1927, p. 182.
[xvi] Gerald Abraham, 1944, p. 46.
[xvii] Joseph de Marliave, 1925, (reprint 1961), p. 116.

[xviii] Marion M. Scott, 1940, p. 260.
[xix] William Kinderman, 1997, p. 111.
[xx] Romain Rolland, 1917, p. 185.
[xxi] Robert Simpson, *The chamber music for strings*, in: Denis Arnold and Nigel Fortune, editors, *The Beethoven companion*, 1973, p. 258.
[xxii] Gerald Abraham, 1944, pp. 45–6.
[xxiii] Philip Radcliffe, 1978, p. 74.
[xxiv] Rebecca Clarke, *The [Beethoven] quartets as a player sees them*, in: *Music & Letters, Beethoven*, Special Issue: Vol. VIII, No. 2, 1927, p. 182.
[xxv] Basil Lam, *Musical Pilgrim*, p. 46, cited in: Joseph Kerman, *The Beethoven quartets*, 1967, p. 140.
[xxvi] Basil Lam, 1975, p. 58.
[xxvii] Beethoven House, Digital Archives Document HCB Mh 72 and Document BH 100.
[xxviii] Beethoven House, Digital Archives Document, BH 62.
[xxix] Barry Cooper, 1990, p. 118.
[xxx] Joseph Kerman, 1967, pp. 139–40.
[xxxi] Marion M. Scott, 1940, pp. 256–7.
[xxxii] Misha Donat, *Notes to the BBC Radio Three Beethoven experience*, Tuesday 7 June 2005, www.bbc.co.uk/radio3/Beethoven
[xxxiii] The pioneer in Beethoven studies Gustav Nottebohm first made the discovery of the symphonic *allegretto* theme in a sketchbook from 1806. See: Gerald Abraham, 1944, p. 49, note 1. See also: Philip Radcliffe, 1978, p. 76 and Joseph de Marliave, 1925 (reprint 1961), p. 59.
[xxxiv] Basil Lam, 1975, p. 60.
[xxxv] Robert Simpson, *The chamber music for strings*, in: Denis Arnold and Nigel Fortune, editors, *The Beethoven companion*, 1973, p. 258.
[xxxvi] Joseph de Marliave, 1925, (reprint 1961), pp. 124–5.
[xxxvii] Heinz Becker, Liner notes to The Amadeus Quartet, *Beethoven: The string quartets*, 1974.
[xxxviii] Robert Winter and Robert Martin editors, 1994, p. 193.
[xxxix] David Wyn Jones: *Beethoven and the Viennese legacy* in: Robin Stowell, editor *The Cambridge companion to the string quartet*, 2003, pp. 214–6.
[xl] William Kinderman, 1997, p. 108.
[xli] Joseph Kerman, 1967, pp. 149–50.
[xlii] Arthur Shepherd, 1935, p. 35.
[xliii] Joseph de Marliave, 1925, (reprint 1961), p. 128.
[xliv] See: David Milsom, *Theory and practice in late nineteenth-century violin performance: an examination of style in performance, 1850–1900*, 2003, p. 85.
[xlv] David Blum, *The art of quartet playing: the Guarneri Quartet in conversation with David Blum*, 1986, p. 95.
[xlvi] David Wyn Jones: *Beethoven and the Viennese legacy* in: Robin Stowell, editor *The Cambridge companion to the string quartet*, 2003, pp. 214–6.
[xlvii] Romain Rolland, 1917, p. 185.
[xlviii] Robert Winter and Robert Martin editors, 1994, p. 194.
[xlix] Misha Donat, *Notes to the BBC Radio Three Beethoven experience*, Tuesday 7 June 2005, www.bbc.co.uk/radio3/Beethoven
[l] Quoted in Philip Radcliffe, 1978, p. 78.
[li] Alan Tyson, *Sketches and autographs*, in: Denis Arnold, and Nigel Fortune, editors. *The Beethoven companion*, 1973, pp. 443–58.

[lii] Joseph de Marliave, 1925, (reprint 1961), p. 129.
[liii] Gerald Abraham, 1944, p. 51.
[liv] Joseph Kerman, 1967, p. 144.
[lv] Heinz Becker, Liner notes to The Amadeus Quartet, *Beethoven: The string quartets*, 1974.
[lvi] Robert Simpson, *The chamber music for strings*, in: Denis Arnold and Nigel Fortune, editors, *The Beethoven companion*, 1973, pp. 259–60.
[lvii] Robert Winter and Robert Martin editors, 1994, p. 194.
[lviii] Philip Radcliffe, 1978, p. 79.
[lix] With acknowledgement to Gerald Abraham, 1944, pp. 53–4.
[lx] Arthur Shepherd, 1935, p. 36.
[lxi] Basil Lam, 1975, p. 62.
[lxii] Joseph de Marliave, 1925, (reprint 1961), pp. 131–2. The quotation from Hans von Bülow is derived from this source; it originally appeared in von Bülow's critical edition of the Beethoven Piano Sonatas.
[lxiii] Heinz Becker, Liner notes to The Amadeus Quartet, *Beethoven: The string quartets*, 1974.
[lxiv] Daniel Brandenburg, Liner notes to The Alexander String Quartet, *Beethoven: String Quartets*, Arte Nova Classics.
[lxv] Marion M. Scott, 1940, p. 260.
[lxvi] Quoted in Joseph de Marliave, 1925 (reprint 1961), pp. 139–40.
[lxvii] As mentioned by Romain Rolland, 1917, p. 185.
[lxviii] Paul Griffiths, 1983, pp. 88–9.
[lxix] The words quoted are derived from David Wyn Jones: *Beethoven and the Viennese legacy* in: Robin Stowell, editor *The Cambridge companion to the string quartet*, 2003, pp. 214–6.
[lxx] Paul Griffiths, 1983, pp. 88–9.
[lxxi] Denis Matthews, 1985, p. 136.
[lxxii] John Daverio, *Manner, tone and tendency in Beethoven's chamber music for strings*, in: Glenn Stanley, editor, *The Cambridge companion to Beethoven*, 2000, p. 150.
[lxxiii] Rebecca Clarke, *The [Beethoven] quartets as a player sees them*, in: *Music & Letters, Beethoven*, Special Issue: Vol. VIII, No. 2, 1927, p. 183.
[lxxiv] Heinz Becker, Liner notes to The Amadeus Quartet, *Beethoven: The string quartets*, 1974.
[lxxv] Sacheverell Sitwell, 1932, pp. 108–9.
[lxxvi] Basil Lam, 1975, p. 62.
[lxxvii] David Wyn Jones: *Beethoven and the Viennese legacy* in: Robin Stowell, editor *The Cambridge companion to the string quartet*, 2003, pp. 214–6.
[lxxviii] Igor Stravinsky and Robert Craft, 1968, p. 113.
[lxxix] Quoted in Joseph de Marliave, 1925 (reprint 1961), pp. 143–5.
[lxxx] Basil Lam, 1975, p. 64.

STRING QUARTET IN E-FLAT MAJOR, OP. 74, *THE HARP*

'The subject is the victory of a sheer delight in creative power over a restless search for fresh knowledge, and here [in Op. 74] the artistic expression is so finished and absolute that once more a phase in Beethoven's development as a man and artist is rounded off and brought to a close.'

Paul Bekker, *Beethoven*, 1925, p. 318.

'The Op. 74 Quartet was written only two years after the Op. 59; nevertheless, it reveals a fundamental change of thought as well as of form. Here we find none of the outward brilliance of effect, the deliberate objectivity, and pure technical beauty of the three quartets of the earlier group. Here one sees mirrored in the music the dark places of the artist's soul; here at last Beethoven finds expression for all the pent-up love and sorrow, plumbing the depths of his unsatisfied longings, laying bare the secret beauty of his inmost thoughts. At the same time he evokes a fuller expressive richness from the genre of the quartet than ever hitherto ... In Op. 74 there is so perfect a union between the thought of the artist and its expression through the medium of the string quartet, that one can imagine no other medium to take its place.'

Joseph de Marliave, *Beethoven's Quartets*, 1925 (1961 reprint), p. 148.

'The so-called *Harp* Quartet, Op. 74 in E flat, is one of which I have always been particularly fond, though I sometimes rather wish it had some other name; the passages in question sound so lacking in resonance if compared to the notes of a harp, yet are so characteristic and effective when looked upon as the plain everyday *pizzicato* that they are.'

Rebecca Clarke, *The [Beethoven] quartets as a player sees them*, in: *Music & Letters, Beethoven*, Special Issue: Vol. VIII, No. 2, 1927, p. 183.

'A gallant work, a great work, but not one of his greatest because in its outward panoply of music there is a little more of the glory of this world than of the glory of the spirit.'

Marion M. Scott, *Beethoven: (The Master Musicians)*, 1940, p. 260.

> 'The Quartet in E flat is not one to raise deep questions and great issues ... Liberation from necessity to raise and meet them, indeed, helps give the piece its special *élan*, as does also a sense of quiet exhilaration in artistic processes circumscribed and carried through with elegance and tact and perfect accuracy ... Unlike any of the quartets of Op. 59, this Quartet in E flat is ostentatiously at peace with itself.

Joseph Kerman, *The Beethoven Quartets*, 1967, p. 158 and p. 168.

> 'Op. 74 is an underrated masterpiece of deep, consummate beauty of thought and execution.'

Robert Simpson, *The Chamber Music for Strings* in: Denis Arnold and Nigel Fortune, editors, *The Beethoven Companion*, 1973, p. 260.

> 'Of all Beethoven's quartets this is perhaps the most subjective, inasmuch as its contrasts seem not altogether integrated except by reference to the composer's personality. This, it may be objected, is true of all works created by a major artist, but there is a sense in which the perfectly realised idea of a work liberates it from its creator, so that it becomes "seraphically free from taints of personality" [*The Lark Ascending*, George Meredith] ... Perhaps there is a phase in the development of certain supreme artists when the awareness of total mastery prompts a serious playing with the sheer range of expression.'

Basil Lam, *Beethoven String Quartets*, 1975, pp. 64–5.

'[The] E-flat Quartet, Op. 74, called *Harp* because of the striking *pizzicato* arpeggios in the opening *Allegro*, is a lyrical contemplative, and expressive work which — despite its unusual and climactic Scherzo — retreats from the innovative thrust of the *Razumovsky* Quartets and returns to the central vocabulary of the Viennese high-Classical style.'

Maynard Solomon, *Beethoven*, 1977, p. 210.

'The three works that comprise Op. 59 are the most exuberant and richly scored of Beethoven's quartets; the next two move gradually in the direction of the sparer texture and more withdrawn manner of the last works. The Quartet in E-flat major, Op. 74, is full and mellow in sound, but for the most part more intimate and thoughtful than any of the *Razumovsky* Quartets.'

Philip Radcliffe, *Beethoven's String Quartets*, 1978, p. 82.

'No doubt it was to distinguish himself from what the quartet had become that he called his F minor work Op. 95 (1810) *Quartetto Serioso*, though this has had the unfortunate effect of suggesting that its immediate predecessor, Op. 74 in E flat (1809), does not have to be taken seriously ... In fact the ostentatious seriousness of Op. 95 is implicit in Op. 74, and the two works together inhabit a quartet style quite different from that of the *Razumovsky* triptych.'

Paul Griffiths, *The String Quartet*, 1983, pp. 92–3.

> 'The terse Op. 95 is in every sense difficult Beethoven; by comparison, Op. 74 is genial and inviting of access, though at no sacrifice of the personal and original.'

Michael Steinberg, *The Middle Quartets*, in: Robert Winter and Robert Martin editors, *The Beethoven Quartet Companion*, 1994, pp. 196–7.

> 'Then: the *Harp* Quartet, an undervalued piece but very significant and peculiar piece. The association of chords in the introduction contains the idea of Schumann's *Der Dichter spricht* even in its details. The slow movement points towards the *late* Schubert in details such as the use of the chord of the sixth as if this were a new, separate stage. Furthermore, the whole quartet is like a premonition of Beethoven's *late* style. A passage from the slow movement quotes the later *Arioso*.'

Theodor W. Adorno, *Beethoven: the philosophy of music; fragments and texts*, 1998, p. 82.

> 'Lyricism takes a somewhat different turn in Op. 74 ... The varied treatment of the *harp* music in the first movement, the alternation of refrain and episodes in the second movement, and the Scherzo and Trio of the third, the rich embellishments of the hymnic main theme of the second movement – all of these traits foreshadow the design of the finale.'

John Daverio, *Manner, Tone and Tendency in Beethoven's Chamber Music for Strings*, in: Glenn Stanley editor, *The*

Cambridge Companion to Beethoven, 2000, p. 157.

> 'Beethoven's next quartet, Op. 74 in E flat, is probably his most neglected work in the genre, despite its appealing nickname ... A major reason for its comparative neglect is that it does not seem to embrace the progressive agenda evident in Op. 59 ... Also, had it belonged to a set of three or six it might have commanded more attention; as a single work it has tended to be forgotten.'

David Wyn Jones, *Beethoven and the Viennese Legacy* in: Robin Stowell, editor, *The Cambridge Companion to the string quartet*, 2003, p. 218.

> 'We can reckon this quartet among the most remarkable products of the years from 1808 to 1812, the romantic twilight of Beethoven's second maturity ... From the beginning of Op. 74 we are in a new world of Beethoven's quartet writing, and as the work progresses it reveals an increasingly complex aesthetic profile. From movement to movement, the work displays unusual extremes of character. This juxtaposition of contrasts is evident in the larger relationship of the four movements, and also in the thematic organization of the first movement.'

Lewis Lockwood, *Beethoven's "Harp" Quartet*, in: William Kinderman, editor, *The String Quartets of Beethoven*, 2005, pp. 91–2.

> 'To chart the critical reception of Beethoven's String Quartet in E-flat, Op. 74, from its publica-

tion in 1810 — some twelve months after its composition — to the present is, very broadly speaking, to observe a twofold mutation in its perception: firstly, from a "modernistic" work into one that stands as a monument to Beethoven's classical heritage; secondly, from a serious, even dark work of deep personal feeling into one that is open, conventional, and unchallenging.'

Nicholas Marston, *Fantasy and Farewell in the Quartet in E-flat, Op. 74*, in: William Kinderman, editor, *The Stri-Quartets of Beethoven,* 2005, p. 109.

Beethoven's String Quartet in E-flat major, Op. 74 is the tenth in the sequence of his sixteen works composed for the genre. The work is familiarly known by its nickname *The Harp* arising from the use made by the composer of a sequence of arpeggiated *pizziacati* that are heard near the start of the first movement. The soubriquet was not sanctioned by Beethoven who conferred few titles on his compositions. Although long established, not all are convinced the nickname is appropriate. Robert Simpson declared it to be 'rather silly'[i]. Gerald Abraham condemned the work to be 'foolishly nicknamed' for what he considered to be 'a not very harp-like passage in its first movement'.[ii] Joseph Kerman remarks: 'This passage ... earned the quartet its nickname "The Harp" — for no very commanding reason, we may think today, with the Bartók quartets twanging in our ears. But at the time probably no quartet had ever employed *pizzicato* so brashly.'[iii] Notwithstanding such reservations as these, as musicologist Wilfrid Mellers has remarked, nicknames persist and serve a purpose. They help to identify a work, are more readily recalled than opus numbers and reveal something about the impression a composition made on its first audiences — from which period nicknames usually derive.[iv] Unlike its three predecessors the *Razumovsky* Quartets, Op. 74 was not composed in response to a commission. We discuss the impulses that disposed the composer to return to the quartet genre in due course.

Writing in his characteristically expressive manner, the French musicologist Joseph de Marliave considered the E flat Quartet sprang from a twofold inspiration: 'the intimate consciousness of [Beethoven's] tenderest and saddest emotions, and the resolute determination to resist the bitter realities of life'.[v] De Marliave is alluding here to such extra-musical influences, bearing on the composer at the period in question, as the irretrievable loss of his hearing, the death of two of his closest teachers and his personal physician, the pain of unrequited love, the insecurity of his financial position — and with it the prospect of leaving Vienna for good, and the harrowing experience of the French bombardment followed by the occupation of Vienna — with its attendant upheavals and deprivations. We make further reference to these considerations in their appropriate chronological sequence.

In his estimation of the quartet Paul Bekker is amongst those who consider that extra-musical influences, of the kind to which we have just made reference, may have conditioned the character of the work. He finds several points of resemblance, 'both external and internal', between the E-flat major Quartet and its predecessor that in C major. Both, he argues, express 'a glad sense of power' but in the Op. 74 Bekker sees this idea 'more fully developed and established with greater wealth of detail'. For him 'the spiritual roots' of the C major Quartet are to be found in the two preceding *Razumowsky* Quartets in F major and E minor. The E-flat major Quartet on the other hand, he asserts, stands alone 'with no close connection with any other work'. He elaborates, de Marliave fashion: 'Now the battle with Fate has been fought to a finish, the C minor phantoms have been exorcised, and the victorious composer has awakened afresh to the joy of creation.'[vi]

In his commentary to the composition, David Wyn Jones calls to mind its predecessor: 'If Op. 59 No. 3 in C looks over its shoulder to some notable works by Haydn and Mozart, from the 1780s and 1790s, this retrospective air, even more apparent in Op. 74, seems to focus on Haydn and Beethoven's own music from the 1790s.' However, he qualifies this observation: 'As often in Beethoven's output, retrospection does not produce a dated, characterless work, but promotes a new coherence.'[vii] Maynard Solomon identifies with much of what Jones has to say: 'Here, as in most of the other chamber and sonata works of this period, one senses that Beethoven was attempting to re-establish contact with styles from which he had largely held aloof after 1802.'[viii] Like Jones though he also finds Beethoven feeling his way to a future style of expression: 'There are powerful intimations of late Beethoven in the Violin Sonata, Op. 96, the Sonata Op. 90, and the String Quartets, Op. 74 and Op. 95.'[ix] Other authorities also consider the E-flat major Quartet looks to the future: 'The Quartet, Op. 74 ... already shows a reaction from the brilliant, almost symphonic style of the three *Razumovsky* Quartets: the idiom points rather in the direction of the intimate, personal manner of the late quartets.'[x] 'Op. 74, while sounding just as much a second-period work as a whole, as Op. 95 sounds a third period, has many passages which are directly third-period expression.'[xi] 'The *Harp* ... is as serious in its own way, as any other Beethoven quartet.'[xii]

Beethoven's debt to Haydn may have emotional connotations that some authorities believe found their way into the E-flat major Quartet. The much-venerated composer died on 31 May 1809 aged 77 and was honoured in a memorial service at which Mozart's Requiem was performed. Op. 74 was the first large-scale composition to occupy Beethoven since Haydn's death and may have been commenced as an act of homage to his former teacher.[xiii] Curiously, Beethoven does not appear to have left any written expression of feeling concerning Haydn's passing — none such appears in his extensive correspondence or recollections of conversations between him and his contemporaries. Perhaps Beethoven felt more disposed to give expression to his feelings through the medium of his music, as Paul Griffiths explains: '[The] two quartets [Op. 74 and Op. 95] might be construed as a homage to Haydn ... The key of E flat, common in Beethoven but not used by him before in a quartet, was the one that Haydn had favoured above all others in his quartets, and there was also a precedent in Haydn for a profound A flat slow movement in an E-flat quartet: Haydn had done that in Op. 20, No. 1, a work which Beethoven had copied out in the middle 1790s.'[xiv]

At the period in question, the key of E flat had particular significance for Beethoven. It has been described as his 'heroic key par excellence'[xv] and the key of his 'E flat phase'.[xvi] In this context he had pioneered the way in 1805 with the epochal *Eroica* Symphony, Op. 55 and during the first three months of 1809 he was at work of the Fifth Piano Concerto, Op. 73 the *Emperor* — whose very nickname proclaims its heroic character. Mention may also be made of the Piano Trio, Op. 72, No. 2 and the Piano Sonata *Les Adieux*, Op. 81a with its highly charged expression suggestive of the feelings of sorrow of parting and of the joy of reunion, enshrined within its three movements titled *Lebewohl, Abwesenheit,* and *Wiedersehen.* When the E-flat major

Quartet, Op. 74 is added to the sequence, in the words of Lewis Lockwood: '[There] is no other time in his career when Beethoven composed three major works in the same key.'[xvii]

If we reflect on the number of compositions Beethoven composed in the three years that separate the completion of the *Razumovsky* Quartets and the commencement of *The Harp* Quartet (1806–09), we cannot help but be astonished by their diversity. In the words of one authority: '[Each] new project raised much great and imaginative technical issues ... [in] ... This era of superb, surpassing fecundity'.[xviii] By way of illustration, we have: the Fourth, Fifth and Sixth (*Pastoral*) Symphonies; three concertos, namely, the Fourth, the already mentioned Fifth (*Emperor*) — both for piano — and the Violin Concerto — also reworked by the composer as a piano concerto. To these may be added: the chamber works in the form of the Cello Sonata in A, Op. 69, the two Trios, Op. 70; works for solo piano including the Variations, Op. 76, the Fantasia, Op. 77 and the Sonatina, Op. 79; the Mass in C; and the Overture *Coriolan*. Moreover, in the winter of 1809–10, Beethoven commenced work on the incidental music to Goethe's drama *Egmont* that portrays the heroism of the nobleman Count Egmont who resisted tyranny at great personal cost. We can easily imagine Beethoven identifying with Egmont in his own personal struggle with misfortune.

From the foregoing it is apparent that the String Quartet in E-flat major, Op. 74 was nurtured in close proximity to companion works of a rich and diverse kind. Reflecting on this body of work, Beethoven's biographer Alexander Thayer felt disposed to remark: 'The close of 1809 terminated in a decade (1800–09) during which — if quality be considered, as well as number, variety, extent and originality — Beethoven's works offer a more splendid exhibition of intellectual power than those of any composer produced within a like term of years.'[xix]

Before proceeding directly to a consideration of the creation origins of the Op. 74 Quartet, we pause for a moment and turn our attention to the reasons for Joseph de Marliave making reference to 'the dark places of the artist's soul' and of Beethoven finding expression in the music of *The Harp* Quartet 'for all [his] pent-up love and sorrow' (see our opening quotations). Thereby, we will establish a framework of reference within which the Op. 74 Quartet came into being and learn something of the composer and his circumstances through the accounts of his contemporaries.

1809 was inauspicious for Beethoven in a number of ways. The death of Haydn has been mentioned. On 7 March his former teacher the theorist Johann Georg Albrechtsberger also passed away; he had taught Beethoven the rudiments of harmony and counterpoint. Beethoven must have felt the loss personally since, on completion of his studies, he had noted alongside them, 'patience, diligence, persistence, and sincerity will lead to success' – a reflection on Albrechtsberger's own compositional philosophy. Of greater significance to Beethoven must have been the death of Johann Adam Schmidt on 19 February. He had been the composer's physician since 1801, endeavoring to bring about improvements to his hearing by, amongst other things, the application of galvanic current – an innovation at that time. Such was Beethoven's trust in, and appreciation of, Schmidt's effort's that he dedicated to him the Trio for Piano and Cello in E-flat major, Op. 38 – an arrangement of the immensely popular Septet Op. 20.

A measure of the depression Beethoven was experiencing as a consequence of his loss of hearing can be judged from a letter he wrote on 2 May 1810 to the German physician Franz Gerhard Wegeler; the two had been friends from their school days together in Bonn. In his letter he laments how beautiful life would be for him had it not been 'poisoned forever'. He remarks how for the last two years he had sought respite by trying to lead a quiet life away from society and concludes, with a combination of despair and fortitude: 'If I had not read somewhere that a man should not voluntarily quit this life so long as he can still perform a good deed, I should have quit this earth long ago.'[xx]

Just how withdrawn from society Beethoven had become, as a consequence of his deafness, is apparent from an account left by the German composer and music critic Johann Friedrich Reichardt. On 30 November 1808 he called on Beethoven but had much difficulty in locating his address. He eventually tracked down the composer in what he describes as a large, desolate and lonely apartment. Of his eventual meeting with the composer he writes: 'His is a powerful nature, like a Cyclops in appearance but at the same time very intimate, hearty and good ... But he has become quite estranged from Prince Lichnowsky [his former patron] who lives in the upper part of the same house, although some years ago they were on very intimate terms.'[xxi]

A further recollection of Beethoven, from the time he was at work on the Op. 74 String Quartet, comes from an unlikely source in the guise of the French army officer Baron Louis-Philippe Trémont. He had been made a member of Napoleon's *Conseil d'État*, in 1808, and was responsible for delivering the Council's despatches to Napoleon during the French invasion of Austria; Bonaparte had by then established his headquarters in Schönbrunn Palace. Trémont called on Beethoven in 1809 and to his great surprise was cordially received. Doubtless this was made possible since he bore a letter of introduction from the composer and theorist Antoine Reicha. He was then resident in Paris but had known Beethoven from their days together in Bonn. Perhaps the rapport between the two was aided by the fact that Trémont was an informed and ardent music-lover. When he eventually located the composer he found him living in reduced circumstances: 'Picture to yourself the dirtiest, most disorderly place imaginable – blotches of moisture covered the ceiling; an oldish grand piano, on which the dust disputed the place with various pieces of engraved and manuscript music ... under the piano an unemptied *pot de nui* [chamber pot]!' To Trémont's delight, he was privileged to hear Beethoven improvise: 'His tempestuous inspiration poured forth lovely melodies, and harmonies unsought because, mastered by musical emotion, he gave no thought to the search for effects that might have occurred to him with pen in hand; they were produced spontaneously without divagation.'[xxii]

Following the death of Dr. Johann Schmidt, Beethoven sought the advice of the physician Dr. Johann Malfatti.[xxiii] He was of Italian extraction and had studied with the celebrated Luigi Galvani – the pioneer the electro-bio-galvanism practiced by Dr. Schmidt. Beethoven consulted with Malfatti on several occasions and it was he who advised him to seek the curative power of mineral springs – both bathing and imbibing – to ease his recurrent abdominal pains – usually referred to by the composer as 'colic'. Beethoven soon established a close relationship with the Malfatti family and, relevant to our narrative, developed an affection for Malfatti's cousin Therese; she was twenty-two years younger than Beethoven. Some authorities consider Beethoven wished to marry Therese, a circumstance that alarmed the family – doubtless because of the difference in their age and, not least, an awareness of the composer's unorthodox ways.[xxiv] Beethoven learned of his 'rejection' from his friend and assistant Baron Ignaz von Gleichenstein. His disappointment can be inferred from a letter he wrote to Gleichenstein sometime in April 1810 in which he laments: 'Your news has plunged me from the heights of the most sublime ecstasy down into the depths.' He resolved to find happiness in his own heart and not to seek it from outside; 'You must create everything for yourself in your own heart.'[xxv] The enduring legacy of Beethoven's relationship with Therese was his much-loved Bagatelle No. 25 in A minor, WoO 59, better known as *Für Elise*. The manuscript of the composition was discovered amongst Therese's papers following her death and was not published until some 60 years after its composition in 1810. It is believed Therese was the intended dedicatee but was deprived of her immortality by someone's misreading of Beethoven's handwriting on the manuscript.[xxvi]

To add to Beethoven's woes, in April 1809 the beleaguered Austrian regime declared war on France. The consequences for Vienna and its residents were serious and far-reaching. The Austrian army was soon overcome and driven back across the Danube. Beethoven's disquiet, and doubtless that of all the residents of Vienna, was heightened when the French began to bombard the city on 11 May. The windows of Haydn's apartments were shattered and a shell exploded in the grounds of the school then attended by the eleven-year old Franz Schubert. At this time Beethoven resided near the defensive city-wall (*Wasserkunst Bastei*) that became a specific target and blasts were discharged close to the windows of his own apartment. Thayer comments: 'Every shot directed ... was liable to plunge into Beethoven's windows.' He eventually sought refuge in the basement of the house of his brother Karl, protecting his remaining hearing with cushions that he placed over his ears.[xxvii]

Vienna surrendered to the French on 12 May, but Beethoven's misfortunes were only just beginning. Punitive taxes were imposed; inflation took hold – affecting Beethoven's income; food was scarce, poor and expensive. All the while the summer heat was intolerable and Beethoven, confined to the city, could not enjoy the strolls into the countryside that were so essential to his creative process. Illustrative of the extent to which the populace were subjugated is that Vienna's principal newspaper, the *Wiener Zeitung*, was obliged to display the Napoleonic eagle on its masthead. On 26 July Beethoven wrote of the disruption to his publisher Breitkopf and Härtell based in Leipzig: '[We] have been suffering misery in a most concentrated form ... I have produced very little coherent work ... The whole course of events has in my case affected both body and soul ... Heaven knows what is going to happen ... What a destructive, disorderly life I see and hear around me, nothing but drums, cannons, and human misery in every form.'[xxviii]

With the threat of the French occupation of Vienna, the Royal Household sought refuge by fleeing the city to take up residence on their estates in Hungary. This had personal significance for Beethoven and contributed to his sorrows. He had just entered into a formal teaching arrangement with the youthful Archduke Rudolph. He was the composer's only composition pupil and would become one of Beethoven's staunchest patrons. In due course Rudolph received the dedication to many of Beethoven's works – in particular we recall the Piano Trio, Op. 97 that bears the subtitle *The Archduke*. Despite their difference in age – Rudolph was 18 years younger than Beethoven – a close bond appears to have formed between the two. This is all the more surprising since theirs was no conventional master-pupil relationship. Rudolph was the youngest son of the Grand Duke of Tuscany, later Emperor Leopold II, and brother of the Emperor Francis II; Rudolph later became

Archbishop of Olmültz. Not surprisingly, Beethoven's many notes and letters to his pupil were always styled with the utmost courtesy and respect.

Beethoven gave expression to his feelings on Rudolph's departure through his music in the form of the Piano Sonata Op. 81a, known variously as *Das Lebewohl – Les Adieux – The Farewell*. Reflecting on this work, Edwin Fischer remarked: 'Thanks to the breadth of Beethoven's emotions, the grief of parting and the joy of reunion have acquired a universal human reference and application in this sonata, which is an example of the kind of programme music of which Beethoven himself said (referring to the *Pastoral* Symphony): "Not painting, but the expression of feeling".'[xxix] Donald Tovey regarded the Piano Sonata Op. 81a as 'an instance of purely artistic organisation on certain materials of emotion and contrast characteristic of deep friendship', namely that between composer and pupil.[xxx] With this work in mind, Alfred Brendel has reminded us: '[We] must not forget ... that Beethoven was well aware of human situations and psychological reactions when he composed.'[xxxi]

With the death of Beethoven's teachers and physician, the realization that his deafness was permanent, the mortification of unrequited love, the terror of the French invasion, the occupation of Vienna and its curtailment of freedom, and with Rudolph's departure, we can appreciate Joseph de Marliave making reference to 'the dark places of the artist's soul' and of Beethoven finding expression in the music of *The Harp* Quartet 'for all [his] pent-up love and sorrow'.

Our discussion of the circumstances bearing on Beethoven at the period under consideration would not be complete with making reference to his resolve to leave Vienna altogether and to accept the offer of employment elsewhere. Comments by his piano pupil Carl Czerny shed light on Beethoven's feelings at this time and put them into perspective. He writes: 'It has often been said abroad that Beethoven was despised and repressed in Vienna. The truth is that even as a young man he received all possible support, attention and encouragement from our great aristocracy which could have been given to a young artist ... It is true that, as an artist, he had to deal with intrigues, but the public were not to blame for that. He was always admired as an unusual character, and his greatness was assumed by everyone who didn't really know him.'[xxxii]

Beethoven's resolve to quit Vienna was precipitated by an invitation he received on 1 November 1808 from Napoleon's younger brother Jérôme, then recently installed as the King of Westphalia. He invited Beethoven, through the diplomatic offices of his High Chamberlain, to consider an offer of appointment as his Senior Kapellmeister in Kassel. Despite the somewhat archaic-sounding title, the post held distinct attractions for Beethoven. His duties would not be onerous; he would merely be required to play for Jérôme's personal pleasure and to conduct occasional concerts. Moreover, he was offered a salary of 600 gold ducats (the equivalent of about 4000 gulden/florins or 200 pounds sterling) and an additional 150 ducats for travelling expenses.[xxxiii] Although the title of Kapellmeister was becoming somewhat antiquated in the first decade of the nineteenth century, it may have had a particular resonance for Beethoven. His grandfather had held such an appointment, and this, combined with childhood memories may have exerted an influence on his subconscious mind.

Beethoven was immediately attracted by the invitation and was disposed to accept it. On 24 November he wrote in enthusiastic terms to his new confident and general factotum Baron Ignaz von Gleichenstein: 'I have received the offer of a fine appointment as Kapellmeister to the *King of Westphalia*. I am to be paid handsomely — I have been asked to state how *many ducats* I should like to have — and so forth.'ˣˣˣⁱᵛ In the New Year of 1809, Beethoven appears to have made up his mind regarding Jérôme Bonaparte's offer of employment. In a further letter of 7 January, this time to his to his publisher Breitkopf & Härtel, he intimated how attractive the position appeared to him regarding the steady income he would receive and the post's other advantages. He complained of the standard of musicians in Vienna, some of whom he accused of hardly being able to read an orchestral score; he was still resentful of the poor standard of playing they had displayed at his mammoth concert on the previous 22 December. He also believed the composer Antonio Salieri intrigued against him — echoes of 'Mozart and Salieri' — disposing him to exclaim: 'At last, owing to intrigues and cabals and meannesses of all kinds, I am compelled to leave my German fatherland.ˣˣˣᵛ

News of Beethoven's planned departure appears to have reached the ears of the Countess Anna Maria Erdödy. She was a competent pianist, an admirer of the composer's music and given to holding frequent musical soirées in her Vienna town house — her family also owned estates in the country. Beethoven for a time occupied rooms in her apartments, held her in high esteem and dedicated to her his two Piano Trios Op. 70 and the two Cello Sonatas Op. 102. By virtue of her social standing the Countess had the ear of Vienna's nobility, the outcome of which was she made known Beethoven's intended departure to a privileged inner-circle that included the Archduke Rudolph, Prince Ferdinand Kinsky and Count Franz Joseph Lobkowitz. In order to secure Beethoven's continuing presence in Vienna, they resolved to take immediate action and collectively agreed to settle upon him an Annuity of 4000 gulden/florins — the equivalent offered to him by Jérôme Bonaparte. Part of their Contract reads: 'The daily proofs that Herr Ludwig van

Beethoven gives of his extraordinary talents and genius as a musician and composer awaken the desire that he surpass the greatest expectations that are justified by his past achievements. Since it has been demonstrated, however, that only a person who is as free from care as possible can devote himself to one profession alone and create great works that are exalted and that enable art, the undersigned have made the decision to place Herr Ludwig van Beethoven in a position where the most pressing circumstances shall not cause him embarrassment or impede his powerful genius.'[xxxvi] Thayer remarks that the three signatories to Beethoven's Annuity Contract were doubtless motivated to assist the composer on the grounds: 'What an inexcusable, unpardonable disgrace to Vienna would be the departure of Beethoven under such circumstances!'[xxxvii]

Although Beethoven was to remain in Vienna for the rest of his life, the financial reassurance his Annuity Contract offered proved to be relatively short-lived. In 1811 devaluation, resulting from the Napoleonic wars, reduced his 4000 gulden to about 1,600 gulden. Moreover, on 11 September 1811, Count Lobkowitz was obliged to stop his payments for four years because he was declared bankrupt and on 3 November 1812 Prince Kinsky died suddenly as the result of an accident, compelling Beethoven to legally challenge his heirs to maintain Kinsky's share of the annual payment that he considered was due to him. It was not until around 1815 that his Annuity was restored to something like its original value – about 3,400 gulden.[xxxviii] These experiences conferred in Beethoven a lasting mistrust of 'paper money' and he was adamant ever after to transact his business affairs in terms of the coinage of the day, namely, gulden, florins, ducats and Louis d'or.

It is against this backdrop of personal circumstances that Beethoven worked on the String Quartet in E-flat major,

Op. 74. It occupied him between the summer and autumn of 1809, following immediately after the E flat Piano Concerto and preceding the Piano Sonata, Op. 81a. The earliest intimation we have from Beethoven that he had turned once more to the genre of the string quartet comes from a letter he wrote to his Leipzig publisher Breitkopf and Härtell on 19 September 1809. He first vents his spleen: 'We are short of money in Vienna, for we need twice as much as formerly [a reference to inflation and the mounting cost of living].' He expostulates: 'Curse this war.' Turning to business affairs, he informs Gottfried Härtell (head of the music firm): 'I will write to you soon about quartets which I am composing — I don't like to spend much time composing sonatas for pianoforte solo, but I promise you a few.'[xxxix] He was exaggerating when he suggested he was at work on 'quartets' — in fact he was devoting himself exclusively to the E-flat major Quartet. Regarding the sonatas, however, he was as good as his word. Since the composition of his F major Sonata, Op. 57, written in 1804–05, Beethoven had composed no piano sonatas. But in 1809 he composed the Sonata in F-sharp major, Op. 78, dedicated to Therese Brunsvik alongside the Sonatina in G major, Op. 79, and in 1809–10 the Sonata in E flat, Op. 81a composed, as we have seen, in response to the Archduke Rudolph's departure and absence from Vienna.

Beethoven adopted a four-movement structure for *The Harp* Quartet that was typical of his quartet writing up to this time; his more radical innovations were some years distant. James Webster likens Op. 74 to Op. 59, No. 3 for being 'modest in scale and expressive force'.[xl] Op. 74 and its successor Op. 95 are relatively short, concentrated works shaped in Haydn-style dimensions making the quartet 'a convening of different equals'.[xli] Abraham singles out for praise the work's 'intimacy and lyricism and fine workmanship'.[xlii] 'It is glitteringly effective; the first violin part touches concerto technique and the second violin has a thrilling prominence.'[xliii]

The compositional origins of Op. 74 are recorded in the extant sketches preserved in the so-called Landsberg 5 sketchbook. Its name derives from the collector of Beethoven memorabilia Ludwig Landsberg from whom it was acquired in 1862 by the Deutsche Staatsbibliothek Kulturbesitz, Berlin. Amongst its 56 leaves are sketches for Op. 74 together with ideas for Opp. 73, 75, 76, and 81a — confirmation of the composer's preference to turn his mind from one work to another.[xliv] Following his detailed study of Landsberg 5, Lewis Lockwood suggests Beethoven composed Op. 74 between May and September but most probably concentrating on it between August and September.[xlv] One of the first detailed studies of the sketches for Op. 74 was undertaken by Gustav Nottebohm (*Second Beethoveniana* 1887) who proposed that all four movements were commenced and finished in their order.[xlvi] Preliminary sketches fill thirty pages of the sketchbook, ten for the first movement (pp. 65–75) and twenty for the other three (pp. 76–95).[xlvii] A facsimile edition of Landsberg 5 has been published as *Ludwig van Beethoven: Ein Skizzenbuch aus dem Jahre 1809* (Landsberg 5) under the editorship of Clemens Brenneis (Bonn: Beethoven Haus, 1995). Since some sketches are advanced and others are only partial, Brenneis believes this suggests that, in edition to Landsberg 5, Beethoven also worked on Op. 74 in a preliminary draft on separate papers; 'a document that has not been preserved'.[xlviii] In his study of the compositional history of Op. 74, Lockwood similarly states: 'The sketches cover all four movements, but at different stages of development. Those for the first movement are already fairly advanced, whereas the sketches for the other movements range from embryonic drafts and revisions. As to the slow introduction, we have no sketches for it at all, suggesting it was written late and worked out elsewhere.' He adds: 'Beethoven was still revising it in the Autograph, which also has alterations of significant details for all four movements.'[xlix]

The history of the Autograph to Op. 74 is of interest. Following the auction of Beethoven possessions in 1827, it was acquired by the Viennese collector and dealer Heinrich Beer. From him it was purchased by Paul Mendelssohn-Bartholdy, brother of the composer, from whom it was inherited by his son Ernst von Mendelssohn-Bartholdy. He generously donated it in 1908 to the Berlin Royal Library together with other Beethoven manuscripts; the Mendelssohns (a wealthy family) owned one of the most prized private nineteenth-century collections. Following the upheavals of the Second World War it now resides in Kraków — Biblioteka Jagiellońska.[l]

On 3 July 1809, Beethoven despatched the text of the E-flat major String Quartet to Kunz and Co., merchants in Vienna, for onward transmission to his publisher Breitkopf and Härtell. His mailing also included the Fantasia for Piano, Op. 77, the Piano Sonata in F major, Op. 78 and the six songs Op. 75. Once more he complained about the stress of life in Vienna, the imposition of levies and of not being able to enjoy 'a change of scene and air'. As a consequence of his reduced financial position, he requested payment of 250 gulden for the sets of compositions adding: 'I consider this is by no means an excessive sum; and just now I do need it.' Of passing interest in this letter is Beethoven's request for copies of the scores of various compositions by other composers. In particular, he wanted the keyboard works of Emmanuel Bach 'for enjoyment and study' and 'to play at the homes of some true friends of music'.[li]

We next learn of *The Harp* Quartet in a letter

Beethoven wrote towards the end of the year (probably in December) to Nikolaus Zmeskall von Domanovecz. He was a civil servant employed in the Hungarian court chancellery and a close friend of the composer to whom he rendered many services. A fine cellist, he held regular musical evenings in his home earning Beethoven's respect for him as a musician and in recognition of which he dedicated to him his next string quartet, Op. 95. Concerning Op. 74, he informed Zmeskall: 'The Quartet is to be rehearsed at [Prince] Lobkowitz's at half past ten or perhaps even at ten o'clock today.' Doubtless the players performed from manuscript parts as was the custom of the day before a composition appeared in print.[lii]

1809 was not all doom and gloom for Beethoven. In recognition of his growing fame and international reputation, on 9 August he received a letter from the Royal Institute of Science and Fine Arts of Amsterdam appointing him a member of that body. He could not refrain from communicating this to Breitkopf & Härtel, with a touch of irony: 'So I now have a title — Ha, Ha, Ha, that makes me laugh.' [liii] Perhaps Beethoven was disposed to mirth when he discovered he had been made a member — *Fourth Class*! Despite his irony, Beethoven replied to the Institute on 20 December with a fulsome expression of his appreciation.[liv]

On 14 October 1809, France signed a Peace Treaty with Austria at the Palace of Schönbrunn. This prompted Beethoven to write to Gottfried Härtell the following month expressing relief that Vienna was enjoying 'a little peace after violent destruction [and] after suffering every hardship'. At last, he explains, he has been able to work for a few weeks in succession — we can infer making progress with Op. 74. He took up a complaint with Härtell that recurs throughout his correspondence with publishers, namely that of errors occurring in his printed compositions. He chastised Härtell:

'Errors creep into every copy, but they are errors that any competent proof-reader can correct.' He further reproached him by stating he could not be expected to be 'on the spot' when his works were being produced and he expected Härtell to the care required on his behalf.[iv]

The following year Beethoven resumed his negotiations with Breitkopf and Härtell. On 4 February 1810 he sent the manuscript copy of the E-flat String Quartet to be prepared for publication. He informed his publisher that his health had improved but had not yet 'become sound and vigorous'. Notwithstanding, together with the text to Op. 74 he also sent Härtell the manuscripts of the following works — testimony to his creativity and industry: Piano Concerto in E-flat major, Op. 73 *The Emperor*; Lieder Op. 75 and Op. 82; Six variations for solo pianoforte, Op. 76; Fantasia for pianoforte, Op. 77; Fantasia for pianoforte, orchestra and choruses, *The Choral Fantasia*, Op. 80; and Three piano sonatas, Op.78, Op. 79 and Op. 81a. For these creations he requested payment of 1,450 florins. He justified himself to Härtell: *'I don't think I am making excessive demands if ask for a fee of 1450 gulden.'* [Beethoven's italics] He further explained that he wanted these compositions also to be published in England (London) that raised the question of copyright. Beethoven therefor asked Härtell to hold back publication until September to facilitate negotiations with his London publisher.[vi]

On 20 June Gottfried Härtell responded to Beethoven's concerns regarding the copyright of his works and aired anxieties of his own concerning the problem of the nefarious actions of unscrupulous publishers. Härtell was particularly anxious about the consequences that might follow from publication overseas: '[Very] soon thereafter, following the London edition, they will also appear from all the [pirate] German publishers, who will take care not to offer you an adequate fee, because they are really accustomed to paying none at all.' He cites his recent experience: 'Thus, as a legal publisher of Haydn's last Quartet [Op. 103 in D minor, published in 1806] (as I can prove at the moment), I have sold, up to this time, no more than about 250 copies; while perhaps two or three times as many of the cheap pirate reprints were sold.' Setting aside his doubts, Härtell offered 250 ducats in gold for the works he had received, mindful that Beethoven was now wary of transacting business in paper money because of the effects of inflation. He stipulated the works should not appear in London before they did in Leipzig – the location of Breitkopf and Härtell's business address. Having been rebuked by Beethoven for errors that had appeared in previous works which they had published on behalf of the composer, Härtell took the precaution of concluding his letter: 'I would like to receive your original manuscripts for greater accuracy in the engraving.'[lvii]

On 2 July Beethoven agreed to sell his latest works to Härtell for the agreed sum of 250 gold ducts. He proposed to send these in three lots linking each with a delivery and publication date. He requested the first lot to be published by 1 September. This consisted of the String Quartet, Op. 74 – that actually appeared in November; Op. 77 (Fantasia); Op.78 and Op. 79 (Piano Sonatas) – all of which also appeared in November; Op. 75 (Lieder) and Op. 76 (Piano Variations) – that appeared in October. The second lot was to be published by 1 November and contained the Fifth Piano Concerto, Op. 73, the Choral Fantasia, Op. 80, and three Lieder Op. 83. The third and last lot was to be published by 1 February the following year and comprised the Piano Sonata Op. 81a, the four Ariettas and a Duet, Op. 82 and the score of the Incidental music to *Egmont*, Op. 84.[lviii]

Following his negotiations with Beethoven on 20 July Härtell wrote to Christian Hasse, a musician and dealer in music with British connections in London. Härtell was clearly still worried about the possibility of pirate editions undermining his business transactions with Beethoven. Moreover, Härtell was aware that Beethoven's publisher in London, Clementi and Co., had received much the same offer as his firm to publish the compositions to which we have made reference, including the E-flat major String Quartet. He informed Hasse: 'Several new and interesting works by Beethoven will appear from us shortly, of which we notify you ... You do not lack for musical acquaintances in London. You would therefore greatly oblige me if you would be so kind as to commission an acquaintance in London to be on the watch, and to send us anything about these items as soon as it comes out.' With a conspiratorial touch he asks for Hasse's discretion in this matter. In the event Härtell received the Op. 74 Quartet in Leipzig in November and Clementi in London in September.[lix]

On 21 August Beethoven wrote a letter to Breitkopf and Härtell of some twelve quarto-pages — testimony to his diligence in business matters. He had given further thought as to how he wished the E-flat Quartet should be presented. First he alluded once again to his financial insecurity, complaining of the effect inflation was having on his Annuity: 'Last year, before the arrival of the French, my 4000 gulden were worth something. This year they are not even worth 1000 gulden [an exaggeration].' He adds: '[My] purpose in life is not to become a profiteer in musical art ... God forbid! ... But I like to live independently; and that I cannot do without a small income.' Concerning the Quartet, he requested 'a practical presentation ... so that the musicians can turn the pages comfortably'. He also provided further detailed instructions: 'Furthermore, add '*Adagio ma non troppo'* [Beethoven's italics] to the second movement. In the third movement in C minor 3/4 time after the major *Più presto quasi prestissimo*, at the point where the minor is resumed — the first part is played twice the first time, as is, moreover indicated'. He informed Härtell of his intention to dedicate the composition to his patron Prince Lobkowitz: 'Make a note of the following dedications ... the Violin Quartet to Prince Lobkowitz; you can look up his unmusical titles in some other work.' These duly appeared on the Title Page — see later. Beethoven had already dedicated to the Prince his Opp. 18, 55, 56, and 68.[ix]

In response to Beethoven's reflections concerning his financial affairs, Gottfried Härtell wrote to him on 24 September about his own and the parlous state into which music-publishing had fallen as a result of the Napoleonic wars: '[You] may have difficulty imaging the paralysis in which northern Germany (to which I am limited as long as the northern shipping remains blocked) finds itself, and the repercussions that this dismal condition has on music.' Härtell complained once more about the problems of pirate editions. To give added testimony to his concerns he cited the unauthorised publication of Beethoven's own works: 'They have not only been published and pirated individually [but also] in France, England, Offenbach, Bonn, Mainz, Augsburg, Berlin, Amsterdam, Hamburg, Munich and even Leipzig.' Härtell concludes his letter by expressing the hope that he can make a mercantile success of selling the composer's works. He was doubly anxious, in part for the reasons just explained but also he was mindful Beethoven's compositions had a reputation for being 'difficult' and, as he put it: '[I] cannot accurately judge of their success.'[lxi]

Since Breitkopf and Härtell were publishers of the widely circulated and influential *Allgemeine musikalische Zeitung*, Gottfried wasted no time in announcing on 3

October 'the coming appearance of a number of Beethoven's works'. These included a reference to the E flat Quartet that was promised to be available in parts, as was the custom of the day.[lxii] Before they were released Beethoven was just in time to intercept their publication in order to incorporate late changes he had made to the score. On 6 October he advised Härtell: 'I will send you on better paper by letter post, in order to avoid delay, the third movement copied out in small writing, that is to say, only the violin part, so that there may be no misunderstanding.'[lxiii] In his letter of 21 August, Beethoven had given instructions as to the rhythm and repeats he required in the Quartet for the purposes of publication. He emphasised this once more, with further exhortations to take care: 'In connection with the second *Adagio* of the Quartet I added a remark about the tempo. Are you sure that that remark was taken to heart? Do be careful and do comply with the request I have often made to you, i.e. to send me not only a proof copy but the manuscripts as well. I hear complaints about the inaccuracy of the engraving; and I have noticed that even the clearest handwriting can be misread.'[lxiv] On 15 October, Beethoven prevailed upon Härtell once more: '*I am letting you know my objection to the Quartet. You see, it is merely the trifling point that whereas the Minore is repeated at once for the first time after the Maggiore, the first part of the Minore must be played twice, but the second part only once, i.e. without a repeat.*' These are Beethoven's italics: in the original letter his words are heavily underlined twice as though for additional emphasis.[lxv]

We have seen that in his letter to Gottfried Härtell of 21 August, Beethoven had intimated that he wanted Prince Lobkowitz to be the dedicatee of the E-flat major Quartet. Franz Joseph von Lobkowitz had been a fulsome supporter of Beethoven soon after the young composer's arrival in

Vienna, on leaving his hometown Bonn in order to receive instruction from Haydn. Of Lobkowitz's support, Anton Schindler remarks: 'The great love this princely family felt for Beethoven was constant and unwavering.' He adds: 'In fact, for ten to twelve years, nearly all Beethoven's works were first tried out in the music circle of Count Lobkowitz.'[lxvi] His mansion house was known as 'the true residence and academy of music' and Lobkowitz himself as 'a true and insatiable music enthusiast'.[lxvii] For example, one of the earliest performances of the *Eroica* Symphony took place in the great salon of Lobkowitz's house that served as a concert hall. It was here, in 1795, that Lobkowitz first heard Beethoven play and later that year he was one of the subscribers to the composer's Piano Trios, Op. 1. It was thereby the start of a long and fruitful relationship with Beethoven who, in recognition of the Prince's support, subsequently conferred upon him the dedications to the *Eroica* Symphony and the Fifth and Sixth Symphonies (jointly with Count Razumowsky); the Triple Concerto, Op. 56; and, central to our discussion, the String Quartet, Op. 74.

Breitkopf and Härtell published the Leipzig edition of the E-flat Quartet in November 1810. Title Page announced: 'QUATUOR/pour/deux Violins, Viola/et Violoncelle/composé et dédié/à Son Altesse/*le Prince regnant de Lobkowitz/Duc de Raudnitz*/par/L. v. Beethoven,/*Propriété des Editeurs*./Leipsic/*Chez Breitkopf & Härtell*.' The edition was offered for the price of one thaler and eight groschen.[lxviii] Beethoven's publisher in London, to whom we have made passing reference, was Muzio Clementi. Clementi may be described as the servant of music's Saint Cecilia *par excellence*. He was variously: a virtuoso pianist; composer – Beethoven admired his piano sonatas; a publisher – Beethoven owned a copy of Clementi's *Introduction to the art of playing on the piano forte* and used it for teaching purposes; and to round out his all-embracing accomplishments, Clementi was a manufacturer of fine pianos.

Clementi met Beethoven whilst on a business trip to Vienna and soon wrote to his partner William Frederick Collard in London: 'By a little management and without committing myself, I have at last made a complete conquest of that *haughty beauty* Beethoven.' [Clementi's italics] Clementi explains how he had persuaded the composer to have his works published in England (London) and how his publishing house would take care of him. Beethoven obligingly gave an undertaking to prepare a list of publications. Clementi tells Collard he had agreed with Beethoven to take in manuscript: the three String Quartets Op. 59; Symphony No. 4, Op. 60; the Overture *Coriolan*, Op. 62; the Concerto for Pianoforte No. 4. Op. 58; and the Violin Concerto that Clementi describes as being 'very beautiful' and which, at his request, Beethoven had offered to adapt for the pianoforte (Op. 61). For all these works, Beethoven was to receive two hundred pounds sterling.'[lxix] It was by means of such an agreement that Clementi secured the publication rights of the String Quartet, Op. 74.[lxx] The Title Page of Clementi's first edition appeared in London styled as follows with Clementi's own opus number: '*Quartet*/FOR TWO VIOLINS/TENOR/and Violincello/Composed by/LEWIS Van BEETHOVEN/Op. 62 – LONDON – P[rice]. 7s 6d [seven shillings, six pence]/Printed by Clementi & Compy. 26 Cheapside/*Where may be had just Published by the above Author, A Concerto/for the Piano Forte, Two Sonatas for Ditto, Therma with Variations for Ditto/A Fantasia for Ditto and a Concerto for the Violin.*'[lxxi]

The String Quartet in E-flat major, *The Harp*, was reviewed in 1811 in issue XIII of the *Allgemeine musikalische Zeitung*. The critic had the temerity to advise

Beethoven: 'He should write more quartets in the manner of Op. 18 and give up the obscurities of his new style.'[lxxii] Maynard Solomon remarks: 'The critic was clearly concerned that the string quartet should adhere to the established and accepted norms of "classical decorum" and was disturbed by this overt preoccupation with "rhetorical subject matter".'[lxxiii] The critic complained 'nothing so difficult had ever been written for a quartet'. He saw the Quartet, Op. 74 'as a powerful blend of the bizarre and the fantastic, an amalgam of heterogeneous elements pervaded by a sombre and even lugubrious spirit'. He reproached Beethoven for trying to express in this quartet 'sentiments alien to the nature of the genre'. He accepted the quartet medium was one 'capable of sweet earnestness and lamenting melancholy' but complained 'it should not have the goal of celebrating the dead or picturing feelings of despair'. This critic believed it was the role of the quartet 'to gladden the heart through the mild, comforting play of the imagination'.[lxxiv]

Nicholas Marston's commentary to the *AmZ* review of 1811 provides a fitting summation of the composer's achievement: 'In short, Op. 74 allied itself much more to Beethoven's previous three quartets (Op. 59) than to his first six (Op. 18): the Op. 18 Quartets exemplified, in their individual movements, qualities of melodiousness, unity and fixed character that raised them to the status of masterworks and enabled them to be placed alongside the works of Haydn and Mozart, whereas Op. 59 breathed the air of a very different planet. Easy intelligibility had given way here to a profundity and learnedness that courted the incomprehensible ... the [*AmZ*] reviewer read Op. 59 and Op. 74 as "modern" music, compared to the "classical" ideal represented by Op. 18.'[lxxv]

With the passing of time, Op. 74 was assimilated into the string quartet repertoire and became recognised for its merits. Something of this is evident in a letter Prince Nikolay Galitzin sent to Beethoven from St. Petersburg on 16 June 1824. Galitzin was a Russian nobleman and accomplished cellist who regularly took part in performing at chamber music recitals. His name is today mostly associated with the commissioning of three of Beethoven's late quartets, for which we reserve discussion as part of our concluding texts in this series. It was whilst waiting to receive the String Quartet, Op. 127, one of the three which he had recently commissioned, that Galitzin relayed to Beethoven: '[We] have played nothing but your Quartets here, and especially the five latest ones [Op. 59, Nos. 1–3; Op. 74; and Op. 95].'[lxxvi]

An early pioneer of Beethoven's string quartets outside of Vienna was the violinist-composer Karl Möser. In 1812 he became concertmaster of the Court Opera in Berlin where the following year he established a regular series of quartet recitals — to rival those of the kind organised in Vienna by Ignaz Schuppanzigh. His chamber series lasted until 1843. Under Möser's sponsorship Beethoven's quartets became familiar repertory pieces. Furthermore, he was adventurous — if not audacious — in his programming. For example, in 1828 he realised a performance of the composer's challenging String Quartet in A minor, Op. 132 and in subsequent concerts performed, Op. 59, Nos. 2 and 3 from the *Razumovsky* set, Op. 74 (*The Harp*) and Op. 95 (*Quartetto Serioso*).[lxxvii]

During the 1837 Dresden concert season, the cellist and composer Friedrich August Kummer presented the E-flat Quartet as an orchestral symphony. It did not, however, find favour with the reviewer of the *Allgemeine musikalische Zeitung* (issue 39). He maintained: 'It was neither a symphony nor even Beethovenian. As an accomplished musician it cannot have escaped Herr F. Kummer's attention that Beethoven's symphonic style relates to his quartet style as an enamel painting relates to a life-sized oil painting. Had Beethoven wished to make this work a symphony he would have written it differently ... The periods [phrases] are longer and the entire colour scale is different, just as the *piano* and *forte* in a quartet are different from those in the symphony, not just quantitatively in terms of the number of instruments but qualitatively according to the idea.'[lxxviii]

Moving on from these contemporaneous accounts, we conclude our opening remarks concerning the creation origins and reception history of *The Harp* Quartet, by citing a selection of observations that musicians and musicologists have made about it over the intervening years since its publication.

From the Diary of Clara Schuman for 30 January 1841 we learn of a musical evening. The entry is more about Felix Mendelssohn but *The Harp* Quartet receives a favourable passing mention: 'In the evening I went to *The Quartet*, which became very interesting because of Mendelssohn's playing ... That was followed by Beethoven's magnificent Quartet in E flat and Mendelssohn concluded with two of his earlier and two more recent *Songs without Words*. I know of no performer whose playing make me feel so good ... he plays everything equally masterfully.'[lxxix]

In 1852, in his *Beethoven et ses trois styles*, Wilhelm von Lenz considered Op. 74 to be a 'capital work' but which for him remained 'severe and grandiose'. He quoted the *AmZ* assessment of it as 'more serious than cheerful, more profound and rich in artistry than agreeable and pleasant'.[lxxx]

In his Ludwig van Beethoven: Leben und Schaffen (1859), the German composer, music theorist and critic Adolph Bernhard Marx placed Op. 74 as the first of Beethoven's last quartets. For him, these compositions emphasized 'the unique power of music to conjure dreamlike states in which nothing is fixed or definite – a twilight zone of fluidity and uncertainty'. In Beethoven last works, Marx wrote, 'the string quartet became the primary medium for the expression of this *dreamlife*'. He considered in Op. 74 'the first signs could be perceived of that self-abandonment to the most intimate and dissolving ... feelings that would dominate the later music'.[lxxxi]

Closer to our own time, the American conductor and writer Robert Craft asked his close friend Igor Stravinsky if he would identify some of his favourite events in the symphonies and quartets of Beethoven. Responding, Stravinsky made the following remarks regarding the Op. 74: '*The Harp* Quartet is slighter than the *Razumovskys*, I think, and its final movement, in spite of the sixth variation with the amazing D flat in the cello, breaks the empyrean flight that began with Op. 59, No. 1.' Mindful that Stravinsky was speaking in the late 1960s, he added: 'I seldom listen to *The Harp* Quartet because of the habitual bad performance of it.' In particular, he did not consider the so-called *fate motif* figure that occurs in the third movement, was played with sufficient expression – 'sloppy' – as he described it. More positively, he concluded: 'My favourite places in the Quartet are measure 110 to the *harp* episode in the first movement, and the modulation at measures 192–3.'[lxxxii]

For our final recollection we enter into the spirit of Alfred Brendel's proposition 'Does Classical music have to be entirely serious?'[lxxxiii] In the spring of 1940 the American musician Dika Newlin was studying composition with Arnold Schoenberg at the University of California; Schoenberg was known affectionately as 'Uncle Arnold'. In one of his classes Schoenberg recalled the occasion when Beethoven's *Harp* Quartet was to be performed. The person responsible for setting out the instrumentalists' seating was clearly unfamiliar with the composition, since he asked 'where the harp was to be placed'![lxxxiv]

Beethoven heads the first movement *Poco Adagio – Allegro*, initially 'a little slowly' then 'fast'. The tempo indication *Poco Adagio* is rare in Beethoven. He used this marking first in his Ballet *Prometheus* (1800–1) – *viz.* the scene in which two inert figures come to life – and later, and for the last time, in the Piano Fantasy Op. 77.[lxxxv] The movement exhibits 'a joyful exuberance and a full consciousness of power' but only after the 'deeply introspective' *Poco Adagio* has been set aside.[lxxxvi] Although cast in conventional sonata form, Beethoven invests the movement with several innovatory features. Musicologist Frank Kämper cites the composer's experiments 'with timbre and sonorities ... vibrating tones, tremoli and pizzicato effects' that 'raise colour and sonority to compositional elements of almost equal weight'.[lxxxvii] Paul Griffiths remarks on the movement's 'exhilarating display of wholly new textures' and Beethoven's string writing that gives the players passages of 'bowed scales and arpeggios' that run from one instrument to another.[lxxxviii]

In opening the movement with a slow introduction Beethoven was following the precedent he had established in his C-major Quartet, Op. 59, No. 3. Before him Mozart had opened his Quartet in E-flat major, K428 with a slow introduction and in 1829 the youthful Mendelssohn paid homage to Beethoven by opening his own String Quartet in E-flat major, Op. 12 with a similar slow introduction.[lxxxix] To some ears Beethoven's introduction is 'a kind of questioning' as the first violin tentatively finds its way by cautious steps.[xc] Commentators have been universally moved by the expressive nature of the movement's simple but affecting opening. Violist Rebecca Clarke described the first bar as 'inimitable', going 'straight into the very heart, making one marvel at the poignancy contained in these few simple chords'.[xci] Basil Lam perceived the opening statements as 'touchingly intimate' and 'worthy of the last quartets'.[xcii] In the same spirit Harold Truscott described the introduction to Op. 74 as 'a wonderful piece of third-period writing'.[xciii]

De Marliave described the short introduction as being 'deeply significant' for revealing 'Beethoven's state of emotional ecstasy, his aspirations and desires'. Consistent with the spirit of the previous remarks we have attributed to him, he declared: 'The veil between the spirit of the artist and our understanding is for a moment drawn aside, and we stand on the threshold of a comprehension that will enable us to divine the secret mystery of the later quartets, and to penetrate the mystery of self-revelation that darkens his work from Op. 127 to the end.' He was unequivocal: 'This short section is so eloquent ... it breathes conviction as a masterpiece of consummate art.'[xciv] De Marliave's near contemporary, the American composer and musicologist Arthur Shepherd responded to the opening of Op. 74 in a similarly reflective fashion: 'Unlike the slow introduction of the third *Razumovsky* Quartet this impressive E-flat opening plays an important role as regards mood and contrast and that inescapable inner psychological drama that pervades these works.'[xcv] Long before both of them, the pioneering Beethovenian Adolph Bernhard Marx had written in his *Ludwig van Beethoven: Leben und Schaffen* (1859): 'The basic mood of the first movement [is] one of deep, intimate feeling and melancholy, albeit occasionally relieved by, for example, the pizzicato "Harp" passages.'[xcvi] Nearer our own time Joseph Kerman likens the opening to 'mystery-making' of a kind he considers typical of the composer's slow introductions. More particularly, he identifies the opening with the slow chords with which Beethoven introduces the closing movement of his last quartet that in F major, Op. 135, above which he wrote the enigmatic words *Muß es sein?*

— 'Must it be?'[xcvii] Robert Simpson attests to the inner feeling that many find is enshrined in the thematic material of the opening theme, describing it as 'majestically lyrical' as though 'lit from within by a deep, quiet, human warmth'.[xcviii] Denis Matthews is content to describe the mood prevailing as not so much mysterious or dramatic but more 'tenderly lyrical'.[xcix]

Some authorities find a measure of 'abstraction' in the opening to the E flat Quartet. This is a proposition the American composer and musicologist Roger Sessions explored in one of his lectures given at the Juilliard School of Music in 1949. He posited: '[There] are compositions ... without, properly speaking, any "themes" at all'. He cited, by way of illustration, passages in the composer's Piano Sonata in F sharp, Op. 78 and, significant for our present discussion, the first movements of Beethoven's Quartets, Op. 74 and Op. 130 in which he argued 'themes are obviously of secondary importance to the movement and structure of the whole'.[c]

It is not surprising that the E-flat major Quartet's pizzicato opening, perhaps its most immediately distinctive and memorable feature, should have received considerable comment — even at its first public appearance. Although the author of the review of the composition that was published in the 11 May 1811 edition of the *Allgemeine musikalische Zeitung* did not find favour with the work as a whole (see previous), and neither did he yet know it as *The Harp* Quartet, he was nevertheless struck by the plucked-string passages. That said he found they 'jarred with the fundamental seriousness of the movement and were but one example of the striking diversity and plenitude of ideas that characterized it'.[ci] More recent commentators, with the advantage of knowing the work more fully, have been more charitable:

Joseph Kerman: 'What is obviously the most striking

special feature of this movement [is] its unusual emphasis on instrumental devices ... The *pizzicato* passages, the brilliant first-violin work, and the rich colouristic mood-effects make their formidable contribution to the overall temper. And the way Beethoven blends them into the quartet texture ... bears witness again to technical control, to compositional virtuosity matching the purely instrumental virtuosity.'[cii]

Michael Steinberg: 'I know of no precedent for so much pizzicato that is not simply accompaniment.'[ciii]

Lewis Lockwood: 'It is safe to say that this extended use of pizzicato as a structural feature is unprecedented in the quartet literature ... As a special closing effect, Haydn and Mozart in their quartets employed pizzicato for such moments as the finale ... cadences of slow movements, especially in soft dynamics, and in Op. 18 Beethoven had done the same. He had expanded its role in Op. 59, above all in the slow movements of Nos. 1 and 3, but always primarily in the cello ... In Op. 74 he was seeking much more than a percussive, colouristic effect.'[civ]

The slow introduction gives way to the *Allegro* in a 'cloud of chromaticism'[cv] that initially speaks 'with blunt cheerfulness'.[cvi] Several authorities applaud Beethoven's compositional skills here. Lockwood writes: 'The *Allegro* shows Beethoven's craft at its rarest, beginning with an exposition that, in a short span of 53 measures, presents a startling variety of differentiated musical ideas.' He identifies as many as nine distinct figures.[cvii] Philip Radcliffe admires the music 'for its continuity of structure and warmth of colour' with a final endorsement: 'In all this passage Beethoven achieves a truly symphonic breadth and spaciousness without any sense of strain on the medium.'[cviii] Harold Truscott finds some of the chordal passages in the *Allegro* foreshadow writing to be found in the five last quartets. In particular, he cites the B-flat Quartet, Op. 130 composed between 1825–6 of which he remarks – of the measures that he illustrates: 'The two passages are so nearly alike that either could have fitted into the movement from which the other comes.'[cix] Joseph Kerman is like-minded, commenting that as the music progresses: 'The quality looks forward to another Quartet in E flat, the Op. 127, whose first movement features an almost continuous process of dreamlike variation.'

In the Coda Beethoven gives the players some 'extended fireworks'.[cx] In particular the first violin is given the *harp* arpeggios in 'a prolonged display of concertante virtuosity from the first violin'.[cxi] It is in effect a brilliant cadenza for the violin and 'Beethoven's only excursion into the virtuoso field in chamber music'.[cxii] 'This passage, like no other in the quartet literature up to this time, may have been a *Beethovenian* gesture toward the French "Quatuor brilliant", a type of string quartet then in vogue in French circles in which the first violin part called for high technical virtuosity and the lower parts were its vassals.'[cxiii] The second violin also has its share of the fireworks: '[It] is thrilling at the end when the pizzicato notes of the three lower instruments, mounting through the fiery arpeggios of the first violin, lead to the triumphant culminating solo for the second violin.'[cxiv]

The second movement is headed to be played *Adagio* – 'slowly' – but with the instruction *ma non troppo* – 'not overly so'. It is sometimes remarked Beethoven had to work hard to extract the theme he desired from the mass of his accumulated sketch materials. This *Adagio* is a case in point. Although the initial concept appears to have occurred to him early on, with more spontaneity than is to be found in the origins of other of his melodies, evidence from the sketches suggests he was uncertain as to its desired final shape and development; he altered and modified his thoughts some ten times before arriving at the final solution.[cxv] The critic discussing the movement in the review of the composition that appeared in the *Allgemeine musikalische Zeitung*, to which we have made reference, perceived the movement as 'a dark nocturne' that breathed 'a dark melancholy' which for him seemed to strain the very fabric of what he *called 'die schöne Kunst'*.[cxvi] Vincent d'Indy in his critical study of Beethoven (1913) designated the slow movement of the E flat Quartet as a *grand lied* – an extended song. Others have characterised the *Adagio* as being 'in the form of a slow rondo with a lovely *cantabile* melody as its refrain'.[cxvii]

Michael Steinberg found 'Mozartian sighs and harmonies' suspended like clouds in the *Adagio* that he considered are not dispelled until the last measures of the poignant coda are heard.[cxviii] For Adolph Bernhard Marx 'it was as though every note were dipped in a tear, as a heart overflowing with feelings laments its anxious suffering in the secrecy of the night' – overtones here of the manner in which de Marliave has written about the poignant character of the E-flat major Quartet.[cxix] Romain Rolland was more succinct: 'The very beautiful *Adagio* is Beethoven at his very best.'[cxx] Heinz Becker discerns the 'gentle modulations' that dominate the *Adagio ma non troppo*, with their 'unexpected turns of harmony', point to the world of Romanticism but nonetheless are so controlled that the movement 'retains the magic of austere tonal beauty, never descending to the level of sentimentality'.[cxxi] The German music scholar Ludwig Nohl, however, chastised Beethoven on the grounds that he considered the *Adagio ma non troppo* was tainted with 'the stale flavour' of the sentimentality that he thought marred the music of his time; he was writing in 1874. Arthur Shepherd believed Nohl was over-reacting and was identifying Beethoven's music with the more 'overladen sweetness' of certain pages of Liszt, Chopin and Mendelssohn. As for himself, he championed the *Adagio* for its 'intense lyricism' and 'pronounced romantic cast'. He expatiates: 'The theme of the *Adagio* is perhaps as near the typical nineteenth century sentimentality as Beethoven ever approached; but who, one may ask, among representative Romanticists would have known how to maintain so satisfying an equilibrium between sentimental emotion and abstract beauty as is manifest by the composer in this *Adagio*?' Casting his eye over Beethoven's construction, he elaborates: 'Beethoven achieves the necessary objectification and abstraction by means of decorative features in the variation design, which serve most admirably to preserve the idiomatic integrity within the quartet medium. In other words, the movement is never in danger of lapsing into a "song without words" à la Mendelssohn.' [cxxii] De Marliave also took up Beethoven's cause, refuting Nohl's assertion: 'If one were looking for traces of sentimentality in Beethoven's music one could perhaps find it in the slow movement of Op. 74, but of a quality so noble and sincere as to transcend criticism, and to lift it out of all possibility of comparison with the false emotion in the works of Beethoven's successors, and even in Mendelssohn.' Regarding Op. 74, he asserts: 'The *Adagio* of the Quartet in E flat is one of the unbroken melodies that characterize the slow movements of the last period ... In the *Adagio*, Beethoven achieved an eloquence that he had never before attained of the bitterness of despair.' [cxxiii]

Mention has been made of the fact that the E flat Quartet was composed in close proximity, chronologically speaking, to several of the composer's other compositions. This circumstance disposed Gerald Abraham to assert: 'One can hardly fail to feel the affinity between the movement as a whole and some of Beethoven's earlier slow movements in the same key'. He identifies, by way of illustration, the theme-and-variations that open the Piano Sonata, Op. 26, and the *Andante* of the Fifth Symphony.[cxxiv] For some authorities passages in the *Pathétique* Piano Sonate, however, provide the strongest connection with the slow movement of Op. 74. For Marion Scott: 'The slow movement is an *adagio* in A-flat major in the mood that once inspired the slow movement of the *Sonate Pathétique*, but now stronger and less sentimental.'[cxxv] For Philip Radcliffe the slow movement of *The Harp* Quartet is: 'One of the most directly appealing movements that Beethoven ever wrote ... [having] affinities with the slow movement of the *Pathétique* Sonata, also in A-flat major.'[cxxvi] For Robin Stowell: 'The slow movement has none of the emotional power of the equivalent movements in Op. 59, Nos. 1 and 2 but returns to the restrained eloquence and rich sonorities like the *Adagio* of the Sonata *Pathétique*.'[cxxvii]

Irrespective of their affinities with other compositions, the beauties of the *Adagio* are justly recognised for their inherent virtues. Kerman enthuses: 'This *Adagio ma non troppo* is a lovely piece of music, relaxed, almost slack by comparison with the serious slow movements of earlier quartets. It banks almost entirely on its opening melody, and this melody makes no effort to generate anything like a sonata dynamic, as usually happened before. It simply appears three times in increasingly rich version (which can be classed as three variations) with episodes between.' For him, the *Adagio* is 'one of Beethoven's best lyric ideas to date' being 'tender' and yet at the same time 'slightly remote in intellectual quality' avoiding 'anything weighty or pretentious'. Referring to the melody heard in the minor mode, Kerman remarks: 'Probably more than one listener has thought of Schubert's *Das Wirsthuas* here.'[cxxviii] This is a reference to song No. 21 from Schubert's Song Cycle *Die Winterreise* where the poet speaks of his steps having led him to the tavern but which takes the unwelcome form of the graveyard. Perhaps it was with such thoughts in mind that disposed the American composer and music critic Daniel Gregory Mason to describe the *Adagio* to be 'unrelieved by its sadness'.[cxxix] Others refer to the music's 'depth of concentration' and 'fervent pensiveness'.[cxxx] With a note of caution, Abraham concedes that at first hearing the *Adagio* may not appear to be such *great* music [his italics] as the slow movements of the *Razumovskys* — he cites the 'vast serenity' of the *Adagio* of Op. 59, No. 2 — but he is unequivocal: '[It] does exquisitely express that masculine tenderness which is almost peculiar to Beethoven in the whole range of music.'[cxxxi]

Mindful of the high emotional level pertaining in the *Adagio*, Rebecca Clarke (herself an accomplished violist) cautions would-be interpreters of the music: 'The sentiment of the second movement can become unbearable if it is overstressed, but is very lovely when left alone and allowed to speak for itself.'[cxxxii] Paul Griffiths expresses related thoughts: '[In] the *Adagio* ... attention is often drawn to the fact that four individuals are involved, with quite separate things to say even if harmonically they are happy to concur.'[cxxxiii] The slow movement disposed the *AmZ* critic also to utter words of caution — but of a sterner kind: 'The harmonic complexities of this movement might provide a useful object of study for younger composers — but should not be taken as a model for imitation [!]'[cxxxiv]

In the third movement the serenity of the *Adagio* is swept aside in a *Scherzo*, fittingly designated *Presto* — 'very fast'. Leaping from the pages, dotted rhythms are heard cast in the guise of the *fate motif* that occurs in other of the composer's works of the period but which here are almost breathless and precipitate. Heinz Becker compares the leaps that are shared between the instruments, to 'the wild beauty of a landscape of jagged rocks'. For him 'disquiet runs through the instrumental parts' gripped with 'pulsating haste' whose power breaks the formal bonds of the movement thereby increasing its dimensions.[cxxxv] It was all too much though for the author of the 1811 *AmZ* review who likened the *Scherzo* 'to a war dance of some uncivilized nation'![cxxxvi]

Beethoven does not designate the third movement as a scherzo but is content to indicate it as *presto*. The *fate motif*, to which we have referred, is of course identified most closely with the composer's Fifth Symphony. Writing of this connection Steinberg comments: 'The C-minor scherzo [of the third movement] is the most boisterously sort of Beethoven.' He adds: 'Its triple upbeat will inevitably recall the Fifth Symphony, completed in the spring of the previous year.' He also considers the piece was the source of inspiration for Schubert's unfinished String Quartet in C minor of 1820 – the so-called *Quartettsatz*, D. 703.[cxxxvii] Notwithstanding the *Scherzo's* intensity, Kerman describes it as the Fifth Symphony's 'benign twin' but he also acknowledges how 'it still sounds violent enough within the framework of this quartet'.[cxxxviii] In his dual role as musicologist and concert pianist, Denis Matthews accepts that the third movement's C-minor scherzo derives its energy from the four-note rhythm, used to such effect in the Fifth Symphony, but draws attention also to the manner in which 'it hammers in unison on the dominant of F minor in the *Appassionata*'.[cxxxix]

Gerald Abraham begs to differ with much of the foregoing: 'This scherzo, being in C minor and almost entirely pervaded by the [*fate motif*], inevitably suggests comparison with the first movement of the Fifth Symphony.' He considered this to be 'absurd' on the grounds that, in his estimation, 'the two movements have nothing else in common'. He does though concede: 'Yet, listening to this scherzo and its incessant-crotchet trio in the major, one becomes conscious of affinities, some superficial, some deeper, with other of Beethoven's finest movements'; he suggests the scherzo and trio of the Ninth Symphony and part of the *Egmont* Overture. He concludes: 'More than that cannot profitably be said; into this movement is poured some of the purest essence of Beethoven's unique spirit. And that spirit, like the essential spirit of all really great music, defies every attempt to condense it into words.'[cxl]

Despite Abraham's reluctance to endorse too close a relationship between the character of the third movement and that of the Fifth Symphony, such an affinity is remarked upon by other authorities. De Marliave For example comments: 'The abrupt turnoff phrase of the *Presto* theme recalls the *Allegro* of the C minor Symphony. Rising at first through intervals the same as in the chord *motif* of the first movement ... The *motif* is hammered out eight times in unison by all four instruments, with fire and intensity that only Beethoven could achieve.'[cxli] Basil Lam also cites the *fate motif* as found in the C minor Symphony and recalls the composer's self-conscious defiance of a few years earlier when, resolved to overcome the disability of deafness, he asserted: 'I will seize *Fate* by the throat: It shall never wholly overcome me.'[cxlii]

Beethoven's construction is set out on the scherzo-trio-scherzo plan that he had already exploited in the second *Razumovsky* String Quartet. This gives him a platform upon which to enjoy what Matthews describes as the music's 'athletic counterpoint' that is expressed in the fullest sonority at its various appearances. 'Could this be', Matthews asks, 'a relic or parody maybe of the "species" exercises Beethoven had once worked for Albrechtsberger?'[cxliii] Kerman is one who agrees. He likens some of the double counterpoint construction to a parody of textbook construction — 'a belly-laugh at all pedants'.[cxliv] And likewise Lam:

'The pedantries of scholastic counterpoint, so amiably parodied in the *thème russe* of Op. 59, No. 2, are here torn apart with exuberant contempt.' He elaborates: 'If the slow movement dwells on frustrated longing for happiness the *Presto* has something of Goethe's *Rastlose Liebe*: 'Dem Schnee, dem Regen/Dem Wind entgegen'; *Restless Love*, set memorably to music by Franz Schubert in which the poet proclaims: 'Into the snow, the rain/and the wind.'[cxlv]

Both de Marliave and Shepherd quote the enthusiasm expressed by Adolph Bernhard Marx for the manner in which Beethoven gives full rein to his creative impulse in the third movement in all its 'force and vitality'. Marx cites the 'abundant energy' in the *Presto* and, moreover, in its 'unusual succession of repetitions' he discerns extra-musical considerations — of the kind to which we have made reference in our prefatory remarks. He states: 'There can be no doubt that in this persistently recurring expression of confident hope, Beethoven deliberately indicted his mastery over uncertainty and despair.' Marx believed this to be nothing less than 'a decisive moment in Beethoven's life'.[cxlvi]

Shepherd has insightful things to say about Beethoven workmanship. He valued the *Presto* for being 'one of the most deft and attractive' of all the composer's quartet scherzos. In considered the manner in which its 'feathery lightness', alternating with 'incisive vigour' and its overall 'compact texture', left their mark on Mendelssohn when writing his own scherzos[cxlvii]. In this connection it is perhaps no coincidence that, as we have seen, the Mendelssohn family had once owned the original manuscript of this music.

An anecdote has a bearing on the origins of the third movement's Trio. In his *Recollections*, Carl Czerny records that around 1809 the composer Ignaz Pleyel came to Vienna bearing his own latest string quartet which was duly performed at the home of Prince Lobkowitz — with Beethoven in attendance. Later in the evening he was asked to play and, as so often, he declined — at least initially. Czerny relates how, overcoming his irritation, Beethoven went to the pianoforte, grabbed the second violin part from Pleyel's Quartet and began to improvise. Czerny enthuses: 'Never had one heard something so ingenious, so captivating, so brilliant from him.'[cxlviii] Of greater relevance to our account, however, is that according to recent research it is believed Beethoven may have incorporated a transformation of Pleyel's theme into the Trio section of the Op. 74.[cxlix]

From her performer's outlook, Rebecca Clarke remarks on one of the particular challenges to be confronted if the composer's directions are to be faithfully observed in performance. Beethoven stipulated a 3—4 rhythm that should not be changed to 6—8. Clarke observes, disarmingly, 'it is all a matter of correct bowing and due emphasis.'[cl] The drama over, 'the scherzo almost vanishes in a muttering *pianissimo*'.[cli]

Almost but not quite. Beethoven appended to the third movement's marking the designation *attacca* — 'go straight on' (Beethoven actually wrote *il seguente* in the score). The closing bars of the Scherzo therefore form an uninterrupted bridge to the fourth and final movement which is an *Allegretto con Variazioni* — an animated movement set out in six variations, the latter interwoven with a coda. After the passion of the *Presto*, a dramatic outburst would be inappropriate so Beethoven ushers in the fourth movement with a smooth flowing melody. In Philip Radcliffe's words: 'This process suggests ... a comparison with the transition from the Scherzo to Finale in the slightly earlier Fifth Symphony, in which subdued and sinister twilight gradually brightens into a triumphant exultation. In the Quartet the sequence is reversed, the hammering energy of the Scherzo slowly subsiding into tranquillity.'[clii] De Marliave's characteristic enthusiasm is not out of place here: 'The Presto sufficed to reveal the hard-won triumph of the artist over the man, and it is in perfect peace of spirit, in the calm after the storm, that Beethoven turns to the composition of this incomparable [fourth] movement, written, like the finale of the first Op. 59 Quartet, in pure ecstasy of musical creation.'[cliii] Robert Simpson is more succinct: 'This finale could not be more right or more unexpected.'[cliv]

This was the first and only time Beethoven adopted a theme and variations in the finale of a string quartet. In his commentary to the movement, Lam sets the scene by inviting the listener to compare the variation form with that of the literary essay in which the writer introduces his subject and 'lets his fancy play upon it'. In this regard he considers the movement to be a good example of the composer's art but 'by no means one of the finest'.[clv] Endorsing Lam's point of view Radcliffe comments: 'The most outstandingly great instances are the magnificent slow finales of the Piano Sonatas Op. 109 and Op. 111. Those of the Third and Ninth Symphonies, though they both contain elements of variation, are difficult to put into any category; the three other remaining instances ... are the Violin Sonatas, Op. 30, No. 1 and Op. 96 [that however] aim mainly at lyrical repose.'[clvi]

In closing the String Quartet Op. 74 with a set of variations, Beethoven may be seen to be casting a backward glance at a practice long established in the eighteenth century. Some authorities consider the presence of Haydn is evident in the closing movement, bearing in mind his former teacher's adoption of the variation form in his String Quartet, Op. 76, No. 6.[clvii] Beethoven, however, holds back from following Haydn too closely and, whereas the grand old man of quartet writing rounded off his variations with a fugue, his former pupil settles for a sixth variation with coda.

More than that, he shows restraint in other ways: 'The substance and style of the six variations which constitute this last movement are light and remindful of the earlier period. They fall within the general classification of the "decorative" variation, and are far removed in style and expressive significance from the subtle idealizations of the "grand" variations, wherewith Beethoven winged his way into the heights of his last period.'[clviii] Simpson describes Beethoven's set of variations as 'simple but far from naïve'.[clix] Kerman characterises them as being 'refined and economical' and 'lucid in the extreme'.[clx] Barry Copper's insights suggest an intellectual dimension is also to be found in Beethoven's workmanship: 'Other unifying forces are also at work ... and behind the elegant unassuming surface of this movement there lurks an intellectual concern with the possibilities of variation form that is nothing if not *serioso*.'[clxi] The Italian-American, scholar-musician John Daverio expressed similar thoughts. He identified what he calls a 'family of strategies' that incorporate 'figural variation, alternation and embellishment' that he considered 'stand in opposition to the dynamic, goal-directed processes that regulate the musical flow over long stretches of the Op. 59 Quartets'. He adds: 'Together [the variations] create a new and deeply felt expressive tone that will continue to inform Beethoven's musical language in the late quartets.'[clxii]

The variations inherit something of the rhythmic motion of the preceding movement, emphasised by the manner in which Beethoven contrasts the mood of one variation against that of another. He does this by designating the odd-numbered variations (I, III and V) *sempre forte* 'always loud/strong' — with a concentration on contrapuntal figuration. For their part, the even-numbered variations (II, IV and VI) are designated *sempre dolce e piano* 'always sweetly and soft' — with a concentration on lyric effects. Lam describes (but does not dismiss) Variations I, III and V as 'studies for strings' whilst for him, Variations II and IV 'reach the heights of Beethoven's incomparable lyrical inspiration'.[clxiii]

Of related interest is that *The Harp* String Quartet is one of the compositions for which Beethoven provided metronome indications. With the advent of Johann Nepomuk Maelzel's new instrument (1816–17), Beethoven seized upon its potential as a means of securing reliable tempi for the performance of his works. A report in the *Wiener Vaterländische Blätter* (*Vienna Patriotic Periodical*) on 13 October stated: 'Herr Beethoven looks upon this invention as a welcome means with which to secure the performance of his brilliant compositions in all places in the tempos conceived by him, which to his regret have so often been misunderstood.'[clxiv] To this end, Beethoven had a pamphlet printed by the publisher Sigmund Anton Steiner that gave his suggested metronome markings for the other string quartets that he had composed to date, namely, Opp. 18, 59, 74 and 95; he also included markings for his first eight symphonies.[clxv]

Typical of Beethoven is that the first thoughts he had for the variations' main theme should differ significantly from what we now hear. Evidence from his sketchbook (p. 70) reveals 'an opening interval strikingly similar to the opening interval-shape of the slow introduction'[clxvi] and of 'quite a different character'.[clxvii] Following his study of the sketches de Marliave recounts: 'The theme for the variations was several times altered, though very simple in character. The original study [which he illustrates] was entirely different from the final form of the melody, which grew slowly into shape after many corrections [amendments]; and many further alterations still were devoted to the variations'.[clxviii] The theme, as finally resolved, 'itself gives the impression of being a variation'[clxix] with its 'quaint syncopated harmonic rhythm and the piquant modulation scheme'.[clxx] Could its short, harmonic and melodic phrases have influenced Brahms in the theme and variations in his String Quartet in B-flat major, Op. 67?[clxxi]

Variation I opens with 'an air of boisterous confidence ... the caprice of a spirit tried to adversity'.[clxxii] The passage is worked in quavers that are expressed in 'staccato scales and stalking arpeggios'.[clxxiii] This variation observes the principle of equal instrumental participation, a reminder of the eighteenth century notion of the string quartet being a form of conversation between instruments. In his estimation of the music, de Marliave sets aside his typical fulsome endorsement of the composer and is more critical: 'Beethoven here breaks no new ground, confining himself entirely within the classical form. The parts move in imitative counterpoint, and it cannot be denied that the part-writing, alternating between similar and contrary movement, is sometimes angular and even crude.'[clxxiv]

Consistent with what we have said about the manner in which Beethoven contrasts the mood of one variation against that of another, Variation II responds to the assertiveness of the opening variation with 'a charming lyrical ... flowing melody' that is set against a harmonic background. Philip Radcliffe, whom we have just quoted, compares the melody to one that Mozart might have written but with the reservation 'the line is less smooth and the chromaticism stands out in stronger relief'. He takes the opportunity here to make a generalisation: 'In Beethoven's later works, though he never lost his love for long, florid sweeps of melody, they become more essentially instrumental in character and proportionally less like Mozart, whose melody had decidedly vocal inflections.'[clxxv] The viola is given the melody — perhaps in doing so Beethoven was momentarily recalling his youthful days in Bonn when he played the instrument in the Court

Orchestra? Its three companions are content to sustain the momentum with accompanying chords. The angular quavers heard earlier give way as the viola sings in triplets a melody that now 'encircles the entire variation like a wreath'.[clxxvi] Beethoven's marking here is *sempre dolce e piano* – 'always sweetly and soft'. 'Not even Brahms glorified the viola as in Variation II'.[clxxvii]

Variation III proceeds with gusto as the second violin and cello go head-to-head in busy semiquavers that sing a tenth interval apart. Although brief, the passage sounds as though it could continue forever in the manner of a *moto perpetuo*.[clxxviii] Eventually, all the instruments join in the breathless pace in figuration that makes use of 'off beats,' staccato scales' and 'stalking arpeggios'.[clxxix]

In Variation IV, Beethoven reprises his marking *sempre dolce e piano* in a passage that slows the tempo once more bringing it into close alignment with the original theme – although also exhibiting a contrapuntal feeling. Whilst Beethoven observes the principle of 'equal instrumental participation'[clxxx], as the four players weave the fabric of the variation, it is the first violin that is given prominence. Its line is 'felicitous beyond description in its irreducible simplicity'.[clxxxi] Beethoven does not, however, neglect the other instruments that elaborate 'a texture of great beauty'.[clxxxii] As de Marliave summates: 'Leisurely and untroubled, the first violin sings the melody in sustained crochets above the soft murmur of a quaver figure in the lower voices. Harmonically, this variation affords glimpses of Beethoven's last period especially in these advanced progressions.'[clxxxiii]

In Variation V, de Marliave believed he could detect echoes of the *Allegro* in J. S. Bach's Violin Concerto in A.[clxxxiv] Prominence is certainly given to the first violin that is brought to the foreground in what is almost a brief solo heard above the accompanying rhythm of the other voices.

It persists in its domination — even a bit showy in its 'upbeat accents' and 'witty play with metrical ambiguity'.[clxxxv]

Beethoven asks for Variation VI to be played *Un poco piu vivace* — 'A little more lively' but throughout to be *pp* — pianissimo — 'very softly'. The cello is heard hovering on a single-note pedal base whilst the other instruments are given quaver chords. To de Marliave's ears, the harmonic colouring here has an almost orchestral tendency in which he suggests the cello's triplets might well have been written for a drum and the upper instruments for woodwind and horns. He presses the proposition further by suggesting: 'The sixth Variation ... contains the germ of many different later developments, heralding the Ninth Symphony and the music of Schubert and Schuman.'[clxxxvi]

The movement concludes in a brief *Allegro* Coda that is a continuation of Variation VI from which it imports fragments of its melody in a manner that suggested to Joseph Kerman 'elegant folk-accents of *An die ferne Geliebte* echoing, or fore-echoing, across the years'.[clxxxvii] There are hints of the beginning of two entirely new variations but these are quickly set aside as all the instruments gather pace in a collective unison passage — *moto perpetuo* style — that leads the music to its close. With passion spent, four quiet chords bring the String Quartet, Op. 74 — *The Harp* — to a close.

So ends a creation that Joseph Kerman characterises as: '[A] work of consolidation rather than of exploration, a work which by no means is content to repeat something that has been done before, is content to move with an expressive framework laid down by its predecessors.'[clxxxviii] For Philip Radcliffe: '[The quartet] is intensely characteristic of Beethoven, especially perhaps in its combination of warmth and richness of sound on the one hand and on the other a feeling that still more could have been said, had the composer so wished.'[clxxxix]

i Robert Simpson, *The chamber music for strings* in: Denis Arnold and Nigel Fortune, editors, *The Beethoven companion*, 1973, p. 260.

ii Gerald Abraham, *Beethoven's chamber music* in: *The Age of Beethoven, The New Oxford History of Music, Vol. VIII*, Gerald Abraham, editor, 1988, p. 292.

iii Joseph Kerman, 1967, p. 161.

iv Wilfrid Howard Mellers, 1957, p. 44.

v Joseph de Marliave, *Beethoven's quartets*, 1925 (1961 reprint), pp. 146–7.

vi Paul Bekker, 1925, p. 318.

vii David Wyn Jones, *Beethoven and the Viennese legacy* in: Robin Stowell, editor, The Cambridge companion to the string quartet, 2003, p. 218.

viii Maynard Solomon, 1977, p. 210.

ix Maynard Solomon, 1988, p. 119.

x Robin Golding, *Liner notes to The Lindsay String Quartet*, undated.

xi Harold Truscott, 1968, p. 19.

xii Barry Cooper, 1991, p. 235.

xiii See, for example, William Kinderman, 2005, p. 6 and Robin Stowell, editor, *The Cambridge companion to the string quartet*, 2002, p. 218.

xiv Paul Griffiths, 1983, p. 94.

xv Arthur Shepherd, 1935, p. 37.

xvi Barry Cooper, 2000, p. 182.

xvii Lewis Lockwood, *Beethoven's Harp Quartet*, in: William Kinderman, editor, *The string quartets of Beethoven*, 2005, p. 91.

xviii Joseph Kerman, 1967, p. 155.

xix Elliot Forbes, editor, *Thayer's life of Beethoven*, 1967, p. 483.

xx Emily Anderson, 1961, Vol. 1, Letter No. 256, pp. 270–71. Franz Wegeler is remembered today for his 1838 biography of Beethoven *Biographische Notizen über Ludwig van Beethoven*, published in collaboration with the composer's former pupil Ferdinand Ries.

xxi Ludwig Nohl, 1880, pp. 58–9.

xxii Oscar George Theodore Sonneck, 1927, pp. 69–75.

xxiii For an authoritative commentary on Beethoven's many illnesses, see: Anton Neumayr, *Music and medicine*, 1994–1997, p. 254.

xxiv Peter Clive, 2001, pp. 222–4.

xxv Emily Anderson, 1961, Vol. 1, Letter No. 255, p. 269.

xxvi *Ibid*, Vol. 1, Letter No. 258, pp. 272–4.

xxvii Elliot Forbes, editor, *Thayer's life of Beethoven*, 1967, pp. 465–6. Some authorities refer to Beethoven seeking refuge in the cellar of the poet and dramatist Ignaz Franz Castelli – see: Anton Neumayr, 1994–1997, p. 254.

xxviii Emily Anderson, 1961, Vol. 1, Letter No. 220, pp. 233–6.

xxix Edwin Fischer, 1959, p. 91.

xxx Donald Tovey writing in the *Encyclopaedia Britannica* of 1914, Vol. 3, in: Michael Tilmouth, editor, 2001, p. 26.

xxxi Alfred Brendel in conversation with David Dubal, in: David Dubal, 1985, p. 108.

xxxii As quoted in: Hans Conrad Fischer and Erich Kock, 1972, p. 32.

xxxiii As discussed by Elliot Forbes, editor, *Thayer's life of Beethoven*, 1967, p. 442 and Peter Clive, 2001.

xxxiv Emily Anderson, 1961, Vol. 1, Letter No. 170, p. 200.

xxxv *Ibid*, 1961, Vol. 1, Letter No. 192, pp. 211–12.
xxxvi Theodore Albrecht, 1996 Vol. 1, Letter No. 134, pp. 205–7.
xxxvii Elliot Forbes, editor, *Thayer's life of Beethoven*, 1967, pp. 453–9.
xxxviii Hans Conrad Fischer and Erich Kock, 1972, pp. 27–9.
xxxix Emily Anderson, 1961, Vol. 1, Letter No. 226, pp. 243–4.
xl James Webster, *Traditional elements in Beethoven's middle-period quartets*, in: Robert Winter editor, *Beethoven, performers, and critics*: the International Beethoven Congress, Detroit, 1977, 1980, p. 120.
xli Paul Griffiths, 1983, p. 93.
xlii Gerald Abraham, *Beethoven's chamber music* in: *The Age of Beethoven, The New Oxford History of Music*, Vol. VIII, Gerald Abraham, editor, 1988, p. 292.
xliii Marion M. Scott, 1940, p. 260.
xliv For a commentary to the contents of Landsberg 5 see: Douglas Porter Johnson, editor, 1985, p. 72, p. 181, p. 188, and p. 191.
xlv Lewis Lockwood, *Beethoven's Harp Quartet*, in: William Kinderman, editor, *The string quartets of Beethoven*, 2005, p. 90.
xlvi Wilhelm Altman, foreword to Eulenberg Edition, *String Quartet, No. 10 in E-flat major, Op. 74*, [undated].
xlvii Joseph de Marliave, 1925 (1961 reprint), p. 149.
xlviii Cited in William Kinderman, editor, 2005, p. 326.
xlix Lewis Lockwood, *Beethoven's Harp Quartet*, in: William Kinderman, editor, *The string quartets of Beethoven*, 2005, pp. 91–2.
l Douglas Porter Johnson, editor, 1985, p. 37.
li Emily Anderson, 1961, Vol. 1, Letter No. 219, pp. 233–6.
lii *Ibid*, 1961, Vol. 1, Letter No. 233, p. 251.
liii *Ibid*, 1961, Vol. 1, Letter No. 226, pp. 243–4. For the text of the letter from the Royal Institute of Science and Fine Arts see: Theodore Albrecht, translator and editor, 1996, Vol. 1, Letter No.143, pp. 216–7.
liv *Ibid*, 1961, Vol. 1, Letter No. 231, pp. 249–50. For a facsimile reproduction of Beethoven's letter of response to the *Gesellschaft Schöner Künst und Wissenschaften* see: Beethoven House, Digital Archives, Library Document, H. C. Bodmer, HCB Br 81.
lv *Ibid*, 1961, Vol. 1, Letter No. 228, pp. 245–6.
lvi *Ibid*, 1961, Vol. 1, Letter No. 245, pp. 260–61. For a facsimile reproduction of Beethoven's letter to Breitkopf and Härtell together with its German text, see: Beethoven House, Digital Archives, Document Sammlung H. C. Bodmer, HCB Br 85.
lvii Theodore Albrecht, 1996 Vol. 1, Letter No. 148, pp. 223–6.
lviii Emily Anderson, 1961, Vol. 1, Letter No. 262, pp. 276–7. For a facsimile reproduction of Beethoven's letter to Breitkopf and Härtell together with its German text, see: Beethoven House, Digital Archives, Document Sammlung H. C. Bodmer, HCB Br 322.
lix Theodore Albrecht, 1996 Vol. 1, Letter No. 151, pp. 231–3.
lx Emily Anderson, 1961, Vol. 1, Letter No. 272, pp. 283–88. For a facsimile reproduction of Beethoven's letter to Breitkopf and Härtell together with its German text and audio recording, see: Beethoven House, Digital Archives, Document Sammlung H. C. Bodmer, HCB Br 322.
lxi Theodore Albrecht, 1996 Vol. 1, Letter No. 152, pp. 233–8.
lxii Wilhelm Altman, foreword to Eulenberg Edition, *String Quartet, No. 10 in*

E-flat major, Op. 74.

[liii] Emily Anderson, 1961, Vol. 1, Letter No. 278, p. 294.

[liv] *Ibid*, 1961, Vol. 1, Letter No. 281, pp. 295–9. For a facsimile reproduction of Beethoven's letter to Breitkopf and Härtell together with the German text, see: Beethoven House, Digital Archives, Document Sammlung H. C. Bodmer, HCB Br 90.

[lv] *Ibid*, Vol. 1, Letter No. 281, pp. 295–7. For a facsimile reproduction of Beethoven's letter to Breitkopf and Härtell together with the German text and audio recording, see: Beethoven House, Digital Archives, Document Sammlung H. C. Bodmer, HCB Br 91.

[lvi] Anton Felix Schindler, *Beethoven as I knew him*, edited by Donald W. MacArdle and translated by Constance S. Jolly from the German edition of 1860, 1966, p. 50.

[lvii] Peter Clive, 2001, pp. 212–13.

[lviii] Beethoven House, Digital Archives, Document, C 240/11. For facsimile reproductions of other first editions by Breitkopf and Härtell, Artaria and André, see Digital Archives Documents: String Quartets, Op. 74.

[lix] Emily Anderson, editor and translator, 1961, Letter No. 142, pp. 167. For an audio version of this letter, together with the German text, see: Beethoven House, Digital Archives, Document Sammlung H. C. Bodmer, HCB BBr 84.

[lx] Barry Cooper, 2000, p. 189.

[lxi] Beethoven House, Digital Archives, Document, C 74/11.

[lxii] Robin Wallace, 1986, p. 18 and p. 36.

[lxiii] Maynard Solomon, *Beethoven: beyond classicism* in: Robert Winter and Robert Martin, editors, *The Beethoven quartet companion*, 1994, p. 68.

[lxiv] Quoted, with adaptations from Leon Botstein, *The patrons and publics of the quartets: music, culture, and society in Beethoven's Vienna* in: Robert Winter and Robert Martin editors, *The Beethoven quartet companion*, 1994, p. 91.

[lxv] Nicholas Marston, *Fantasy and farewell in the Quartet in E-flat, Op. 74*, in: William Kinderman, editor, *The string quartets of Beethoven*, 2005, p. 110.

[lxvi] Theodore Albrecht, 1996 Vol. 1, Letter No. 370, pp. 41–3.

[lxvii] Robert Winter, 1994, pp. 41–2.

[lxviii] *Ibid*, pp. 43–4.

[lxix] Nauhaus Gerd editor, *The marriage diaries of Robert & Clara Schumann*, 1994, pp. 56–7.

[lxx] Quoted in: Nicholas Marston, *Fantasy and farewell in the Quartet in E-flat, Op. 74*, in: William Kinderman, editor, *The string quartets of Beethoven*, 2005, p. 110.

[lxxi] *Ibid*, p. 110 (quoted with adaptations).

[lxxii] Igor Stravinsky and Robert Craft, 1968, p. 114.

[lxxiii] Alfred Brendel, *Alfred Brendel on music: collected essays; Lecture I*, 2001.

[lxxiv] Dika Newlin, 1980, p. 52.

[lxxv] With acknowledgement to Lewis Lockwood, *Beethoven's Harp Quartet*, in: William Kinderman, editor, *The string quartets of Beethoven*, 2005, p. 91.

[lxxvi] Arthur Shepherd, 1935, p. 37.

[lxxvii] Frank Kämper, *Liner notes to The Alexander String Quartet*, undated.

[lxxviii] Paul Griffiths, 1983, p. 93.

[lxxxix] James Webster finds 'a reminiscence' of Mozart's *Die Zauberflöte* in Beethoven's slow introduction, significantly also in the same key of E flat. See: James Webster, *Traditional elements in Beethoven's middle-period quartets*, in: Robert Winter editor, *Beethoven, performers, and critics: the International Beethoven Congress, Detroit, 1977*, 1980, p. 120.

[xc] As suggested by Michael Steinberg, in: Robert Winter and Robert Martin, editors, 1994, p. 198.

[xci] Rebecca Clarke, *The [Beethoven] quartets as a player sees them*, in: *Music & Letters, Beethoven*, Special Issue: Vol. VIII, No. 2, 1927, p. 183.

[xcii] Basil Lam, 1975, p. 65.

[xciii] Harold Truscott, 1968, pp. 33–4.

[xciv] Joseph de Marliave, 1925 (reprint 1961), p. 152.

[xcv] Arthur Shepherd, 1935, p. 37.

[xcvi] Quoted in: Nicholas Marston, *Fantasy and farewell in the Quartet in E-flat, Op. 74*, in: William Kinderman, editor, *The string quartets of Beethoven*, 2005, p. 110.

[xcvii] Joseph Kerman, 1967, p. 158.

[xcviii] Robert Simpson, *The chamber music for strings* in: Denis Arnold and Nigel Fortune editors, *The Beethoven companion*, 1973, p. 260.

[xcix] Denis Matthews, 1985, p. 136.

[c] Original source: Lecture 3: Summer 1949 at the Juilliard School of Music, New York City, reproduced in: Roger Sessions, *The musical experience of composer, performer, listener*, 1950 (reprint 1966), p. 52.

[ci] As quoted by Nicholas Marston, *Fantasy and farewell in the Quartet in E-flat, Op. 74*, in: William Kinderman, editor, *The string quartets of Beethoven*, 2005, pp. 109.

[cii] Joseph Kerman, 1967, p. 161.

[ciii] Derived form Michael Steinberg, in: Robert Winter and Robert Martin, editors. *The Beethoven quartet companion*, 1994, p. 199.

[civ] Lewis Lockwood, *Beethoven's Harp Quartet*, in: William Kinderman, editor, *The string quartets of Beethoven*, 2005, p. 93.

[cv] Philip Radcliffe, 1978, p. 82.

[cvi] Basil Lam, 1975, p. 65.

[cvii] Lewis Lockwood, *Beethoven's Harp Quartet*, in: William Kinderman, editor, *The string quartets of Beethoven*, 2005, p. 93.

[cviii] Philip Radcliffe, 1978, p. 84.

[cix] Harold Truscott, 1968, pp. 35–6.

[cx] Joseph Kerman, 1967, p. 161.

[cxi] Denis Matthews, 1985, p. 136.

[cxii] Romain Rolland, 1917, p. 186.

[cxiii] Lewis Lockwood, *Beethoven's Harp Quartet*, in: William Kinderman, editor, *The string quartets of Beethoven*, 2005, p. 101. In support of his contention, Lockwood also remarks: 'We should also remember that 1809 [was] the year in which Beethoven composed a whole series of cadenzas for his first four piano concertos, intending them for his virtuoso student and patron the Archduke Rudolph.'

[cxiv] Rebecca Clarke, *The [Beethoven] quartets as a player sees them*, in: *Music & Letters, Beethoven*, Special Issue: Vol. VIII, No. 2, 1927, p. 183.

[cxv] According to the studies of the sketches made by Joseph de Marliave, 1925 (1961 reprint), p. 150. The same observation is made by Philip Radcliffe, 1977, p. 84.

[cxvi] Quoted by Nicholas Marston, *Fantasy and farewell in the Quartet in E-flat, Op. 74*, in: William Kinderman, editor, *The string quartets of Beethoven*, 2005, p. 110.

[cxvii] Robin Golding, *Liner notes to The Lindsay String Quartet*, undated.

[cxviii] Michael Steinberg, in: Robert Winter and Robert Martin, editors, 1994, p. 200.

[cxix] Quoted in Nicholas Marston, *Fantasy and farewell in the Quartet in E-flat, Op. 74*, in: William Kinderman, editor, *The string quartets of Beethoven*, 2005, p. 110.

[cxx] Rolland, Romain, 1917, p. 186.

[cxxi] Heinz Becker, *Liner notes to Beethoven's string quartets*, The Amadeus String Quartet, 1974.

[cxxii] Arthur Shepherd, 1935, pp. 37–8.

[cxxiii] Joseph de Marliave, 1925 (1961 reprint), p. 160.

[cxxiv] Gerald Abraham, 1944, p. 60.

[cxxv] Marion M. Scott, 1940, p. 260.

[cxxvi] Philip Radcliffe, 1978, p. 84.

[cxxvii] Robin Stowell editor, *The Cambridge companion to the string quartet*, 2003, p. 218.

[cxxviii] Joseph Kerman, 1967, pp. 162–3.

[cxxix] Quoted in Phillip Radcliffe, 1978, p. 88.

[cxxx] As remarked in the foreword to the Philharmonia score [anon], *Ludwig van Beethoven, String Quartet, Op. 74*, Wien, [undated], No. 319.

[cxxxi] Gerald Abraham, 1944, p. 60.

[cxxxii] Rebecca Clarke, *The [Beethoven] quartets as a player sees them*, in: *Music & Letters, Beethoven*, Special Issue: Vol. VIII, No. 2, 1927, p. 183.

[cxxxiii] Paul Griffiths, 1983, p. 93.

[cxxxiv] Nicholas Marston, *Fantasy and farewell in the Quartet in E-flat, Op. 74*, in: William Kinderman, editor, *The string quartets of Beethoven*, 2005, pp. 109–10.

[cxxxv] Heinz Becker, Liner notes to Beethoven's string quartets, The Amadeus String Quartet, 1974.

[cxxxvi] Quoted by Nicholas Marston, *Fantasy and farewell in the Quartet in E-flat, Op. 74*, in: William Kinderman, editor, *The string quartets of Beethoven*, 2005, pp. 110.

[cxxxvii] Michael Steinberg, in: Robert Winter and Robert Martin, editors, 1994, p. 200.

[cxxxviii] Joseph Kerman, 1967, p. 164.

[cxxxix] Denis Matthews, 1985, p. 137.

[cxl] Gerald Abraham, 1944, p. 62.

[cxli] Joseph de Marliave, 1925 (1961 reprint), p. 165.

[cxlii] Basil Lam, 1975, p. 68.

[cxliii] Denis Matthews, 1985, p. 137.

[cxliv] Joseph Kerman, 1967, p. 165.

[cxlv] Basil Lam, 1975, pp. 67–8.

[cxlvi] Joseph de Marliave, 1925 (1961 reprint), p. 165 and p. 168 and Arthur Shepherd, 1935, p. 39.

[cxlvii] Arthur Shepherd, 1935, p. 39.

[cxlviii] As quoted in Paul Badura-Skoda, Carl Czerny: *On the Proper Performance*

cxlix See: William Kinderman, editor, 2005, p. 6.

cl Rebecca Clarke, *The [Beethoven] quartets as a player sees them*, in: *Music & Letters, Beethoven*, Special Issue: Vol. VIII, No. 2, 1927, pp. 183–4.

cli Robert Simpson, *The chamber music for strings* in: Denis Arnold and Nigel Fortune, editors, *The Beethoven companion*, 1973, p. 261.

clii Philip Radcliffe, 1978, p. 87.

cliii Joseph de Marliave, 1925 (1961 reprint), p. 170.

cliv Robert Simpson, *The chamber music for strings* in: Denis Arnold and Nigel Fortune editors, *The Beethoven companion*, 1973, p. 261.

clv Gerald Abraham, 1944, p. 64.

clvi Philip Radcliffe, 1978, p. 87.

clvii As suggested, for example, by James Webster, *Traditional elements in Beethoven's middle-period quartets*, in: Robert Winter, editor, *Beethoven, performers, and critics: the International Beethoven Congress*, Detroit, 1977, 1980, p. 122 and Robin Stowell, editor, 2003, p. 218.

clviii Arthur Shepherd, 1935, p. 39.

clix Robert Simpson, *The chamber music for strings* in: Denis Arnold and Nigel Fortune editors, *The Beethoven companion*, 1973, p. 261.

clx Joseph Kerman, 1967, p. 166.

clxi Barry Cooper, 1991, p. 235.

clxii John Daverio *Manner, tone and tendency in Beethoven's chamber music for strings*, in: Glenn Stanley editor, *The Cambridge companion to Beethoven*, 2000, p. 157.

clxiii Basil Lam, 1975, p. 68.

clxiv Elliot Forbes, editor, *Thayer's life of Beethoven*, 1967, p. 544.

clxv With acknowledgment to Barry Cooper, 1991, p. 282.

clxvi Lewis Lockwood, *Beethoven's "Harp" Quartet*, in: William Kinderman, editor, *The string quartets of Beethoven*, 2005, p. 100.

clxvii Wilhelm Altman, foreword to Eulenberg Edition, *String Quartet, No. 10 in E-flat major, Op. 74*, [undated].

clxviii Joseph de Marliave, 1925 (1961 reprint), p. 151.

clxix Heinz Becker, Liner notes to *Beethoven's string quartets*, The Amadeus String Quartet, 1974.

clxx Joseph Kerman, 1967, p.166.

clxxi As suggested by Philip Radcliffe, 1978, p. 87.

clxxii Joseph de Marliave, 1925 (1961 reprint), p. 170.

clxxiii Robin Golding, *Liner notes to The Lindsay String Quartet*, undated.

clxxiv Joseph de Marliave, 1925 (1961 reprint), p. 170.

clxxv Philip Radcliffe, 1978, p. 87.

clxxvi Joseph de Marliave, 1925 (1961 reprint), p. 170.

clxxvii Basil Lam, 1975, p. 68.

clxxviii Gerald Abraham, 1944, pp. 63–4.

clxxix As singled out for mention in their commentary to the composition by Joseph de Marliave and Robin Golding.

clxxx Heinz Becker, *Liner notes to Beethoven's string quartets*, The Amadeus String Quartet, 1974.

clxxxi Basil Lam, 1975, p. 68.

[dxxxii] Philip Radcliffe, 1978, p. 88.
[dxxxiii] Joseph de Marliave, 1925 (1961 reprint), p. 171.
[dxxxiv] *Ibid.*
[dxxxv] Michael Steinberg, in: Robert Winter and Robert Martin, editors, 1994, p. 200.
[dxxxvi] Joseph de Marliave, 1925 (1961 reprint), p. 172.
[dxxxvii] Joseph Kerman, 1967, p.167.
[dxxxviii] *Ibid*, p. 168.
[dxxxix] Philip Radcliffe, 1978, p. 88.

STRING QUARTET IN F MINOR, OP. 95
QUARTETTO SERIOSO

'Not only is there interpenetration of themes, but they are treated as veritable personages, coming and going and expressing their opposing sentiments. It is in effect, a drama which looms through the symphonic warp and woof. Always, contrary to what we often perceive in the modern or romantic *Poème symphonique*, this symphonic texture remains, with Beethoven, firm and logical. Never does passion run riot, nor does it intrude into the structure an element of disorder.'

Vincent d'Indy, *Beethoven: A Critical Biography*, 1913.

Quoted in Arthur Shepherd, *The String Quartets of Ludwig van Beethoven*, 1935, p. 42.

> 'Here in this work which stands on the borderline between Beethoven's second and third styles, we have the gruff and brooding Beethoven.'

Romain Rolland, *Beethoven and Handel*, 1917, pp. 186–7.

> 'The quartet in F minor, Op. 95, the *Quartetto Serioso*, affords a magnificent prelude to [the Seventh and Eighth Symphonies]. Of the sixteen it is the most compressed in form and most full of Beethoven's characteristic effects of expressive contrast; passion and sorrow, despair and exultation follow each other with a quick succession that recalls in a sense the *Prometheus* of Goethe ... and is finally dispelled by a shout of joy.'

Joseph de Marliave, *Beethoven's Quartets*, 1925 (reprint 1961), p. 175.

> 'The F minor Quartet is a compound of defiant power and tender pathos. There were many tragic circumstances in the composer's life at this period which might have found echoes in this amazingly trenchant utterance. Beethoven was in the afterthroes of his disrupted love affair with Thérèse von Brunswick, his *Immortal Beloved*. It was also the period of friendship with Bettina Brentano, whose remarkable nature had the power of eliciting from Beethoven some of the most illuminating avowals concerning his own creative process.'

Arthur Shepherd, *The String Quartets of Ludwig van Beethoven*, 1935, p. 40.

> 'To enjoy the full flavour of this serious, passionate, hard-bitten work, with its rough humour, grimly pointed wit and strange flashes of trendiness, it should be studied in conjunction with Beethoven's letters to Zmeskall [the work's dedicatee] — the similarity in tone is striking. It is very much a man's quartet. It is also remarkable as belonging to both Beethoven's middle period and his last.'

Marion M. Scott, *Beethoven: (The Master Musicians)*, 1940, p. 261.

> 'Never before in the history of chamber music can so much power and passion have been packed into so small a space, and without once overstepping the ill-guarded boundary into the territory of the symphonic. The greatness of Beethoven's music is a greatness *sui generis* ['of its own kind'].'

Gerald Abraham, *Beethoven's Second Period Quartets*, 1944, pp. 69–70.

> '[The] F minor Quartet — *Quartetto Serioso*, Beethoven called it, very remarkably — takes its point of departure not in availability but in introspection. This for Beethoven was expressed in terms of complex technical problems ... With this work, the quartet becomes for the first time Beethoven's private workshop. For an unusually

long period of time he withheld the piece from publication and even from performance — one would like to say, exactly on account of its problematic and personal nature ... [The] Quartet in F minor stands at the highest summit of Beethoven's artistic achievement up to the end of the second period.'

Joseph Kerman, *The Beethoven Quartets*, 1967, p. 156 and p. 184.

'The F minor Quartet is often regarded as a kind of anticipation of the "third period"; decidedly its elisions and compressions, and its dissociations, freed him for new courses of action, but that work remains a special case nevertheless. The later works take advantage of ground broken by the F minor, but they go further in the direction of consolidation of a vaster past than he had hitherto been able to reach.'

Robert Simpson, *The Chamber Music for Strings* in: Denis Arnold and Nigel Fortune, editors, *The Beethoven Companion*, 1973, p. 264.

'Op. 95 is sometimes called a transitional work, but if this epithet has a meaning it must carry the implication of diverse elements not perfectly integrated. This has been said of Op. 74, but its successor of 1810, the bitter fruit of a barren year, belongs neither with the earlier quartets nor with those of Beethoven's final maturity ... The designation on the autograph, *Quartetto Serioso*, is as strange as the work itself which could easily be

considered frivolous; did Beethoven in a mood
of angry disillusion regard the previous quartets
as too brilliant to satisfy him?'

Basil Lam, *Beethoven String Quartets*, 1975, pp. 69–70.

'The sense of reserve is still more pronounced
in the next Quartet, Op. 95, in F minor where
it is allied to a remarkable power of concentration ... Fourteen years elapsed between Op. 95
and Op. 127, but in certain ways the F minor
Quartet is strongly prophetic of the later quartets.'

Philip Radcliffe, *Beethoven's String Quartets*, 1978, p. 89
and p. 97.

'[Op. 95] marked a new departure, already hinted
at in the Piano Sonata Op. 78 and to be further
fulfilled in the works of the next decade: the Cello
Sonatas Op. 102 and the Piano Sonatas Op. 90
and Op. 101. To set the opening bars of Op. 95
alongside those of the *Appassionata* ... is to grasp
the Quartet's speed of action. Both are intensely
dramatic, but the terse resolute subject of the
Quartet establishes a new time-scale.'

Denis Matthews, *Beethoven, (The Master Musicians)*, 1985,
p. 117.

'The F minor Quartet is a strange work, its first
movement violent and wilful, the others enigmatic
and restless, till suddenly at the end of the finale
comes light — even dazzling light — in the shim-

mering coda: a passage quite different thematically from anything else in the Quartet.'

Gerald Abraham, *Beethoven's Chamber Music* in: *The Age of Beethoven, The New Oxford History of Music, Vol. VIII,* Gerald Abraham, editor, 1988, p. 292.

'Just how seriously Beethoven took his Op. 95 Quartet in F minor is shown not only by [his designation of it as *Quartetto Serioso*] but also his delay in having it published, and his curious reticence about its performance: "The Quartet is written for a small circle of connoisseurs and is never to be performed in public." Perhaps he was aware of the work's extraordinary character, even dimly conscious that it was stylistically ahead of its time.'

Barry Cooper, *The Beethoven Compendium: a guide to Beethoven's life and music*, 1991, p. 236.

'The self avowed difficulty of the quartet [Op. 95] as a whole invites comparison with the late quartets, but the later works find a cohesion that is more satisfying than evident in Op. 95. Rather than looking forward, perhaps it is more profitable to look back and view the work as a disintegration of middle-period Beethoven, not into empty gestures but into a fiercely channelled, deliberately provocative expression. It may not convince but it is utterly absorbing.'

David Wyn Jones, *Beethoven and the Viennese Legacy* in: Robin Stowell editor, *The Cambridge Companion to the*

String Quartet, 2003, p. 220.

> '[Beethoven] called [Op. 95] *Quartetto Serioso* and it lives up to its name, packing a lifetime's worth of struggle into what is his shortest string quartet. But *serioso* could also mean *for connoisseurs*, and the name was perhaps intended as an indication that this might not be a crowd-pleaser like his previous quartet, Op. 74 ... While it stands alone, Op. 95 bridges the gap between the experimental Op. 59 Quartets and the intensely spiritual late quartets that begin with Op. 127 (1824) — a serious work indeed,'

Alison Bullock, *Notes to the BBC Radio Three Beethoven Experience*, Thursday 9 June 2005, www.bbc.co.uk/radio3/Beethoven

> 'If the *Razumovsky* Quartets are explorers in expansive ways, the F minor Quartet breaks new ground with its terse, elliptical concentration and its handling of sharp contrasts. The pithy density of the *Quartetto serioso*, as it was dubbed by Beethoven, poses special challenges, and he was clearly aware that this music would not be readily understood by audiences. The uncompromising character of the piece is encapsulated in his provocative comment that it "is written for a small circle of connoisseurs and is never to be performed in public" ... The remarkable Op. 95 in F minor is a harbinger of Beethoven's last quartets, which have long been regarded as some of the most complex and demanding works of his entire oeuvre.'

William Kinderman editor, *The String Quartets of Beethoven*, 2005, pp. 6–7.

> 'In the wealth and grandeur of inspiration, in the intenseness of expression and in the beauty of its architecture, this Quartet surpasses even the preceding ones. It reveals the very essence of Beethoven's demonical greatness just as the *Appassionata*, Op. 57 does among the piano sonatas.'

Preface to Philharmonia Score, *Ludwig van Beethoven, Streichquartett*, Op. 95, Wiener Philharmonischer Verlag A. G. Wien (undated).

In the years preceding the composition of the String Quartet in F minor, Op. 95, Beethoven had composed a number of works that are noteworthy for their expansive scale – when compared, for example, with similar compositions by Haydn and Mozart. Mention may be made of the Fifth and Sixth Symphonies, the Violin Concerto, the first version of *Fidelio* and the pioneering *Waldstein* and *Appassionata* Piano Sonatas. However, as Michael Steinberg has remarked, there was also alive in Beethoven a desire to impart to his music what he describes as 'an appetite for compression' and 'tight packing' that was as unprecedented in its manner as was the expansive nature of the works just mentioned.

Much of the character of Op. 95 is implicit in its sub-title – *Quartetto Serioso*. This is one of the few occasions when Beethoven conferred an interpretative title on one of his compositions. Others of the period include the *Pathétique* Sonata, the *Eroica* Symphony and the *Pastoral* Symphony; later on such designations appear in the *Farewell* and

Hammerklavier Piano Sonatas. Of interest is that *serioso* is a Beethoven-invented word, albeit a derivative of the more correct Italian *sèrio*. At the risk of overstating the case, this can be seen as an early attempt on Beethoven's part to depart from the strictly formal conventions of Italian musicological terminology — a procedure he would, in due course, take further in favour of styling expressive markings and tempo directions in his own native language (*Hammerklavier* being the most enduring example).

Beethoven did not compose the F minor Quartet in response to a commission the inference being the work came into being through the promptings of some inner conviction. In this regard musicologist David Wyn Jones suggests it is possible to view the Op. 95 Quartet in much the same light as we perceive the *Sonate Pathétique, Sinfonia Eroica and Sinfonia Pastorella* as indicating 'an exploration of *seriousness* in the same way as the piano sonata had explored the world of the *pathétique* and the two symphonies *heroism* and the *pastoral* respectively [italics added]'.[ii] We may then ask what disposed Beethoven to explore the realm of seriousness in music of such decisive energy and expressive language? The answer, some consider, is to be found in the composer's personal circumstances to which we therefore briefly direct our attention.

As we shall see, the F minor Quartet had its creation origins in the year 1810. This was a difficult time for Beethoven who was entering a period of solitude and self-examination. Moreover, he was now forty years of age and saw his hopes of finding a partner in marriage fading. In particular his affection for Therese Malfatti — a young woman to whom he had been introduced by his friend Baron Ignaz von Gleichenstein — had come to nothing.[iii] In the spring of 1810 he wrote to Gleichenstein of the 'wounds inflicted on his soul' and of how he could only find the means of going on within the deepest feelings of his music.[iv] Doubtless his sense of loss was heightened when he learned that Gleichenstein was engaged to Therese's younger sister Anna. Notwithstanding, he congratulated his friend on 'sailing on a calm sea' and finding 'a perfect haven' but as for himself he lamented: 'You do not feel the anguish of a friend who is struggling against a tempest.'[v]

Beethoven's solitude was in part self-imposed as a consequence of his deafness. A measure of the depression he was experiencing due to his loss of hearing can be judged from a letter he wrote on 2 May 1810 to the German physician Franz Gerhard Wegeler; the two had been friends from their school days together in Bonn. In his letter he laments how beautiful life would be for him had it not been 'poisoned forever'. He remarks how for the last two years he had sought respite by trying to lead a quiet life away from society and concludes, with a combination of despair and fortitude: 'If I had not read somewhere that a man should not voluntarily quit this life so long as he can still perform a good deed, I should have quit this earth long ago.'[vi] Just how withdrawn from society Beethoven had become is apparent from an account left by the German composer and music critic Johann Friedrich Reichardt. On 30 November 1808 he called on Beethoven but had much difficulty in locating his address. He eventually tracked down the composer in what he describes as 'a large, desolate and lonely apartment'. Of his eventual meeting with the composer he writes: 'His is a powerful nature, like a Cyclops in appearance but at the same time very intimate, hearty and good.'[vii]

To add to the composer's woes were the upheavals created by Napoleon's invasion of Vienna that had implications for his loss of income as his aristocratic patrons fled the city — not to mention the terror of the bombardment with its inherent threat to his remaining hearing. A cryptic entry from Beethoven's diary reveals he came to realize the only way to deal with his misfortunes was to fall back on his self-reliance and self-belief in his art: 'Submission, the deepest submission to your fate.' Beethoven's self-injunction may have been influenced by his reading of Zacharias Werner's Tragedy *The Templars of Cyprus*. In the copy in his possession he annotated passages where the hero of the work has to accept his fate — such as: 'He can be defeated but not destroyed.'[viii]

Basil Lam has likened Beethoven's suffering to that of Goethe's *Werthe*, as set forth in *The sorrows of young Werthe* in which a sensitive artist of romantic and passionate temperament gives expression to his innermost feelings. That said, Lam cautions against attaching too much significance to the extra-musical circumstances of the composer's life and their bearing on the music itself. He writes: 'Any attempt to relate a composer's work to what is known of his life is bound to be a crude over-simplification, if only because music has a complex life of its own that resists verbalisation; but a style in which ideas expand in cumulative rhythmic patterns reflects a state of mind in which it is possible, in Elliot's phrase, to construct something upon which to rejoice.'[ix]

A clue to the reason why Beethoven included the epithet *serioso* in the title to the F minor Quartet was doubtless his realisation that, for the period in question, it was out of character with his audiences' expectations. His audiences, and for that matter those of his composer-contemporaries, can be arranged into three groups. First and foremost were the aristocracy who held musical soirees in their great salons; next came the wealthy class of bankers, manufacturers and professionals; and thirdly was the rising class of the less affluent such as musicians, civil servants and shop keepers (Beethoven's older brother was an apothecary) who would in the course of time dominate the musical scene — especially as hearing string quartets played in public became more common with the inception of professional string quartets such as that pioneered by Beethoven's friend Ignaz Schuppanzigh.[x]

When Beethoven issued the caution 'not to be played in public' relating to the F minor String Quartet, he was doubtless aware that his new musical style was too in advance of the musical conventions of the day — even by his own daring standards. He was beginning to explore compositional techniques that he would develop even further in his last string quartets such as, discordant outbursts of sound juxtaposed with silence pregnant with meaning, quirky tempos and metric ambiguity, unorthodox groupings of movements, and ever greater freedom with tonality. Writing about these innovations Joseph Kerman observes: '[The] Quartet in F minor seems to foreshadow aspects of the technique of the of the last quartets in its dominant qualities of conciseness, directness, and instant confrontation of contrast.'[xi] 'The Quartet is as violent as it is serious. Everything is concise, rapid, without respite or relaxation.'[xii] Others have felt disposed to make similar observations. The American musicologist Arthur Shepherd considered the Op. 95 to be a 'superb quartet' not only for its anticipations of the composer's later contribution to the genre but also for what he believed to be its 'premonitions' of the works of later romantic composers. He cites how for him the first and second movements reveal fore-shadowings of Brahms and how the *Larghetto espressivo* introduction of the last movement anticipates feelings found in Schumann's C major Symphony.[xiii] Shepherd's compatriot, the musician-musicologist John Daverio, alludes to the composition's traits 'that resonate with the late quartets'. In particular he singles out what he describes as the work's gnomic (cryptic-epigrammatic) quality that he too associated with the early Romantics.[xiv] For Harold Truscott: '[Op. 95] is as much pure third period throughout as anything actually composed during that late period; in fact, in sheer compression, one of the attributes which comes very much to the fore in the last period, this quartet outdoes any work composed during the last years.'[xv]

Discussing the F minor Quartet's terseness Kerman states: 'Everything unessential falls victim, leaving a residue of extreme concentration, in dangerously high tension ... But strength, not strain, is the commanding impression.' Of the work's construction he adds: 'All through the Quartet in F minor one senses Beethoven's impatience (or fury) with conventional bridge and cadential passages of every kind — the more-or-less neutral padding material of the classic style In the E flat Quartet [Op. 74] he enjoyed stylizing them. Now he will do without them.'[xvi] Elaborating on the difference between the F minor and E flat Quartets, he notes that although they were composed within a short period of one another, like two siblings, they could not be more different: '[Between] the two there is a cleavage in aesthetic stance ... The E flat Quartet is an open, unproblematic, lucid work of consolidation ... The F minor Quartet is an involved, impassioned, highly idiosyncratic piece, problematic in every one of its movements, advanced in a hundred ways. One work looks backward, perhaps, and the other forward. Or, to put it better, one work looks outward, the other inward. It would be hard to imagine any composer grouping these antipodes together in a single opus.'[xvii] Philip Radcliffe is more succinct: 'In general character [Op. 95] is as different as possible from Op. 74, being much sparer in texture and, [notably] much more explosive in manner.'[xviii] Here we have an example of Beethoven's contention that he never repeated himself.

It is well known Beethoven typically worked on several compositions at the same time, turning from one to the other in his sketchbooks and often exchanging ideas between them. This assumes relevance when we consider the incidental music he composed for Goethe's drama *Egmont*. It shares the same musical chronology as the Op. 95 Quartet and both works share the same key of F minor — an uncommon key for Beethoven. Barry Cooper suggests these compositions are illustrative of the composer's 'F minor phase' that briefly succeeded those of his C and E flat phases of the preceding years.[xix] The underlying theme of Goethe's drama must have appealed intuitively to Beethoven, dealing as it does with the portrayal of a fearless hero (Count Egmont) who strives for moral victory at his personal cost — shades of the hapless Florestan in the composer's opera *Fidelio*. In his study of the two compositions, Seow-Chin Ong has demonstrated not only do they share a common genesis but also the extent to which musical bonds unite them. In the music drama, assuming the likeness of Klärchen (Egmont's beloved) Liberty appears before him as an apparition expressed in music of a restrained manner. Ong draws a parallel between this and way Beethoven introduces a slow movement in the Quartet juxtaposed, as it were, between two movements of drama and conflict.[xx] In his comparison of the two compositions, Robert Simpson makes the following evaluation: 'The whole Quartet is concerned (perhaps like *Egmont*) with two worlds, the real and the ideal, the first embodied in the harsh F minor (Beethoven's *barbarous* key), and the other imagined in remote keys, or keys deliberately made to seem unreal, such as the D flat in the first movement, the D major in the second, or the marvellous translations into distant keys in the two trios of the scherzo.' Simpson reflects: 'It may be that *Egmont* did not give him the outlet he needed to explore the nature of the revolutionary mentality; the F minor Quartet certainly did.' He asks: 'Is it possible that in composing the Quartet Beethoven expressed the inner thoughts of *Egmont*, as opposed to the public effect displayed in the Overture?'[xxi] Paul Bekker expresses similar thoughts: 'The powers of darkness which he conjures up here [in the music for *Egmont*] have no longer full power over him, and he can therefore deal with them [in the F minor Quartet] imaginatively as a subject of artistic expression.'[xxii]

The French musicologist Joseph de Marliave was uncharacteristically aloof in his estimation of the F minor Quartet. In his study of Beethoven's quartets *Les Quatuors de Beethoven* (1925 posthumous) he first pays tribute to the work by quoting the views of the German music scholar Ludwig Nohl (*Beethoven* 1887) who regarded the work as 'the most intimately individual of all [Beethoven's quartets]' and who placed it 'in the front rank' of Beethoven's work. As for himself, however, he comments: '[One] cannot honestly say that it deserves so high a place, for the Op. 95 has neither the symphonic grandeur of Op. 59, nor the depths of Op. 74.' He does though acknowledge: 'It is characterised by an attempt to express a condensed idea in the simplest, though also the most expressive, *thematic* form, and by restraint of method.' Regarding Beethoven's craftsmanship de Marliave is equally positive: 'Technically the work is a pure piece of *quartet writing*, and never oversteps the limits of the genre.' In support of his contention he quotes his fellow French musicologist Jean Chantavoine (who was among the first to publish Beethoven's manuscript sketches): 'The less complex character of this work [Op. 95] reveals only the intention of the composer to write a quartet on less symphonic lines than the foregoing [Op. 59], one unencumbered with obscure meaning ... where the purely musical aspect was to predominate.'[xxiii]

Kerman is uncompromisingly candid in his estimation of Beethoven's Op. 95: 'The F minor Quartet is not a pretty piece, but is terribly strong – and perhaps rather terrible. One does not hear it with joy and the *Mitgefühl* [compassion] that the E flat Quartet should evoke; the piece stands aloof, preoccupied with its radical private war on every fibre of rhetoric and feeling that Beethoven knew or could invent.' Kerman considered the work to be Beethoven's 'most self-absorbed and uncompromising and fraught with energy, the energy turned squarely on itself'. He believed Op. 95 differed so radically from what the composer had previously achieved in the genre of the string quartet 'that one almost imagines him setting himself some sort of spiritual exercise'. Here, he asserts, is Beethoven 'at his most quirky' and 'Beethoven possessed'. In this quartet Kerman believed considers Beethoven 'evokes that almost tangible sense of the artist assaulting a demon of his own fancying'.[xxiv] Cooper acknowledges the 'extraordinary compressed intensity' of Op. 95 that he conjectures must have bewildered his contemporaries at its first hearing, not least for its 'overall mood ... of extreme anguish'.[xxv] He also has words of caution arguing it would be wrong 'to set Op. 95 apart as a kind of early late quartet'. He reminds us that many of the composition's distinctive features occur in other of the composer's works of the period. By way of illustration he cites the 'dramatic compression' found in the String Quartet Op. 59, No. 2 and the sometimes 'violent, even grotesque contrast' found in the String Quartet Op. 18, No. 6. Setting aside his reservations he accepts: '[There] is something about the overall tone of Op. 95 that makes it difficult to avoid looking ahead into the mid-1820s.'[xxvi]

It is on record Benito Mussolini was an admirer of Beethoven's F minor String Quartet. He was himself a violinist, although not the accomplished musician he sought to portray himself as being. Contemporary accounts tell of him 'sitting listening intently to Beethoven's Op. 95 Quartet being played to him, overwhelmed by the musical experience'.[xxvii] In his personal recollections, Benjamin Britten enthused how between the ages of thirteen and sixteen he knew every note of Beethoven and Brahms; for his fourteenth birthday he received the full score of *Fidelio*. Later in life he would disavow this youthful enthusiasm for Beethoven. However, a diary entry of his for 16 October 1932 – when Britten was age nineteen – reveals he was still in thrall to the composer. He recalls hearing the Spencer Dyke String Quartet performing the Op. 95; the Spencer Dyke Quartet became well known from the 1920s onwards for its pioneering recordings brought out by the National Gramophone Society. On hearing their rendering of the F minor Quartet Britten described it as being 'a wonder of the world'.[xxviii] A poignant circumstance connects the Romanian pianist Dino Lipatti with Beethoven's Op. 95; he died at the height of his powers at the age of just thirty-three. In his last hours he sought consolation by listening to the radio with his wife – the F minor String Quartet was being broadcast. As it came to an end (with what Gerald Abraham has called 'perhaps the most brilliantly pure and luminously quartet writing ever conceived by a musician'), Madame Lipatti said to her husband: 'It seems as if the whole world is in the pages of that wonderful music.' 'Yes', responded Lipatti, 'but to write such music one must be a chosen instrument of God.' According to his wife, these were amongst his last coherent words.[xxix]

In April 1959 the American composer and pedagogue Aaron Copland was invited to contribute to *The Distinguished Lecture Series* at the University of New Hampshire. Copland did not mention the String Quartet Op. 95 directly but his remarks are well suited to the nature of the work:

'Beethoven brought three startling innovations to music: first, he altered our very conception of the art by emphasizing the psychological element implicit in the language of sounds. Secondly, his own stormy and explosive temperament was, in part, responsible for a dramatization of the whole of music. Third, and possibly [the] most original achievement: the creation of musical forms dynamically conceived on a scale never before attempted and of an inevitability that is irresistible.'[xxx]

Beethoven dedicated his String Quartet Op, 95 to Nicholas Zmeskall von Domanovez (Domanovecz). He became acquainted with the composer in the 1790s soon after Beethoven's arrival in Vienna; the two became close friends. Zmeskall was an excellent cellist and regularly performed in the string quartet sessions convened by Beethoven's patron Prince Karl Lichnowsky. Although Zmeskall was employed as a civil servant in the Hungarian Court Chancellery in Vienna, such was his standing in music that Haydn dedicated to him the 1800 edition of his so-called *Sun* Quartets. For this, Beethoven subsequently teased his friend with the nickname *Comte di Musica* in friendly acknowledgment of his patronage. Zmeskall had to endure much similar leg-pulling and badinage from Beethoven as is evident from the many notes the composer sent to his long-suffering friend. Of particular interest is that the Op. 95 was Beethoven's first quartet to originate outside the traditional patronage and publication system. Clearly, the dedication to Zmeskall may be interpreted as a special mark of respect and affection to a trusted friend.[xxxi]

Beethoven worked on the F minor Quartet in 1810, returning to it again in 1811. The origins of the composition survive today in the form of five sources. A primary source is the so-called Landsberg 11 sketchbook, named after its original owner Ludwig Landsberg. Its present-day size consists of fifty leaves (one-hundred oblong pages) on which Beethoven worked from the winter of 1809 until the autumn of 1810. Sketches for all four movements for Op. 95 are found on pp. 30—35 and 37—54 alongside sketches for the incidental music to Goethe's *Egmont*, Op. 83 and the Piano Trio in B-flat major, Op. 97, *The Archduke*. Beethoven's workings-out are in a mixture of pencil and ink.

Landsberg 11 passed from private ownership to the Berlin Royal Library in 1862 and since World War II it is housed in the Biblioteka Jagiellońska, Kraków, Poland. A second source is what was originally an improvised sketchbook that the composer used from late 1810 until the summer of 1811. Its surviving contents are now preserved in various locations with some thirty-nine leaves so far identified. These once formed part of a larger gathering that Beethoven would have stitched together as was his custom; he variously ruled the pages with 10, 12, 14 or 16 staves to a page. In this source he continued to work on the String Quartet in F minor, Op. 95 and the Trio in B-flat major, Op. 97; as noted both begun in Landsberg 11 together with the music to *Die Ruinen von Athen*, Op. 113. The Berlin State Library (*Staatsbibliothek zu Berlin*) possesses a bifolium bearing sketches for the first movement of Op. 95. The Pierpont Morgan Library, New York has two bifolia (formerly on loan to the Library of Congress, Washington) that reveal a draft, in score, of sections of the third movement and sketches for the fourth movement (*Larghetto* to the *Allegretto agitato*). The Royal Musical Library Stockholm (*Musikaliska Akademien*) has one leaf of sketches for Op. 95, namely the third movement and the transition to the fourth movement. Four further leaves have been traced to a private collection in Paris containing sketches for the *Larghetto* and ideas for the theme of the *Allegretto agitato*.[xxii]

The manuscript of the F minor Quartet bears the

following title: '*Quartetto Serioso* – 1810 im Monat Oktober Dem Herrn von Zmeskall gewidmet von Freunde L. v. Bthvn, und geschrieben im monat Oktober.' ['*Quartetto serioso* – October 1810 – dedicated to Herrn von Zmeskall by his friend Ludwig van Beethoven, and written in the month of October.'][xxxiii] Beethoven's attribution to the work's composition 'in the month of October' is now considered to be an oversight, given that he is known to have worked on it in 1811 and later in 1814. The autograph score is preserved today in Vienna's *Nationalbibliothek*.

With regard to the performing time of the F minor Quartet, it is instructive to consider it in relation to its predecessors; these reveal Beethoven striving to expand the medium. The six Op. 18 Quartets have a performing time of typically 20–25 minutes. With the three Op. 59 Quartets the performing time extends to 30 minutes – that for No. 1 in the set approaches 40 minutes. Op. 74 plays for more than 30 minutes. With Op. 95 expansion gives way, as remarked, to compression; it is the shortest of all his string quartets.[xxxiv] Maynard Solomon observes: 'Beethoven was no longer at pains to apply symphonic ideas to the genres of chamber music, nor was he seeking to create heaven-storming compositions.'[xxxv] Comparing the F minor Quartet with other of the composer's later compositions, Gerald Abraham comments: 'In some of Beethoven's works, for instance his last-period fugues and the finale of the *Choral* Symphony, he seems to be engaged in the colossal struggle with intractable material which defies even his power to mould it completely and quite satisfactorily; he has rough-hewn it as none could, but the shaping has beaten him.' Here, however, in Op. 95 he maintains 'despite the heterogeneity of the material' Beethoven has achieved 'perfect unity of form' and has allowed himself 'to be extremely wilful and yet has held the result under perfect control'.[xxxvi]

Beethoven achieves terseness by disposing with conventional transitions and repeats to enable the music to make its inexorable forward-progress.

Interestingly, Op. 95 shares the key of F with his very first work in the quartet genre, namely, Op. 18, No.1. (F minor) and his very last Op. 135 (F major).

What we have called the terseness (q.v. *compression*) in Beethoven's F minor String Quartet had a direct influence on composer Michael Tippet's structural procedures as he himself has acknowledged: '[The] musical forms deployed in my Double Concerto were those of Beethoven: a succinct dramatic sonata allegro, a slow movement virtually modelled on the song-fugue-song layout of the *Andante* of Beethoven's String Quartet in F minor, Op. 95, and finally a sonata rondo with coda.'[xxxvii]

We take our discussion forward now by considering the creation origins of the String Quartet in F minor, Op. 95 as they unfolded between the period of its creation in 1810 and eventual publication in 1816. Along the way we make mention of contextual circumstances bearing on the composer and how he appeared to his contemporaries.

Although 1810 is regarded as being, by Beethoven's standards, a relatively lean year — compositionally speaking, as he was at work with his sketchbooks drafting ideas for Op. 95 he found time to negotiate on 4 February with Breitkopf & Härtel for the publication of 'some new works' — evidence of his previous creativity and productivity. These included: Piano Concerto, Op. 73; String Quartet, Op. 74; Fantasia for piano, Op. 77; Piano Sonatas, Opp. 78, 79; Choral Fantasia, Op. 80; and Piano Sonata, Op. 81a. He asked for payment of 1450 gulden, 'to be paid in assimilated coinage' — reflecting his growing mistrust of paper money and bankers' drafts.[xxxviii] These pioneering achievements, now so much a part of our musical inheritance, were not readily assimilated even by some of Beethoven's more gifted and enterprising composer-contemporaries. This is evident from the response the Swiss publisher Hans Georg Nägeli received when he wrote to Carl Maria von Weber on 21 May 1810. Nägeli had remarked that one of Weber's compositions (not identified) reminded him of Beethoven. Weber was neither flattered nor amused and his reply illustrates how far in advance of musical convention Beethoven's music appeared, even to so imaginative a musical mind as Weber's. Weber responded: '[My] views differ far too much from those of Beethoven ever to come into contact with him. The fiery, almost incredible inventive faculty which inspires him is attended by so many complications in the arrangement of his ideas that it is only his earlier compositions that interest me; the later ones appear to me a confused chaos, unintelligible struggle after novelty from which occasionally heavenly flashes of genius dart forth, showing how great he might be if he chose to control his luxuriant fancy.' What, we may ask, would Weber have thought of the composer's Op. 95 then being gestated in the very manner that gave him such discomfort?[xxxix] Mention has been made of the *Egmont* music. On 21 August Beethoven wrote to Breitkopf & Härtel informing that he wished the work to be dedicated to his composition pupil the Archduke Rudolf.[xl]

The following year, as Beethoven resumed work on his Op. 95, he experienced periods of ill health. In late March he had occasion to write to Rudolph: 'For over a fortnight now I have been afflicted with a headache which is plaguing me. I have hoped that the pain would subside, but in vain.'[xli] By 12 April things had improved. He was able to write to his celebrated contemporary, Johann Wolfgang von Goethe, to inform him he would shortly receive from Breitkopf and Härtell a copy of his music for *Egmont*, 'that glorious

Egmont on which I have again reflected through you, and which I have felt and reproduced in music as intensely as I felt when I read it'. In fact Goethe did not received his copy until 23 January 1812 when the songs and entr'acte music were published; Breitkopf and Härtell published the Overture in December 1810.[xlii] A few weeks later Beethoven produced a piano arrangement of the *Egmont* Overture that was also published by Breitkopf and Härtell but not apparently to his satisfaction; the edition contained errors. This earned Gottfried Härtell, head of the firm, a characteristic withering reprimand: 'Mistakes — you yourself are a mistake.'[xliii] In early summer Beethoven turned his attention to a subject that was to preoccupy him for much of his life, namely, finding a suitable subject for an opera — to follow on from *Leonora-Fidelio* that, as it turned out, was to be his only work for the lyric theatre. In a letter of 11 June 1811 he set out his views on the subject to Count Ferdinand Pálffy, a Hungarian nobleman and administrator of the Burgtheater and one of the Directors of the Imperial Opera. He explained to Pálffy: 'It is very difficult to find a good libretto for an opera. Since last year I have turned down no less than twelve or more of them. I even paid for them out of my own pocket and yet was not able to fine one I could use.'[xliv]

Thoughts about a future opera project continued to occupy Beethoven as is evident from a further letter he wrote on this subject in 28 January 1812 to August von Kotzebue, manager of Vienna's Burgtheater. He informed Kotzebue he would consider a libretto 'Whether it be romantic, quite serious, heroic, comic or sentimental ... I must admit that I should like best of all some grand subject taken from history, and especially from the Dark Ages, for instance, from the time of Attila or the like.'[xlv] In 1812 the composer-violinist Louis Spohr was in Vienna where he was scheduled to conduct some of his oratorios. In his *Autobiography* he writes how he wished to meet Beethoven at one of Vienna's many musical parties but learned the composer had withdrawn from such reunions 'for his deafness had so much increased that he could not hear music readily or clearly, and he had become exceedingly shy of society'. Spohr eventually encountered Beethoven by chance in a restaurant. He recalls: 'One had to shout loud enough to be heard three rooms off.' He describes Beethoven as being somewhat abrupt 'but a pair of sparkling eyes gleamed under his shaggy eyebrows'. Spohr then expresses his opinion of Beethoven's music that he states was current at the time, and with which he concurred for many years afterwards: 'His ear could no longer guide him in his constant strivings after originality and new forms. Was it, then, wonderful [not surprising] that his works should become more and more strange, incoherent and incomprehensible?' He concludes: 'I freely confess that I have never been able to acquire a taste for Beethoven's later works.'[xlvi]

Two further descriptions of Beethoven from the period under consideration arise from meetings with him when he was seeking respite for abdominal pains by taking the waters at the spa town of Teplitz. Beethoven experienced abdominal pains throughout his adult life, frequently described as *colic*, which he sought to remedy at health spas such as that at Teplitz and Baden. In August 1812 he was encouraged to take a course of hydrotherapy by Dr. Jacob Staudenheim, a distinguished physician who attended upon members of the Imperial Court. Of his treatment Beethoven remarks: 'My doctor chases me from one spot to another to enable me to recover good health ... I must splash about again in the water. Hardly have I performed the duty of filling my inside with a large quantity of this water when again I must have my outer surface washed down with it several times.'[xlvii] The German diplomat and Biographer Karl August von Ense was also at

Teplitz at the same time as Beethoven and appears to have made the composer's acquaintance. Writing of this to his friend, the poet and philologist Ludwig Uhland, he confided: 'I soon was on intimate terms with him ... He lives only for his art ... On his walks he seeks out distant places along lonely paths ... finding peace in the contemplation of the great features of nature and thinking in musical tones.' The second of our encounters worthy of mention was that between Beethoven and none other than Germany's celebrated man of letters Johann Wolfgang von Goethe who also met the composer at Teplitz. This was perhaps the only occasion in Goethe's life when he came face to face with an artist of his own stature. He wrote to his wife: 'I have never before seen a more comprehensive, energetic or intense artist. I understand very well how strange he must appear to the outside world.' A few days later he wrote to his friend Carl Friederich Zelter: 'His talent astounded me; but unfortunately he is a quite intractable person ... he does not make things enjoyable either for himself or for others.'[xlviii] For his part, Beethoven was far from being in awe of the great man of letters and disapproved of his courtly demeanour. He could not help remarking: 'Goethe delights far too much in the court atmosphere, far more than is becoming to a poet.'[xlix]

Perhaps the most enduring visual image of the composer dates from 1812 arising from the following circumstance. The Viennese pianoforte manufacturers Nannette and Andreas Streicher adorned their music salon in Vienna with the busts of celebrated composers. Accordingly, they commissioned the sculptor Franz Klein to take a likeness of Beethoven that required his face to be covered with gypsum plaster. Klein had earlier perfected this technique when preparing anatomical models. Beethoven had first to be persuaded to have his face lubricated with oil, to prevent his whiskers from adhering to the plaster, then to have his eyebrows covered with paper strips — for the same reason. Finally, before his face was covered with plaster, quills were inserted into his nostrils to enable him to breath. The ordeal proved too much for Beethoven and the taking of his likeness almost ended in disaster. Finding the process too uncomfortable, and fearing he would suffocate, he tore the cast from his face and dashed it to the floor. Fortunately for posterity, Klein was able to reassemble the broken pieces that were later used to create the well known bust that is considered to be a particularly authentic likeness of the composer — resolute expression, pock marks and all.[i]

We take leave of Beethoven in 1812 with a remarkable letter he wrote to a little girl known only as 'Emilie M'. She is thought to have been between just eight and ten years of age and was learning to play the piano. She sent Beethoven a gift of a wallet, woven in her own handiwork, with an accompanying letter expressing her admiration of the composer's compositions — she must have been have been possessed of remarkable insight for one so young. Beethoven replied to Emilie saying he would treasure her gift among other tokens of regard that he had received. He encouraged his young admirer: 'Persevere, do not only practise your art, but endeavour also to fathom its inner meaning; it deserves this effort. For only art and science can raise men to the level of the gods.'[ii]

In 1813 the health of Beethoven's younger brother Kaspar (Caspar) Karl (Carl) began to fail, placing the composer under an obligation to assist him and his family financially; Carl eventually died in 1815. In May 1806 Caspar Carl had married Johanna Riess who was pregnant at the time with their son Karl. Beethoven disapproved of Joanna and, remarkably, secured the boy's custody — at least in part. Carl's deposition to the legal authorities reads: 'Since I am convinced of the openhearted disposition of my brother Ludwig van Beethoven, I desire after my death, he undertake the guardianship of my surviving minor son Karl Beethoven. I therefore request the honourable Court to appoint my said brother to undertake this office and, like a father, to assist my child with word and deed in all circumstances.'[lii] Karl's guardianship continued to be contested by Johanna and led to much bitterness and encroachment on the composer's capacity to compose.[liii]

More positively, 1814 was a good year for Beethoven. With the opening of the Congress of Vienna it would see him reach the very zenith of his fame. Before the Congress, on 27 February he gave the final of four *Akademie* (benefit) Concerts at Vienna's Grosser Redoutensaal. The series had commenced on 8 December 1813. For the February concert in 1814 an orchestra of 123 members took part; each received two florins for the rehearsal and a further three florins for the actual performance. The concert included: Symphony No. 7; the Trio *Tremate empi, tremati,* Op. 116 (featuring the soprano Anna Milder-Hauptmann who had a close association with the premier of *Fidelio*); *Wellington's Victory*, Op. 91; and the first performance of the Symphony No. 8. Mounting these concerts entailed considerable financial expense to Beethoven. For example, for copying out the violin and wind orchestral parts of the Trio and the two Symphonies — a total of 452 sheets — Beethoven paid his copyist Wenzel Schlemmer (his favourite and most reliable) 90 florins — a sum comparable to the fee he might expect to receive from one of his more substantial compositions. Consider also that Schlemmer's bill for copying out the orchestral parts for *Der glorreiche Augenblick* — a total of 1,468 sheets at 15 kreuzer per sheet — came to 367 florins and 17 kreuzer.[liv]

In the early months of the year Beethoven was occupied revising his Opera *Fidelio*, a work close to his heart. Of the endeavours entailed he was wont to remark 'This work will earn for me a martyr's crown'. The task included writing a new overture – his fourth. *Fidelio* appeared in its revised form on 23 May but Beethoven had not had time to complete the new Overture, so that to *Die Ruinen von Athens*, Op. 113 was performed in its place. By the time of the second performance on 26 May, the new Overture '*Fidelio*' found its rightful place. Of the experience in creating the new music he enthused: 'As the wind often does, so harmonies whirl around me, and so do things often whirl about too in my soul.'[lv] The poet and playwright Georg Friedrich Treitschke – Assistant Director of the Theater an der Wien – assisted the composer with the necessary textual revisions. Of the work's reception he wrote: 'This opera appeared several weeks ago at the Imperial Royal Court Opera here [in Vienna] and had the good fortune to find more than the usual applause and always to attract full houses ... The whole opera has been revised in accordance with altered conceptions of that which are more in keeping with theatrical effects, and over half of it is newly written.'[lvi]

In the same month that he was revising *Fidelio*, Beethoven took part in a performance of the Trio in B-flat major, Op. 97, *The Archduke*. He had premiered the work previously on 11 April at a charity concert sponsored by the violinist Ignaz Schuppanzigh. In the May performance the composer's new Quartet Op. 95 received its first public performance. Sadly, as a consequence of his deteriorating hearing, this was Beethoven's last appearance in public as a pianist – the once near-incomparable virtuoso of the keyboard was finally silenced.[lvii]

On 16 June Beethoven's originality as a composer was publicly recognised in the pages of the *Allgemeine musikalische Zeitung*. The Journal's music critic stated: 'Originality is such a rare advantage, even with artists, that it might well be attributed to only a few chosen ones, geniuses of the first rank. Which contemporary artist would indeed possess this divine gift to a higher degree than Beethoven?' The next passage has particular significance: 'Perhaps the originality of his *completed* works can be compared only with the originality of Shakespeare. The most profound humour and most tender romantic feeling are completely united in them.' Recognising the challenge the composer's works posed for many of his contemporaries the author continues: 'In the works of great poets there is an irony that gently hovers over the entire piece, but also frequently breaks forth incisively, making itself easily noticeable to the judiciously attentive ... For a long time Beethoven's compositions have not been considered enough from this point of view. But precisely from this vantage many things that *appear* to be harsh and strange in him are recognised as exquisite and necessary.'[lviii][lix]

At the period of the Vienna Congress the French portraitist Louis Letronne, then resident in the capitol, was called upon to create portraits of the various monarchs and statesmen who had come to the imperial city to participate in this event — what today would be called 'a summit'. During this time Letronne also took a likeness of Beethoven. His portrait was intended to be the draft for a copper engraving to be undertaken by Blasius Höfel — a member of Vienna's Academy of Fine Arts. In the event Höfel was dissatisfied with Letronne's sketch and requested the composer to sit for second time — no small undertaking given Beethoven's irascible nature. The publishing house Artaria & Co. subsequently published Höfel's portrait in connection with releases of some of the composer's works — further evidence of Beethoven's popularity and fame. This new popularity derived mainly from the success of the two compositions Beethoven had composed and performed on the occasion of the Vienna Congress, namely: the Cantata *Der glorreiche Augenblick* (*The Glorious Moment*), Op. 136 and the Symphony *Wellingtons Sieg* (*Wellington's Victory*) or the *Schlacht bei Vittoria* (*Battle near Vittoria*), Op. 91 to which may be added the acclaim accorded to the composer's Seventh Symphony — the only one of the three compositions to remain in today's concert repertoire.[lx]

In considering the events of 1815 we reunite our connection with the progress of the String Quartet in F minor, Op. 95. Sometime between 16–18 March Beethoven enlisted the Viennese businessman Johann von Häring to help him write to Sir George Smart in London to assist him promote several of his publications in England; Beethoven had a working knowledge of the French language but not English whereas Häring had an excellent commend of English. George Smart, a founder member of the Philharmonic Society, was celebrated as a conductor and had been knighted for his services in 1811. Beethoven offered the String Quartet Op. 95 for 40 guineas, describing it as 'Serious Quartetto for 2 violins, tenor and base'. With the many other compositions he also offered Smart, Beethoven described them as 'the produce of four years labour'. He reassured Smart the Quartet had not yet been published and he therefore had copyright priority. [lxi] Beethoven's 'agent' in London was the pianist-composer Charles Neate. The two first became acquainted in 1815 and when Neate left Vienna in February 1816 he took with him several of the composer's unpublished works (see following). For his efforts Beethoven presented Neate with a manuscript copy of his Violin Concerto. Eventually the English music publisher Robert Birchall took four of the publications Beethoven was offering for sale, namely: piano arrangements of *Wellingtons Sieg* and the Seventh Symphony, plus the Violin Sonata, Op. 96 and the *Archduke* Trio. For these works Beethoven received £65 (about 130 Viennese ducats).[lxii]

A few days after writing to George Smart, Beethoven received words of encouragement regarding his string-quartet writing from the clergyman-violinist Karl Amenda. Beethoven had made Amenda's acquaintance years previously in 1799 at the chamber-music sessions held in the household of Prince Lobkowitz where Amenda was then employed. Thereafter he soon became the composer's closest friend; it is a measure of the closeness of the composer's feelings towards Amenda that he was one of the first to whom he confided the onset of his deafness. When Amenda had to return to his native Courland, Beethoven made him a gift of the first version of the F major quartet Op. 18. On 20 March 1815 Amenda wrote to Beethoven encouraging him: 'To bless us violin players again soon with quartets.' Being then resident in his native Latvia, we can assume Amenda was unaware of the existence of the composer's latest addition to the genre, namely his Op. 95.[lxiii]

At about the same time Beethoven was negotiating with George Smart in London, on 29 April he approached the Vienna-based art dealer and music publisher Sigmund Anton Steiner & Co. with the further prospect of securing the publication of several of his compositions in Germany. It so happens that, thereby, Steiner would eventually supplant Breitkopf & Härtell as the composer's principal publisher. The publications in question – 'the produce of four years labour' – included the F minor Quartet, Op. 95 alongside the scores of: *Fidelio*; Cantata der *glorreiche Augenblick*, Op. 136 (not published until 1837); Trio for voices and piano, Op. 116; *Schlacht bei Vittoria* with pianoforte arrangement; pianoforte arrangement of the Symphony in F major; pianoforte arrangement of the Symphony in A major; Trio for pianoforte, violin and cello, Op. 97; Sonata for pianoforte and violin, Op. 96; Overture in E flat, Op. 117; Overture C major, Op. 115; Overture in

G major, Op. 113 (*Die Ruinen von Athens, König Stephan, Namensfeier*); and 12 English songs with pianoforte accompaniment, WoO 157. Having paid Beethoven for these compositions, Steiner was then at liberty to make use of them with the exception of their sale in England, for which, as we have seen, Charles Neate was in negotiations with George Smart.[lxiv] By way of interest, Neate obtained 75 guineas for the three Overtures but they did not prove to be popular with English audiences.

On 20 May Beethoven felt obliged to write to both the publisher Steiner and his friend Zmeskall for the return of the score and parts to the F Minor Quartet explaining: 'Some foreigners have turned up here; I can't refuse to let them see some of my recent compositions.'[lxv] It would seem Beethoven had given Steiner the score to the Quartet and Zmeskall the set of manuscript parts. The foreign visitors probably included Charles Neate who, as we have just seen, ultimately took the Quartet Op. 95 home with him to London in February 1816 with the hope of achieving its simultaneous publication there on the composer's behalf.[lxvi]

Shortly after the proceedings of the Congress of Vienna had come to a close, the painter Joseph Mähler made a portrait of Beethoven, doubtless with his celebrity as a stimulus. Some time around 1800 he had portrayed him in an Arcadian setting striking a lyre with a temple of Apollo situated in the background. This clearly meant a great deal to Beethoven who retained this particular study of his likeness until his death.[lxvii] In August 1815 Mähler painted a second portrait of Beethoven. With the passing of the years it is understandably more severe and some consider it conveys a distant, almost trance-like expression. At least three versions of Mähler's portrait exist, one copy of which is now owned by the *Gesellschaft der Muisk freunde.*[lxviii] Mention may be made of a further portrait of the composer from this period taken by Johann Christoph Heckel. This may not be the most flattering study of Beethoven ever taken but, according to contemporary opinion, it was considered to be one of the best portraits of the composer ever made. In the words of H. C. Robbins Landon it reveals 'the same stubborn, rebellious and square-jawed Beethoven that we know to be truthful from the mask'.[lxix] Landon is of course referring to the plaster likeness taken of Beethoven in 1812 by Franz Klein to which we have made reference.

In November 1815, Beethoven's fame and contribution to Vienna's musical life were recognised by him being awarded the honour of *Bürgerrecht* – 'freedom of the City'. The citation reads: 'By the Magistrat of the Imperial Royal Capital and Residence City of Vienna, Herr Ludwig van Beethoven – upon action of the Public Hospital's Management Commission, and in consideration that in the past years he not only made available the performance of his musical instrumental compositions free of charge for the benefit of the men, women and children in the St. Marx Hospital, but also, with unpretentious willingness, personally took over their leadership, and through this humanitarian endeavour procured for the Public Hospital's Poor Fund such rich proceeds that through it the poor men, women and children, humbled by old age and infirmity, could be provided comfort and alleviation of their destinies – will be granted tax free the *civil rights* [freedom of the city] of this Capitol and Residence City as proof of the acknowledgment of his merit and of the esteem for these good sentiments.'[lxx]

Ii was on 6 February 1816 when Beethoven eventually entrusted Charles Neate with the great number of works he hoped to have published in England (London), namely, Opp. 61, 72, 92, 95, 102, 112, 113, 115, 117, and 136. However, several weeks passed and he became increasingly concerned at Neate's apparent lack of progress; the reason for Neate's tardiness was, as we shall shortly disclose, both touching and disarming. On 18 May Beethoven eventually learned of Neate's safe arrival in London from his former piano pupil Ferdinand Ries. As well as being the highly productive composer of eight symphonies, as many piano concertos, and no fewer than 26 string quartets, Ries held the important position of Director (one of a number) of the London Philharmonic Society. Accordingly, Beethoven wrote to his former protégée on 11 June: 'As for the Quartet in F minor, you may sell it without delay to a publisher, and please signify to me the day of publication as I should wish it to appear here [in Vienna] on the very day [as in London].' Beethoven was clearly anxious to comply with the performing (copyright) conventions of the period. He also expressed the hope Neate would be able to organise a benefit concert on his behalf to promote the compositions in his possession. He left the matter of payment to Neate but on the understanding 'The more the better'.[lxxi]

We pause for a moment in our narrative regarding the progress of the F minor Quartet, to become acquainted with Beethoven as he appeared at this time to the physician Dr. Karl von Bursy. He was a friend of Karl Amenda who had provided Bursy with the letter of introduction necessary to gain access to the reclusive composer. Bursy recalls in his diary: '[Beethoven] is short, but sturdy-looking with grey hair ... and fiery eyes ... full of intense life. He asked me to speak loudly as his hearing is very bad ... He has not been well for some time.' Beethoven told Bursy: 'I always work at several things at once, and take up first one then the other.' Bursy continues: 'He often strikes the piano with his first so violently that the room resounds ... Beethoven seems very anxious about money ... He was pleased to hear that *Fidelio* had been so well received in Berlin ... I saw but little music; some pieces of paper lay on the table.' Bursy remarks how publishers complained 'Beethoven charged monstrously for his compositions'. On a later visit (27 July) Beethoven was not at home and so Bursy left him a message, then temptation overtook him; he left with Beethoven's quill as a souvenir. He confessed, the *corpus delicti* was 'a constant memorial to his moment of weakness'.[lxxii]

In August Beethoven was in negotiations with Sigmund Anton Steiner over the publication of the F minor Quartet. He had found errors in the printing that he wanted correcting. Adopting his typical sense of humour he threatened to wake Steiner up by appearing in person in the guise of 'thunder and lightening'.[lxxiii] Over the next weeks the situation had not improved prompting Beethoven to write once more to Steiner urging him to make progress with the printing of the score of the Quartet and to ensure the text was error-free. He urged: 'I recommend the most thorough investigation [proof reading]'. *I have had a look at it here, and it cannot be corrected without the score.*' [Beethoven's italics][lxxiv] Notwithstanding these exhortations, Beethoven clearly trusted Steiner in business matters. The previous month he deposited 10, 000 florins with his firm for which he was to receive interest at the rate of 8%. The source of this newfound wealth was the royalties he had received from the concert series he gave during the Congress of Vienna.

Sigmund Anton Steiner & Co eventually published the F minor Quartet, Op. 95 in September 1816 under the titile: 'Eilftes Quartett für Zwey Violinen, Bratsche und Violincelle. Seinem Freunde dem Herrn Hofsekretär Nik. Zmeskall von Domanovetz gewidmet von Ludwig van Beethoven. 95tes Werk. Eigenthum der Verleger. Wien, im Verlag von S. A. Steiner und Comp., Vienna.' ['Eleventh Quartet for two violins, viola, and 'cello, dedicated by Ludwig van Beethoven to his friend Nicolas Zmeskall von Domanovetz, Court Secretary. Op. 95. Copyright of the publishers, S.–A. Steiner & Co., Vienna.']^{lxxv}

Concerning the publication of the F minor Quartet overseas, Beethoven wrote to George Smart on 11 October explaining how he had sent Charles Neate with several of his publications with a view to their publication in England. He complains Neate had been dilatory in this regard. By now though Beethoven had discovered the reason; Neate had fallen in love and had allowed his business obligations to fall by the wayside! Neate's affections were clearly well founded since he married the young woman concerned soon afterwards. Concerning the Quartet Op. 95, Beethoven prevailed upon Smart to add to the score the frequently cited words: 'The Quartet is written for a small circle of connoisseurs and is never to be performed in public.' He added: 'Should you wish to have some quartets for public performance I would compose them to this purpose occasionally.' This promise, however, came to nothing.[lxxvi]

According to Cecil Bernard Oldman, sometime Keeper of Books at the British Museum, a London edition of the F minor Quartet appeared soon after by Clementi & Co.[lxxvii] As was the custom of the day, the Vienna edition was published in parts incorporating revisions that Beethoven had made since the work's first performance in 1814.[lxxviii] Given that the composition belongs essentially to the period of its creation, 1810–11, its opus number '95' may be regarded, in the strict terms of the composer's musical chronology, as being deceptively late. A contemporaneous manuscript exists in which the parts of the F minor Quartet are copied out in score form. This was formerly attributed to the work's dedicatee Nikolaus Zmeskall von Domanovez but is now considered to be the work of the musician Ferdinand Piringer who is known to have scored several contemporary string quartets in this manner.[lxxix] Zmeskall received his dedicatory copy of the Quartet from Beethoven on 16 December with words of affection from the composer: 'Well my dear Zmeskall, you are now receiving my friendly dedication. I want it to be a precious memento of our friendship which has persisted here so long; and I should like you to treat it as proof of my esteem ... for you are one of the earliest friends I made in Vienna.'[lxxx]

Beethoven magnanimously forgave Neate for his tardiness that had caused him such anxiety. He wrote to him on 18 December: 'What can I say to your warm-felt excuses? Past ills must be forgotten and I wish you heartily joy that you have safely reached the long wished-for port of love.'[lxxxi]

The formal announcement of the publication of the F minor String Quartet, Op. 95 duly appeared in the *Wiener Zeitung* on 21 December 1816.[lxxxii]

The *Quartetto Serioso* String Quartet is one of the compositions for which Beethoven provided metronome indications. With the advent of Johann Nepomuk Maelzel's new instrument (1816–17), Beethoven seized upon its potential as a means of securing reliable tempi for the performance of his works. A report in the *Wiener Vaterländische Blätter* (*Vienna Patriotic Periodical*) on 13 October 1817 stated: 'Herr Beethoven looks upon this invention as a welcome means with which to secure the performance of his brilliant compositions in all places in the tempos conceived by him, which to his regret have so often been misunderstood.' To this end, Beethoven had a pamphlet printed by the publisher Sigmund Anton Steiner that gave his suggested metronome markings for the string quartets that he had composed to date, namely, Opp. 18, 59, 74 and 95, together with those for his first eight symphonies.'[lxxxiii]

With the passing of time, Op. 95 was assimilated into the string quartet repertoire and became recognised for its merits, despite its inherent musical challenges and Beethoven's injunction that the composition should be performed only within a small circle of connoisseurs. Something of the composition gaining a place in the repertoire is evident in a letter Prince Nikolay Galitzin sent to Beethoven from St. Petersburg on 16 June 1824. Galitzin was a Russian nobleman and accomplished cellist who regularly took part in performing at chamber music recitals. His name is today mostly associated with the commissioning of Beethoven's late quartets. It was whilst waiting to receive the String Quartet, Op. 127, which he had recently commissioned, that Galitzin relayed to Beethoven: '[We] have played nothing but your quartets here, and especially the five latest ones [Op. 59, Nos. 1–3; Op. 74; and Op. 95].'[lxxxiv]

On 23 January the following year a recital had been reserved for the premiere of Beethoven's newly composed String Quartet, Op. 127; this was part of Ignaz Schuppanzigh's quartet concert series. It transpired, however, that the Op. 127 Quartet was not ready to receive its first performance – Beethoven still had work to do on the final movement. In the event, the String Quartet, Op. 95 was performed in its place.[lxxxv] In January 1899 Gustav Mahler arranged a concert performance of the Op. 95 Quartet that was played by the whole string section of the orchestra. He justified his action to the music critic Edward Hanslick in the following terms: 'Chamber music by definition is intended [ideally] for performance in a domestic setting ... Once it is transferred to the concert hall, the intimacy is lost ... in a large space the four parts are weakened and do not reach the listener with the strength intended by the composer. I give this strength by reinforcing each part ... The sound volume of a work must be adapted to the dimensions of the hall.' In this context mention may also be made of Mahler's orchestration of the *Grosse Fuge* in B flat, Op. 133.[lxxxvi]

The first movement's opening bars of the *Allegro con*

brio are conceived to secure the immediate attention of the listener – much as the rap of a chairman's gavel brings a gathering to order. All the instruments are voiced as one, speaking in agitated, unison octave-registers that are made all the more dramatic by being followed by an abrupt silence. In half a dozen bars, or so, Beethoven establishes the manner of what is to follow with recourse to scarcely more than simple tonic and dominant harmony – 'a beautiful instance of the amount of melodic and rhythmic interest that Beethoven could infuse into a single passage'.[lxxxvii] In a moment the listener is transported from 'maelstrom' to 'tranquillity'.[lxxxviii] Beethoven's procedures have been compared with the manner in which, ten years earlier, he had opened the String Quartet in F major, Op. 18 No. 1 'but the advance in Beethoven's expressive power is clearly shown'.[lxxxix] 'The difference is amazing; the F major was clean and chiselled; but this F minor cuts like an acetylene flame.'[xc]

The character of this movement is far remote from the serenity of the composer's Op. 18. Beethoven's first entry into the genre of string-quartet writing had been preoccupied with contented music-making – albeit suffused with occasional Beethovenian flourishes. Here, in the Op. 95 Quartet, the concept of the string quartet being a polite interplay between the four instruments – in the style of informed conversation – is swept aside. Beethoven is not in a mood for polite prolixity – compression holds sway: 'The music exudes a sense of having been ruthlessly pared down until all that remains is the very essence of the musical material involved.'[xci] In this movement Beethoven says all he has to say in well under five minutes, less than half the performing time of the work's predecessor the *Harp Quartet*.

Commentators have likened the character of the first movement to passages in other of the composer's works of the period. For Cooper the music's 'sudden short and angry outbursts' call to mind the *Appassionata Sonata* from 1804.[xcii] For Kerman there are echoes (no pun intended) of the storm in the *Pastoral* Symphony from 1807 (significantly also in F minor): 'Lighting strokes, rainy hushes, soughing branches, roars of thunder – all are manoeuvred with much verve and with instrumental virtuosity.'[xciii] Given the discomforting nature of the music, some authorities find in this composition anticipations of the future Beethoven. The work has been described as 'a link between the middle- and late-period quartets' In particular, the abrupt manner of the first movement is considered to approximate to that of certain movements in the posthumous works. At the same time the gestures are 'explosive' with some of the 'highly strung rhetoric of the *Appassionata* Sonata and the E minor Quartet'.[xciv] In Beethoven's determination to cow the listener, rather than to charm him or her, was he giving expression to the pain and suffering of his personal experiences – to which we have made earlier reference?[xcv]

In his constructional procedures Beethoven sets convention aside. 'Everything that makes for connection – grading and shading of theme into theme, the art of subtle transition – all this is deliberately abandoned; the tonality is even violently dislocated'.[xcvi] 'Beethoven dispenses with all the usual compositional niceties whirling through ideas and keys in an amazingly condensed outpouring.'[xcvii] 'It is difficult to find the traditional formal landmarks in the midst of this impassioned music: exposition, development and recapitulation seem to be drawn together into a single vast paraphrase.'[xcviii] The music's aphoristic concentration has suggested to some musicologists the manner of the scherzo of the *Hammerklavier* Sonata.[xcix] What is unequivocal is Beethoven's studies for the movement are interwoven with ideas for the dramatic music planned for *Egmont* – with the inference of the transfer of like-minded feeling between the two. The *Allegro con brio* encompasses a mere 151 measures and yet 'The peculiarity of its greatness is that the elements are compressed as though by a more than gravitational force of the mind so that the impression of magnitude is strengthened.'[c] It is as though Beethoven were invoking one of his favourite authors: 'I could be bounded in a nutshell and count myself a king of infinite space.'

In Friedrich Blume's words: 'In no other composer does such perfect sovereignty dominate the building of themes as in Beethoven.' In Op. 95 he sees the composer setting aside his earlier propensity for what he describes as 'strictly periodic and homogeneous themes' in favour of 'aphoristically abbreviated theme structures that at times consist of only one or two motifs and without any real thematic delimitation pour their energies directly into the movement'.[ci] 'Everything is condensed and elliptical; the modulations are sudden and to unexpected keys; there are constant changes of mood and musical idea ... Yet the whole is melted and cast in a whole by the heat of Beethoven's creative fire, and stamped all over with the fierce little semi-quaver figure with which it opens ... Here, in short, is an isolated and very premature foretaste of Beethoven's *third period.*'[cii] More prosaically, Beethoven eschews conventional repeats and expositions. As Denis Matthews asserts: '[Such] an intensely compact movement, with its explosive mood-changes, abrupt silences, and brief consolatory ideas, could scarcely stand formal repetition.'[ciii]

Of the F minor Quartet's opening *Allegro con brio*, the ardent Beethovenian Donald Tovey enthused: 'The whole movement is a marvel of terseness, and contrives to pack a large symphonic tragedy into five minutes.'[civ] Alongside him Basil Lam likens the movement to 'this brief tragedy in one act' that, notwithstanding its moments of 'calm ... noble pathos,' banishes any hope of a happy ending.[cv] 'Nothing

Beethoven ever wrote is more wilful, more masterful in the violent sense than this movement. And it is a manifestation of triumphant masterfulness.'[cvi] Abraham, whom we have just quoted, adds: 'In the heat of Beethoven's creative imagination not only are the various musical particles fused in a solid whole but the pattern of classical sonata itself begins ... to melt too.'[cvii]

From the recollections of composers and musicologists, it seems the F minor Quartet held a special place in the estimation of Arnold Schoenberg. We learn of this from the philosopher-musicologist Theodor Adorno who happened to be a close friend of Schoenberg's pupil Alban Berg. The latter invited Adorno one evening to hear the Kolisch Quartet; the ensemble had been founded in the 1920s, initially to help promote Schoenberg's chamber works. On the evening in question, however, the Quartet performed the F minor Quartet of Beethoven that had been coached 'in a truly innovative interpretation' by Schoenberg.[cviii] An anecdote from the spring of 1940 connects the first movement of the Op. 95 String Quartet once more with Schoenberg. The American musician Dika Newlin was then studying composition with the composer at the University of California. Schoenberg required his class to analyse the first movement prompting Newlin to recall: '[That] first movement in which nothing is usual and everything is unexplainable (as so often in Beethoven).'[cix] Nearer our own time John Dalley, second violin to the *Guarneri String Quartet*, has shared his performer's view of the music: 'This is one of my favourite quartets. The first movement is unique in its extraordinary terseness, its harmonic boldness, and its rapid changes of mood – fierce one moment, tender the next. No other movement having only a single tempo mark calls out for so many fluctuations of speed within such short spans of time.'[cx]

The second movement is marked *Allegretto ma non troppo* with the additional direction *attacca* indicating Beethoven wanted the third movement to follow directly without a break, thereby departing from his more customary procedure of linking the last two movements. After the drama of the opening movement 'With the *Allegretto ma non troppo* Beethoven gives a real impression of a decent to the depths; it is almost like an initiation rite.'[cxi] The melody heard is 'emotional and fluid',[cxii] possessed of 'extraordinary beauty and sensitiveness',[cxiii] and 'calm, religious and ethereal in tone'.[cxiv] 'In few of his works has there been a more direct tugging at the heartstrings than in this affecting *Allegretto*. Every page seems to bring the hearer closer to the sanctuary of spiritual aspiration.'[cxv] 'It may be doubted whether the posthumous quartets contain anything more delicately subtle than the *Allegretto* of Op. 95.'[cxvi]

In his estimation of the music de Marliave states: 'This slow movement ... provides ample evidence there is no gap or break in the continuity of [the composer's] style. It forms a link that bridges the gulf between the second and the last period'.[cxvii] Matthews considered the slow movement to be no less in its way than the first 'reconciling lyrical expression with intellectual precision'. Of things in the music 'at which to marvel', he singles out for special mention 'the harmonization of the cello's opening scale ... subtle minor-key inflections that disturb the otherwise serene main theme ... [and] ... the setting off of a fugue by the viola on a new theme – a latent counterpoint to the former one'.[cxviii]

Bearing in mind that the work's dedicatee Nikolaus Zmeskall was an accomplished cellist, it is not unreasonable to think that in giving prominence to the cello Beethoven was making a conscious gesture in acknowledgment of his friend's skill. Beethoven appears to have carefully prepared himself for the task of composing the cello part. In his survey of the composer's 1810 sketch sources, the pioneering Beethoven musicologist Gustav Nottebohm found passages written out from Bach's *Chromatic Fantasia and Fugue*. This suggests Beethoven was developing his thoughts along these lines that would ultimately find expression in 'the persistent chromaticism' that is such a feature of the slow movement and of the opening cello passage in particular.[cxix] Whatever was the source of inspiration for the cello passage, as it mysteriously descends 'an instrumental song of touching beauty' emerges.[cxx]

The ensuing music is a cross between 'a lyrical song and a fugue', the flow of the lines of which 'purges the chromatic harmony of subjective emotion'. The spare texture of the writing here has acquired 'that luminosity typical of the slow movements of Beethoven's last years'.[cxxi] A mood of uncertainty is felt, in part conveyed by 'destabilising chordal interruptions'.[cxxii] The atmosphere that prevails has been described as 'enigmatic' perhaps revealing affinities with the *andante con moto* of the third *Razumovsky* Quartet.[cxxiii] The *Allegro ma non troppo*, as Beethoven heads the slow movement, is universally recognised for being 'deeply reflective and poignantly lyrical'.[cxxiv] But it does not offer any sort of 'consolatory relaxation' or respite from the urgency of the preceding movement: 'It does not represent a resting place or a point of reflection but a newly intense stage on the journey that was initiated by the outburst at the very beginning of the quartet.'[cxxv]

Beethoven sets a tempo of an indeterminate kind that is neither slow nor fast and which has been likened to that adopted in such of the Op. 95's immediate neighbours as the Seventh and Eighth Symphonies and the E minor Piano Sonata, Op. 90.[cxxvi] The music's 'gentle and continuous flow', its 'leisurely expansiveness' and 'strange undercurrent of restlessness' are all the more effective following on from the 'extreme terseness' of the opening *Allegro con brio*.[cxxvii] Beethoven's lyricism has disposed commentators to eloquence: '[The] *Allegretto* is far-ranging in harmonic exploration, but instead of conquering new territories by ferocious thrusts, it wanders into them like Keats's knight in arms, "Alone and palely loitering? ... So haggard, and woe-begone?".' [Ballad: *La belle Dame sans Merci*][cxxviii] 'After the passion of the *Allegro*, the *Allegretto* breathes an atmosphere of calm, "apathetic and broken sighs".'[cxxix] '[The] superb *Allegretto ma non troppo* ... deepens the sense of disturbance and tempers it with a very equivocal sweetness.'[cxxx] A sweetness that is also 'pensive'.[cxxxi]

The central section of the slow movement takes the form of a fugal exposition that in some measure anticipates Beethoven's later pre-occupation with fugue in his last works in the quartet genre, notably the *Great Fugue*, Op. 133 and that in the opening movement of the String Quartet in C-sharp minor Op. 131.[cxxxii] Beethoven had already exploited fugal procedures in the *Eroica* Symphony and in doing so in the slow movement of the F minor Quartet he imparts to the work something of the Symphony's contrapuntal figuration and with it a sense of 'troubled oppression' and 'a certain impassioned vigour'.[cxxxiii] It is well known that in adopting fugal procedures Beethoven was prepared to depart from strictly orthodox musicological conventions in favour of artistic expression. He once remarked to Karl Holz, a civil servant of the composer's acquaintance and an accomplished violinist: 'To *make* a fugue requires no particular skill; in my study days I made dozens of them. But the fancy wishes to assert its privileges, and today a new and really poetical element must be introduced into the old traditional form.'[cxxxiv]

In the context of these assertions there are those who consider Beethoven's fugal writing is more orthodox than usual in his fugal movements, especially his expressive chromatic expression.[cxxxv] Lam is unequivocal: 'The central section, on a subject distantly related to the cello phrase in the first bars, is nearer Bach than to anything in Beethoven's own music.' He also found the feeling created to be no less 'haunting and mysterious'.[cxxxvi] Kerman acknowledges that whilst Beethoven's fugal writing may show some allegiance to Bach's Book 1 of *The well-tempered Clavier*, his 'modulatory vicissitudes' extend beyond Bach's expressive range — consistent with his views bearing on the need for a 'really poetical element'.[cxxxvii]

The instruments 'gently sing' their fugato (Marion Scott), first the viola in highly chromatic writing with responses from the other members. 'The cello is treading on razor blades, and the upper instruments are whispering through their teeth memories of the semitone lament, which, indeed, seems to be frozen into the cello line itself.' Beethoven has achieved 'a climax of passion rarely matched by ... himself.'[cxxxviii]

The soft final chord of the slow movement ushers in the scherzo-like third movement *Allegro*. Beethoven gives this the designation *assai vivace ma serioso* — a very alive *Allegro* but serious — a reminder that in the manuscript score he wrote the words *Quartetto Serioso*. The *Allegro* 'bursts upon us, full of Beethoven's fierce energy, reawakened after the twilight of the slow movement with redoubled force'.[cxxxix] Romain Rolland found this movement to be 'dark in feeling and pervaded with gloom'.[cxl] De Marliave, writing in 1925 (in point of fact a few years earlier — the date of his publication is posthumous) saw the music in terms of that of other composers: 'Beethoven here seems to be not so much looking back to the spirit of Gluck as anticipating the spirit of the future; this individual rhythm, striking and clear-cut, is unmistakably modern; it lives again in the music of Weber, Schuman — especially in the Symphony in C, for instance – and Wagner.'[cxli] With its alternation between 'fierceness and tenderness' it makes 'a fitting counterpart to the opening *Allegro*'. [cxlii]

In composition Beethoven never made things easy for himself and the creation of the third movement reveals evidence of this. Shepherd remarks: 'As so often the case with many of the master's most striking ideas, the true saliency of this *Allegro* theme was only achieved after hesitating starts'. By way of illustration he cites Beethoven's early variants of the third-movement theme.[cxliii] Also typical of Beethoven is that his final thoughts are usually the most pared-down and simple. The third movement *Allegro* to the F minor Quartet is no exception, being made out of 'the barest elements possible: a three-note figure and a scale ... both in jagged dotted rhythm'.[cxliv] Its principal character derives from the resulting unsettling, 'spiky dotted rhythm'[cxlv] the rigidity of which 'gives all the parts equal power and determination, no other theme managing to make itself heard'.[cxlvi]

Although the rhythm and structure of the *Allegro* may be suggestive of a scherzo – as it is often described – Beethoven's inclusion *ma serioso* in the movement's heading is indicative of the absence of any humorous intention.[cxlvii] This is an aspect of the music upon which Kerman reflects: 'The third movement of the Quartet in F minor is as surprising as its predecessors, though for an opposite reason: not for its complexities but for its simplicities.' He considers 'it ranks in the familiar category of Beethoven's driving scherzos, which generally set out to strike a gross contrast with their slow movements'. He cautions, the movement must not be called a *scherzo* because Beethoven specifically marks it *Allegro assai vivace ma serioso*. Kerman suggests 'perhaps we may call it a march', calling to mind the *Alla marcia, assai vivace* of the

Quartet in A minor, Op. 132.[cxlviii] Abraham likens the 'scherzo' to those equivalent movements in the second *Razumovsky* String Quartet and Op. 74 *The Harp*.[cxlix] De Marliave invokes some of his characteristic word imagery here: 'As though from another world, the slow march of a solemn melody falls upon the ear, chanted by unseen voices to an accompaniment of harps ... here all is dark, with mysterious shadows.'[cl] 'Beauty is not the aim of this notable manifestation of controlled rage.'[cli] 'The mood is stormy, rather in the manner of the first movement.'[clii] '[Its] unrelenting energy and persistent dotted rhythm stretch the medium.'[cliii] Heinz Becker comments in similar fashion: 'The wrathful undertones of the first movement are again heard in this rugged music, which seems to have been hewn out of stones.'[cliv] To Abraham's ears the principal subject had 'a strangely Mendelssohnian flavour' although he acknowledged 'the music is not at all Mendelssohnian; where Mendelssohn would have given us an elegiacally rustling brooklet, his great predecessor opens up the springs of a deeper fountain'.[clv] Less ambiguous is that Beethoven's String Quartet Op. 95 undoubtedly exerted an influence on the youthful Mendelssohn as found, for example, in his A minor Quartet, Op. 13.

Marion Scott has words of sympathy for would-be performers of this music: 'The *scherzo* is an alternation of recklessness and resignation — extremely hard to hold together in performance.'[clvi]

By the close of the movement Beethoven is in no mood for 'elaborate perorations' of the kind to which he gives such effect at the end of the third *Razumovsky* Quartet and the Fifth and Eighth Symphonies. He is content to end the piece 'unceremoniously'.[clvii]

The fourth and final movement is set in a twofold *Larghetto espressivo — Allegretto agitato*. The former relates to the movement's opening eight bars that have been described variously as 'a last moment of reflection', [clviii] 'a moment of decided relaxation', [clix] and 'a slow, wandering introduction, somewhat reminiscent of the wonderful *La Melancholia* in Op. 18, No.6'.[clx] 'The impression [conveyed] is rather that of a strange dream in the course of which echoes of an earlier age float by and disappear ... an appealing pathos'.[clxi] De Marliave, whom we recall wrote about Beethoven's string quartets (*Quatuors de Beethoven*) early in the twentieth century, considered these introductory measures to have 'a purely modern feeling' and 'the passionate emotional content' of the movement as a whole he believed foreshadowed Schumann's Symphony in C 'and perhaps even *Tristan*'.[clxii] Radcliffe makes a similar observation: 'The F minor Quartet ... left its mark on Schumann, the slow introduction to the Finale must surely have suggested the haunting little piece *Thema* from the *Album for the young*.'[clxiii] Writing of the short *Larghetto* introduction Cooper remarks: '[In] its beginning ... it suggests a passage like the *Adagio ma non troppo con effetto* in the Piano Sonata in A, Op. 101 composed in 1816, the year Op. 95 was published.' He describes the writing as 'extremely expressive, almost vocal [in] quality'.[clxiv]

The *Allegretto agitato* returns to the 'intentional concision' of the first movement in 'an irresistible surge'.[clxv] The character of the music is 'agitated ... highly condensed' and 'maintains the general mood of anguish' that is characteristic of the Quartet as a whole.[clxvi] In support of the expressive nature of the music, de Marliave was moved to quote from Theodor Otto Helm's *Beethovens Streichquartette* (1885): 'A thousand heroic scenes flash before the imagination, evoked by the passion and martial vigour of this passage.'[clxvii] Nearer to our own time other commentators have remarked in similar manner: 'The main part of the movement is *agitato*, and the music touches both the stormy world and the ghostly.'[clxviii] Others detect 'some affinity' with the second movement of Op. 59, No. 2 perhaps suggestive of a sonata rondo?[clxix] As far as Tovey was concerned it was the nature of the music that mattered most, disposing him to expostulate: 'In the case of the F minor Quartet, Op. 95, I frankly do not know, and I do not care what you call the finale. Its theme is midway in style between a rondo theme and a first-movement theme.'[clxx] In Kerman's estimation the final movement avoids 'the harshness that had shadowed earlier parts of the Quartet' and for him it is imbued with a simpler and more direct pathos than that of the opening *Allegro*. Looking back to the Op. 59 set of quartets, he considered the finale to the Op. 95 to be 'less garrulous' than the finale of the E-minor *Razumovsky* Quartet and altogether with less 'bluster'. He concludes: 'This movement, the Quartet as a whole, is not going to end in the oblivion of sheer raging exhaustion.'[clxxi]

The final movement is even terser than the first movement and has a shorter playing time. Tovey likened what he called 'the most haunting phrase in the rondo' to one in the coda of Mozart's C minor Piano Concerto that Beethoven is known to have much admired.[clxxii] Authorities pay tribute here to Beethoven's powers of invention: '[The] construction of the *Allegretto agitato* [does not] fit any textbook prescription; it makes its own combination of sonata and rondo features ... counterpoint and figuration ... are marvellously varied, resulting in an almost Wagnerian overload of rich inflection.'[clxxiii] 'The first theme has two strong components: a leaping rhythmic figure and a short answer. A second theme appears almost at the very end, like a triumphant conclusion to the first theme, only after the latter has passed in an internal development through a real world of terror, dragged on by the frenzied course of its leaping rhythmic figure.'[clxxiv]

In Marion Scott's opinion, the *Larghetto espressivo*, preceding the finale, 'packs as much tragedy into its seven bars as Shakespeare into fourteen lines of a sonnet'.[clxxv] Rolland was content to describe the resulting musical character as 'agitated and restless'.[clxxvi] With regard to the composer's working-out, Lam invites the listener to compare the final sonata-rondo and its introduction with the *Malinconia* and finale of the String Quartet Op. 18, No. 6. This, he asserts, 'is to realize how far Beethoven's art had developed in the decade between, though the earlier work is no less true to experience'. He adds: '[Beethoven] had already written, in the Piano Sonata Op. 31, No. 2, a finale with something of the same undemonstrative fortitude in adversity.'[clxxvii]

The String Quartet in F minor, Op. 95 is known to have been a special favourite of Mendelsohn who regarded it as 'the most characteristic thing Beethoven ever wrote'; to some ears the *Allegretto agitato* 'has a decided foretaste of his music'.[clxxviii] The American musicologist Robert Craft invited Igor Stravinsky to discuss some of his favourite events in the symphonies and quartets of Beethoven. Responding, Stravinsky singled out for special mention Op, 95 remarking: 'As for the *Quartetto Serioso*, the most wonderful event occurs in the measures 47–65 of the *Allegretto*.'[clxxix]

Several commentators draw a parallel between the closing passages of the Quartet and the triumphal conclusion of the composer's *Egmont* Overture that, as we have seen, shared a common creation origin with the Op. 95. However, as Radcliffe points out: '[The mood] is far gayer and more light-handed, and is best understood if we bear in mind that there was in Beethoven a streak of waywardness which delighted in unexpected changes of mood and became increasingly apparent in his later works.' In support of his contention he cites the aphoristic remark of the American composer Randall Thompson: 'No bottle of champagne was ever uncorked at a better time.'[clxxx] Kerman makes related observations: 'One has a distinct impression of an inversion of means, as though the composer had seized upon a single technical idea to see how opposite emotional effects could be wrung out of it.' He further remarks that whereas the Overture closes with an F-minor *Symphony of Victory* — sounding a note of triumph, the Quartet is content to close in a lighter 'evanescent' vein.[clxxxi] Simpson's insights are relevant here: '[The] astoundingly lithe and delicate F major coda to the Quartet's finale could aptly represent the hero's [Egmont's] fleeting sense of justification and sense of release at the moment of his death ... and the music [thereby] has an additional extra-musical motivation.'[clxxxii]

Although Beethoven gave the title *Serioso* to the String Quartet Op. 95, in opting to close the piece in a deft, almost light-hearted manner Bekker likens the composer to finally discarding a mask.[clxxxiii] The American musicologist Rey M. Longyear believes that in choosing to end Op. 95 with 'an opera buffa-like conclusion', Beethoven was consciously destroying the illusion of seriousness that has hitherto prevailed. He believes this ending exemplifies many of the characteristics of romantic irony that the German philosopher and poet Friedrich Schlegel described as 'paradox, self-annihilation, parody, eternal agility, and the appearance of the fortuitous and unusual'.[clxxxiv] Kerman is more succinct and down to earth: 'The seriousness seems kicked in the rear.'[clxxxv] In her study of the F minor Quartet, Alison Bullock comments in similar fashion: '[Suddenly] Beethoven flips, adding a comical ending whose bluster is so unconnected to the pathos of the rest of the music that one suspects an attempt to laugh off the earlier anguish.'[clxxxvi] Perhaps a parallel can be found here in the manner in which Beethoven was known to end one of his typical improvisations at the keyboard. It is on record that after captivating an audience with his technical virtuosity, typically imbued with feeling that had the power to move his listeners to tears, he would leave off with a hearty laugh.[clxxxvii] Be this as it may, the character of the music is 'almost jocular'[clxxxviii], 'the spirit of laughter takes charge and is hailed as the solution to life's problems' [clxxxix] and the music finally attains its freedom in 'a great whirl of animation'[cxc] worthy of a comic-opera coda, 'absurdly and deliberately unrelated to the *Quartetto Serioso*'.[cxci]

Although Vincent d'Indy was one of Beethoven's admirer's and author of *Beethoven: A critical biography* (1913) he was discomforted by the closing pages of the F minor Quartet, pronouncing them to be 'a light Rossinian operatic finale' that he considered 'no interpretation could palliate this error of genius'.[cxcii] Abraham was aware of the French composer's views and remarks: 'The curious fact that the epilogue has no connection with the rest of this powerful and darkly coloured work, either rhythmically or in mood, sadly worried the logical mind of Vincent d'Indy.' In Beethoven's defence, Abraham cites the views of the Indian-born English musician Ernest Walker who remarked 'somehow it does not sound at all alien ... indeed it sounds as exactly right as the similar patch of blue sky at the end of the storm in the *Pastoral* Symphony'. Abraham adds: 'The addition of what is practically a brief independent extra movement is yet another symptom of third-period style.' He enthuses: '[The] music flames into half a minute of perhaps the most brilliant pure quartet writing ever conceived by a musician. The final movements of the *Razumovskys* are brilliant, but their brilliance has symphonic tendencies; this shimmer of quavers, *molto leggieramente* and practically all piano is exquisitely luminous.'[cxciii] Brigitte Massin writes about this passage in terms no less enthusiastic: 'As a final surprise at the end of the Quartet we have the sudden illumination of F major on a sustained chord, played by all four instruments together, but timidly and extremely quietly (ppp): then in this new light achieved after bitter struggle, *molto leggieramente*, [we have] at the very end of such a grave and serious quest, with the first violin soaring high towards the distantly glimpsed light over the support of the lower instruments.'[cxciv] Drawing on her experience as a professional violist, Rebecca Clarke contends: 'A great surprise is the coda of the last movement, which can be made to sound absolutely magical if played *ppp* "with one hair" ...'.[cxcv] 'Everything is effortless and amusing and trite, the texture glistens, it is all over in a second or two (like everything else in this compressed quartet). A perfectly astonishing conclusion.' Kerman, whom we have just quoted, asks: 'Was Beethoven *serious* in calling a piece with such an ending as this *Quartetto Serioso*?'[cxcvi]

In Romain Rolland estimation, the closing pages of Op. 95 offer 'a brilliant gleam of sunlight'.[cxcvii] For Arthur Shepherd they are 'a sparkling epilogue that is one more token of Beethoven's affirmative soul'.[cxcviii] We give the last summative words to Joseph Kerman: '[Some] quartets, much more than others, appear to take substance from a deep and inner process of introspection and emotional synthesis. It is the penetration ... of the inward look that establishes the particular greatness of the Quartet in F minor ... It is, in fact, ultimately the chief signpost to the third period.'[cxcix]

---

[i] Michael Steinberg, *The middle quartets* in: Robert Winter and Robert Martin, editors, *The Beethoven quartet companion*, 1994, pp. 203–4.

[ii] David Wyn Jones in: Robin Stowell editor, *The Cambridge companion to the string quartet*, 2003, p. 220.

[iii] Beethoven's relationship with Therese Malfatti is discussed at length in Elliot Forbes, editor, *Thayer's life of Beethoven*, 1967, Chapter XVIII.

[iv] Emily Anderson, editor and translator, 1961, Vol. 1, Letter No. 252, p. 267

- and Brigitte Massin, translation Frank Dobbins, liner notes to Auvidis Valois *Beethoven's Quatours*, undated.
- Emily Anderson, editor and translator, 1961, Vol. 1, Letter No. 265, p. 279.
- *Ibid*, 1961, Vol. 1, Letter No. 256, pp. 270–71. Franz Wegeler is remembered today for his 1838 biography of Beethoven *Biographische Notizen über Ludwig van Beethoven*, published in collaboration with the composer's former pupil Ferdinand Ries. For a facsimile reproduction of Beethoven's letter to Wegeler, together with the original German text and an audio recording, see: Beethoven House, Digital Archives, Library Document Sammlung Wegeler, W 19.
- Reichardt's recollections are more fully outlined in: Ludwig Nohl, 1880, pp. 58–9.
- See: Beethoven House, Digital Archives, Library Document, BH 57.
- Basil Lam, 1975, p. 70. The Elliot quotation is derived from the writer's *Ash Wednesday* and reads: 'I rejoice, having to construct something/Upon which to rejoice.'
- For an extended discussion of this aspect of music-making in the early part of the nineteenth century, see: Leon Botstein, *The patrons and public of the quartets: Music, culture, and society in Beethoven's Vienna* in: Robert Winter and Robert Martin editors, *The Beethoven quartet companion*, 1994, p. 87.
- Joseph Kerman, 1967, p. 185.
- Brigitte Massin, translation Frank Dobbins, liner notes to Auvidis Valois *Beethoven's Quatours*, undated.
- Arthur Shepherd, 1935, p. 43.
- John Daverio, *Manner, tone and tendency in Beethoven's chamber music for strings* in: Glenn Stanley editor, *The Cambridge companion to Beethoven*, 2000, p. 157–8.
- Harold Truscott, Beethoven's late string quartets, 1968, p. 19.
- Joseph Kerman, 1967, p. 169.
- *Ibid*, p. 156.
- Philip Radcliffe, 1978, p. 89.
- Barry Cooper, 2000, p. 198.
- Seow-Chin Ong, *Aspects of the genesis of Beethoven's String Quartet in F minor, Op. 95* in: William Kinderman editor, *The string quartets of Beethoven*, 2005, pp. 132–167.
- Robert Simpson, *The chamber music for strings* in: Denis Arnold and Nigel Fortune editors, *The Beethoven companion*, 1973, pp. 261–4.
- Paul Bekker, 1925, p. 319.
- Joseph de Marliave, 1925 (reprint 1961), p. 178.
- Joseph Kerman, 1967, pp. 168–9 and p. 187.
- Barry Cooper, 2000, pp. 197–8.
- Barry Cooper, 1991, p. 236.
- Derived from the writings of David Osmond Smith, professor of music at the University of Sussex, in: Michael Oliver editor, *Settling the score: a journey through the music of the twentieth century*, 1999, p. 101.
- Donald Mitchell editor, *Letters from a life: the selected letters and diaries of Benjamin Britten 1913–1976*, 3 Vols., 1991, p. 280.
- Alec Robertson, 1961, p. 214.
- Aaron Copland, 1961, p. 39.

xxi For a silhouette portrait of Nicholas Zmeskall von Domanovez (by an unknown artist) see Beethoven House, Digital Archives, document B 1987.

xxii The sketch origins for the F minor String Quartet are discussed in the following sources: Douglas Porter Johnson, editor, 1985, p.72, pp. 195–200, pp. 201–6 and p. 463; William Kinderman editor, 2005, p. 326; Christoph Wolff and Robert Riggs, *The string quartets of Haydn, Mozart and Beethoven: studies of the autograph manuscripts*: a conference at Isham Memorial Library, March 15–17, 1979. Cambridge, Massachusetts: Department of Music, Harvard University, 1980, pp. 233–4; Barry Cooper, 2000, p. 197; and Seow-Chin Ong, *Aspects of the genesis of Beethoven's String Quartet in F minor, Op. 95* in: William Kinderman editor, 2005, pp. 132–167.

xxiii Arthur Shepherd, 1935, p. 40. See also: Elliot Forbes, editor, *Thayer's life of Beethoven*, 1967, pp. 502–3.

xxiv With acknowledgment to the discussion of this aspect of Beethoven's string quartet writing by David Wyn Jones in: Robin Stowell editor, *The Cambridge companion to the string quartet*, 2003, p. 220.

xxv Maynard Solomon, 1977, p. 208.

xxvi Gerald Abraham, 1944, p. 70.

xxvii Meiron Bowen editor, *Tippett on music*, 1995, p. 92.

xxviii Emily Anderson, 1961, Vol. 1, Letter No. 245, pp. 260–1. For a facsimile reproduction of this letter see: Beethoven House, Digital Archives, Library Document, H. C. Bodmer, HCB Br 85.

xxix Quotation from John L. Holmes, 1990, p. 101. For a facsimile reproduction of this letter see: Beethoven House, Digital Archives, Library Document NE 116.

xl For a facsimile reproduction of this letter see: Beethoven House, Digital Archives, Library Document, H.C. Bodman, HCB Br 88.

xli Emily Anderson, editor and translator, 1961, Vol. 1, Letter No. 300, p. 316.

xlii *Ibid*, Vol. 1, Letter No. 303, p. 318.

xliii *Ibid*, Vol. 1, Letter No. 306, pp. 320–1.

xliv *Ibid*, Vol. 1, Letter No. 312, pp. 324–5.

xlv *Ibid*, 1961, Vol. 1, Letter No. 344, pp. 353–4.

xlvi As recounted in Ludwig Nohl, *Beethoven depicted by his contemporaries*, 1880, p. 12. For further recollections of Beethoven by Louis Spohr see: Oscar George Theodore Sonneck, *Beethoven: impressions of contemporaries*, pp. 94–100.

xlvii Emily Anderson, editor and translator, 1961, Vol. 1, Letter No. 380, pp. 383–4. For a modern-day interpretation of how Beethoven may have appeared, when taking the waters, see the illustration by the artist-sculptor Donna Dralle reproduced in the website text *The unheard Beethoven* to the Theme with Variation in A, Hess 72.

xlviii Elliot Forbes, editor, *Thayer's life of Beethoven*, 1967, p. 521. See also H. C. Robbins Landon, 1970, pp. 143–4.

xlix Emily Anderson, 1961, Vol. 1, Letter No. 380, pp. 383–4. See also: Beethoven House, Digital Archives, Library Document, Sammlung H. C. Bodmer, HCB Br 103.

l For a vivid description of the ordeal Beethoven had to undergo in order to have his facial likeness reproduced, see: John Ella, 1969, Vol. 1, pp. 6–10. For additional information see: Beethoven House, Digital Archives, Library Documents Ley, Band VIII, Nr. 1311; B 257; p 2; B 447; B 448; B 1153;

i and B 450. See also: Peter Clive, 2001, pp. 186–7.
ii Emily Anderson, editor and translator, 1961, Vol. 1, Letter No. 376, pp. 380–1.
iii Theodore Albrecht, 1996, Vol. 1, See also: Beethoven House, Digital Archives, Library Document No. 171, pp. 6–7 and Ley Band VII, Nr. 394a.
iiii In a later codicil possibly added under pressure from Johanna – without Beethoven's awareness – Carl reinstated her as Karl's co-guardian stipulating that his son should continue to live with her. However, in January 1816, the Austrian Court (Landrecht) settled Karl's guardianship in Beethoven's favour. Notwithstanding, the question of Karl's guardianship continued to be contested by the two parties. In 1820 Beethoven pursued the matter once more through the courts. To his humiliation the proceedings were heard this time though a lower court, the civic judicial authority (*Magistrat der Wien*); the reason being Beethoven was not of noble birth. As Schindler remarks: '[Neither] his genius, nor his works of art could have given him his recognised and favoured position in aristocratic circles.' Anton Felix Schindler, *Beethoven as I knew him* edited by Donald W. MacArdle and translated by Constance S. Jolly from the German edition of 1860, 1966. For a more general discussion of Beethoven's standing in society, see: *Beethoven's origins and his relationship with the aristocracy* in: Hans Conrad Fischer and Erich Kock, *Ludwig van Beethoven: a study in text and pictures*, 1972, pp. 25–36.
iv Theodore Albrecht, 1996 Vol. 1, Document 182, pp. 30-1 and Document 193, pp. 50– 3.
v Letter to Count Franz Brunsvik, see: Emily Anderson, editor and translator, 1961, Vol. 1, Letter No. 462, p. 445.
vi Theodore Albrecht, 1996, Vol. 1, Letter No. 184, pp. 34–6. Beethoven and Treitschke offered *Fidelio* to Carlsruhe, Darmstadt, Frankfurt, Hamburg and Stuttgart. None of the opera house in these cities however performed *Fidelio* in the composer's lifetime.
vii Anton Schindler, 1860, English edition: Donald MacArdle, 1966, p. 171.
viii Wayne M. Senner, Robin Wallace and William Meredith, editors, *The critical reception of Beethoven's compositions by his German contemporaries*, 1999, Vol. 1, pp. 41–2. For a detailed study of irony in the music of Beethoven, see: Rey M. Longyear, *Beethoven and romantic irony* in: Paul Henry Lang, *The creative world of Beethoven*, 1971, pp. 145–62.
ix Further evidence of the extent to which Beethoven's hearing had deteriorated, and how it was affecting him socially, is apparent from the recollections of the pianist Johann Wenzel Tomaschek. In 1798 he had heard Beethoven perform the *Adagio* and *Rondo* from his Op. 2 Piano Sonata at a concert in which he also played his recently composed Piano Concerto in C major. The experience had 'stirred him strangely to the depths of his soul'. On 10 October 1814, Tomaschek paid the composer a further visit. The following is an extract from his account: 'The unfortunate man was especially hard of hearing this day, so that one had to scream rather than talk to be understood. The reception room in which he greeted me was anything but splendidly furnished and, incidentally, was as disordered as his hair. Here I found an upright piano and on its music-rack the text of a cantata (*Der glorreiche Augenblick*) by Weissenbach; on the keys lay a lead-pencil, with which he sketched out his work; and beside it on a scribbled sheet of music-paper I found a number of the most divergent ideas, jotted down without any connection, the most heterogeneous individual details elbowing each other, just as they had come to his mind.' As recounted in: Oscar George Theodore Sonneck, *Beethoven: impressions of contemporaries*, 1927, pp. 100–1.

[li] For a reproduction of Höfel's portrait see Beethoven House, Digital Archives, document Sammlung Wegeler, W 25. Höfel's study of the composer also exists in the form of a colour lithography that was considered by his contemporaries to be a faithful likeness.

[lii] Emily Anderson, editor and translator, 1961, Vol. 1, Letter No. 534, pp. 502–4. For a facsimile reproduction of this letter see: Beethoven House, Digital Archives, Library Document Sammlung H.C. Bodmer, HCB Br 237.

[liii] See: Barry Cooper, 1991, p. 24 and Barry Cooper, 2000, p. 238.

[liii] Theodore Albrecht, 1996, Vol. 1, Letter No. 200, pp. 61–5.

[liv] For a facsimile reproduction of Beethoven's Contract with Sigmund Anton Steiner see Beethoven House, Digital Archives, Library Document Sammlung H.C. Bodmer, HCB BS II/2a and II/2b. See also: Emily Anderson, editor and translator, 1961, Vol. 3, Contract No. 6, p. 1423. For a comprehensive account of Charles Neate's dealings on Beethoven's behalf with the London publishers see Elliot Forbes, editor, *Thayer's life of Beethoven*, 1967, pp. 636–7.

[lv] Emily Anderson, editor and translator, 1961, Vol. 1, Letter No. 542, p. 510.

[lvi] Theodore Albrecht, 1996, Vol. 1, Letter No. 206, pp. 73–4. See also Letter No. 606a p. 557. For a facsimile reproduction of Beethoven's letter to Charles Neate see Beethoven House, Digital Archives, Library Document Sammlung H.C. Bodmer Br 175.

[lvii] See: Beethoven House Digital Archives, *Beethoven Gallery* and Library Document B 2388. Although this portrait situates Beethoven in a somewhat idealised pastoral setting, the artist is not considered to have sacrificed his appearance in striving for Romantic effect.

[lviii] See: Beethoven House, Digital Archives, Library Document B 2388a and H. C. Robbins Landon, 1970, pp. 12–13 and plate 9.

[lix] H. C. Robbins Landon, 1970, p. 10, plate 13.

[lx] Theodore Albrecht, 1996, Vol. 1, Letter No. 214, pp. 85–6.

[lxi] Emily Anderson, editor and translator, 1961, Vol. 1, Letter No. 639, pp. 583–4. See also: Beethoven House, Digital Archives, Library Document Sammlung H.C. Bodmer, HCB BBr 107.

[lxii] Dr. Bursy's Diary recollections are given in: Ludwig Nohl, *Beethoven depicted by his contemporaries*, 1880 pp. 150–61.

[lxiii] Emily Anderson, editor and translator, 1961, Vol. 1, Letter No. 649, p. 592.

[lxiv] *Ibid*, 1961, Vol. 1, Letter No. 651, pp. 593–2. For a facsimile reproduction of Beethoven's letter to Steiner together with the text and an audio reading, see Beethoven House, Digital Archives, Library Document Sammlung H.C. Bodmer, HCB Br 242, HCB Br 241.

[lxv] Beethoven House, Digital Archives, Library Documents: J. van der Spek C Op. 95; Sammlung H.C. Bodmer, HCB C Md 79, 6; and Sammlung Schorn 97. See also: Joseph de Marliave, 1925 (reprint 1961), p. 177. De Marliave heads his commentary to the F minor Quartet with the words: *Von Perlen baut sich enine Brüche* – 'Pearls build a bridge' – from the writings of Friedrich von Schiller.

[lxvi] Emily Anderson, editor and translator, 1961, Vol. 1 Vol. 1, Letter No. 664, pp. 604–7.

[lxvii] *Ibid*, 1961, Vol. 1, Letter No. 636, pp. 581–2, footnote 2.

[lxviii] A corrected copy of the manuscript of Op. 95 is preserved today in the Beethoven House Archive in Bonn. See: Barry Cooper, 1991, p. 192 and p. 239.

lxix Beethoven House, Digital Archives, Library Document Sammlung H.C. Bodmer, HCB Bk 5.

lxx Emily Anderson, editor and translator, 1961, Vol. 1, Letter No. 653, pp. 595–6.

lxxi *Ibid*, 1961, Vol. 1, Letter No. 683, pp. 620–1. By the time Beethoven sent his conciliatory letter to Neate he had received the news that his Overtures Opp. 113, 115 and 117 had not been received with enthusiasm by the London audiences. He acknowledged: 'I by no means reckon them amongst my best works ... but still they were not disliked here [in Vienna].' He asks Neate if there was some fault in their execution or perhaps a lack of 'party spirit'? The truth appears to be that Beethoven's English admirers, by now familiar with such orchestral-sounding works as the *Egmont* Overture, had expected the composer's latest works in this genre to be no less stirring.

lxxii Theodore Albrecht, 1996, Vol. 1, Letter No. 206, pp. 73–4.

lxxiii With acknowledgment to Barry Cooper, 1991, p. 282. See also: Elliot Forbes, editor, *Thayer's life of Beethoven*, 1967, p. 544.

lxxiv Theodore Albrecht, 1996, Vol. 1, Letter No. 370, pp. 41–3.

lxxv Barry Cooper, 2000, p. 324.

lxxvi Henry-Louis de la Grange, *Gustav Mahler*, 1995, p. 136.

lxxvii Philip Radcliffe, 1978, p. 90.

lxxviii Alison Bullock, *Notes to the BBC Radio Three Beethoven experience*, Thursday 9 June 2005, www.bbc.co.uk/radio3/Beethoven

lxxix Joseph de Marliave, 1925 (reprint 1961), p. 179.

xc Marion M. Scott, 1940, p. 261.

xci Barry Cooper, 1991, pp. 236.

xcii Barry Cooper, 2000, pp. 198.

xciii Joseph Kerman, 1967, p. 173

xciv Philip Radcliffe, 1978, p. 91.

xcv As suggested, for example, by Gerald Abraham, *Beethoven's chamber music* in: *The Age of Beethoven, The New Oxford History of Music, Vol. VIII*, Gerald Abraham, editor, 1988, p. 292.

xcvi Gerald Abraham, 1944, pp. 70–1.

xcvii Alison Bullock, *Notes to the BBC Radio Three Beethoven experience*, Thursday 9 June 2005, www.bbc.co.uk/radio3/Beethoven

xcviii Heinz Becker, *Liner notes to Beethoven's string quartets*, The Amadeus String Quartet, 1974.

xcix Alec Harman with Anthony Milner and Wilfrid Mellers, *Man and his music: the story of musical experience in the West*, 1988, p. 653.

c Basil Lam, 1975, pp. 70–1.

ci Friedrich Blume, 1972, pp. 51–2.

cii Gerald Abraham, *Beethoven's chamber music* in: *The Age of Beethoven, The New Oxford History of Music, Vol. VIII*, Gerald Abraham, editor, 1988, pp. 292–3.

ciii Denis Matthews, 1985, pp. 137–8.

civ Donald Tovey, 1944, pp. 106–7.

cv Basil Lam, 1975, p. 72.

cvi Gerald Abraham, 1944, p. 70.

cvii *Ibid*, pp. 70–1.

cviii Theodor W. Adorno translator, *Alban Berg: master of the smallest link*, 1991,

p. 29.
[cix] Dika Newlin, *Schoenberg remembered: diaries and recollections (1938–76)*, 1980, p. 215.
[cx] David Blum, *The art of quartet playing: The Guarneri Quartet in conversation with David Blum*, 1986, p. 93.
[cxi] Brigitte Massin, translation Frank Dobbins, liner notes to Auvidis Valois *Beethoven's Quatours*, undated.
[cxii] Joseph Kerman, 1967 p. 176.
[cxiii] Philip Radcliffe, 1978, p. 92.
[cxiv] Rolland, Romain, 1917, p. 187.
[cxv] Arthur Shepherd, 1935, pp. 41–2.
[cxvi] Philip Radcliffe, 1978, p. 178.
[cxvii] Joseph de Marliave, 1925 (reprint 1961), p. 183.
[cxviii] Denis Matthews, 1985, p. 138.
[cxix] As discussed by Bail Lam, 1975, p. 72.
[cxx] Heinz Becker, *Liner notes to Beethoven's string quartets*, The Amadeus String Quartet, 1974. See also: Michael Steinberg, *The middle quartets* in: Robert Winter and Robert Martin, editors, *The Beethoven quartet companion*, 1994, p. 208.
[cxxi] Alec Harman with Anthony Milner and Wilfrid Mellers, *Man and his music: the story of musical experience in the West*, 1988, p. 654.
[cxxii] Alison Bullock, *Notes to the BBC Radio Three Beethoven experience*, Thursday 9 June 2005, www.bbc.co.uk/radio3/Beethoven
[cxxiii] Gerald Abraham, 1944, p. 71.
[cxxiv] Arthur Shepherd, 1935, p. 41.
[cxxv] Joseph Kerman, 1967, p. 176. A point of view also shared by Philip Radcliffe, 1978, p. 92.
[cxxvi] Michael Steinberg, *The middle quartets* in: Robert Winter and Robert Martin, editors, *The Beethoven quartet companion*, 1994, p. 208.
[cxxvii] Philip Radcliffe, 1978, p. 92.
[cxxviii] Michael Steinberg, *The middle quartets* in: Robert Winter and Robert Martin, editors, *The Beethoven quartet companion*, 1994, p. 208.
[cxxix] Joseph de Marliave, 1925 (reprint 1961), p. 183.
[cxxx] Joseph Kerman, 1967, p. 186.
[cxxxi] Marion Scott, 1967, p. 186.
[cxxxii] As mentioned, by way of illustration, by Jörgen Ostman, Liner notes to Arte Nova Classics, *String Quartets, Beethoven*, Vol. 6 (undated) and Barry Cooper, 1991, p. 236.
[cxxxiii] Joseph de Marliave, 1925 (reprint 1961), p. 186.
[cxxxiv] Quoted in: Arthur Shepherd, 1935, p. 42.
[cxxxv] See, for example, Arthur Shepherd, 1935, p. 42.
[cxxxvi] Basil Lam, 1975, p. 73.
[cxxxvii] For example Joseph Kerman, 1967, pp. 176–7.
[cxxxviii] Joseph Kerman, 1967, p. 177.
[cxxxix] Joseph de Marliave, 1925 (reprint 1961), p. 186.
[cxl] Romain Rolland, 1917, p. 187.
[cxli] Joseph de Marliave, 1925 (reprint 1961), p. 186.
[cxlii] Philip Radcliffe, 1978, p. 95.

cxliii Arthur Shepherd, 1935, p. 42.
cxliv Basil Lam, 1975, p. 74.
cxlv Alison Bullock, *Notes to the BBC Radio Three Beethoven experience*, Thursday 9 June 2005, www.bbc.co.uk/radio3/Beethoven
cxlvi Heinz Becker, *Liner notes to Beethoven's string quartets*, The Amadeus String Quartet, 1974.
cxlvii 'The movement is constructed on the *Grand* scherzo plan with the usual oscillations of theme and *alternativo*.' Arthur Shepherd, 1935, p. 43.
cxlviii Joseph Kerman, 1967, pp. 180–1.
cxlix Gerald Abraham, *Beethoven's chamber music* in: *The Age of Beethoven, The New Oxford History of Music, Vol. VIII*, Gerald Abraham editor, 1988, p. 293.
cl Joseph de Marliave, 1925 (reprint 1961), p. 187.
cli Basil Lam, 1975, p. 74.
clii Michael Steinberg, *The middle quartets in*: Robert Winter and Robert Martin editors, *The Beethoven quartet companion*, 1994, p. 212.
cliii Denis Matthews, 1985, p. 138.
cliv Heinz Becker, *Liner notes to Beethoven's string quartets*, The Amadeus String Quartet, 1974.
clv Gerald Abraham, 1944, p. 78.
clvi Marion M. Scott, 1940, p. 261.
clvii Philip Radcliffe, 1978, p. 95.
clviii Brigitte Massin, translation Frank Dobbins, Liner Notes to Auvidis Valois *Beethoven's Quatours*, undated.
clix Joseph Kerman, 1967, p. 181.
clx Alison Bullock, *Notes to the BBC Radio Three Beethoven experience*, Thursday 9 June 2005, www.bbc.co.uk/radio3/Beethoven
clxi Philip Radcliffe, 1978, p. 96.
clxii Joseph de Marliave, 1925 (reprint 1961), p. 189.
clxiii Philip Radcliffe, 1979, p. 182.
clxiv Barry Cooper, 1991, pp. 236.
clxv Brigitte Massin, translation Frank Dobbins, liner notes to Auvidis Valois *Beethoven's Quatours*, undated.
clxvi Barry Cooper, 2000, pp. 198.
clxvii Joseph de Marliave, 1925 (reprint 1961), p. 190.
clxviii Michael Steinberg, *The middle quartets* in: Robert Winter and Robert Martin editors, *The Beethoven quartet companion*, 1994, p. 214.
clxix Gerald Abraham, *Beethoven's chamber music* in: *The Age of Beethoven, The New Oxford History of Music, Vol. VIII*, Gerald Abraham editor, 1988, p. 293.
clxx Donald Tovey, 1944, p. 121.
clxxi Joseph Kerman, 1967, p. 182.
clxxii Cited by Denis Matthews, 1985, p. 138.
clxxiii Joseph Kerman, 1967, p. 182.
clxxiv Brigitte Massin, translation Frank Dobbins, liner notes to Auvidis Valois *Beethoven's Quatours*, undated.
clxxv Marion M. Scott, 1940, p. 261.
clxxvi Romain Rolland, 1917, p. 187.

[clxxvii] Basil Lam, 1975, p. 74.
[clxxviii] Philip Radcliffe, 1978, p. 96.
[clxxix] Igor Stravinsky and Robert Craft, 1959, p. 114.
[clxxx] Philip Radcliffe, 1978, p. 97.
[clxxxi] Joseph Kerman, 1967, p. 184.
[clxxxii] Robert Simpson, *The chamber music for strings* in: Denis Arnold and Nigel Fortune editors, *The Beethoven companion*, 1973, p. 262.
[clxxxiii] Paul Bekker, 1925, p. 319.
[clxxxiv] Rey M. Longyear, *Beethoven and romantic irony* in: Paul Henry Lang, *The creative world of Beethoven*, 1971, pp. 145–62.
[clxxxv] Joseph Kerman, 1967, p. 183.
[clxxxvi] Alison Bullock, *Notes to the BBC Radio Three Beethoven experience*, Thursday 9 June 2005, www.bbc.co.uk/radio3/Beethoven
[clxxxvii] Beethoven's piano pupil Carl Czerny recalls such moments in his writings about the composer.
[clxxxviii] Jörgen Ostman, Liner notes to Arte Nova Classics, *String Quartets, Beethoven*, Vol. 6 (undated).
[clxxxix] Paul Bekker, 1925, p. 319.
[cxc] Heinz Becker, *Liner notes to Beethoven's string quartets*, The Amadeus String Quartet, 1974.
[cxci] Basil Lam, 1975, pp. 74–5.
[cxcii] As quoted in Marion M. Scott, 1940, p. 261.
[cxciii] Gerald Abraham, 1944, pp. 78–9.
[cxciv] Brigitte Massin, translation Frank Dobbins, liner notes to Auvidis Valois *Beethoven's Quatours*, undated.
[cxcv] Rebecca Clarke, *The Beethoven quartets as a player sees them, Musical Times*, Special issue [Beethoven's Death Centenary], Vol. VIII, No. 2, 1927, 184.
[cxcvi] Joseph Kerman, 1967, p. 183.
[cxcvii] Rolland, Romain, 1917, p. 187.
[cxcviii] Arthur Shepherd, 1935, p. 43.
[cxcix] Joseph Kerman, 1967, p. 187.

BIBLIOGRAPHY

The author has individually consulted all the publications listed in this bibliography and can confirm that each makes reference, in some way or other, to Beethoven and his works. It will be evident from their titles which of these are publications devoted exclusively to the composer. Others that make only passing reference to Beethoven and his compositions, nevertheless unfailingly bear testimony to his genius and humanity. The diversity of the titles listed also testifies to the centrality of Beethoven to western culture and, indeed, beyond; the mere survey of these should be of itself a rewarding experience for the typical lover of so-called classical music. The entries are confined to book publications only, reflecting the scope of the author's researches. The cut-off date for this was 2007; consequently no works after this date are listed, notwithstanding the author is mindful that Beethoven musicology, and related publication, continue to be a major field of endeavour.

Abraham, Gerald. *Beethoven's second-period quartets*. London: Oxford University Press: Humphrey Milford, 1944.

Abraham, Gerald. *Essays on Russian and East European music*. Oxford: Clarendon Press: New York: Oxford University Press, 1985.

Abraham, Gerald, Editor. *The age of Beethoven, 1790-1830*. London: Oxford University Press, 1982.

Abraham, Gerald. *The tradition of Western music*. London: Oxford University Press, 1974.

Abse, Dannie and Joan. *The Music lover's literary companion*. London: Robson Books, 1988.

Adorno, Theodor W., Translator. *Alban Berg: master of the smallest link*. Cambridge: Cambridge University Press, 1991.

Adorno, Theodor W. *Beethoven: the philosophy of music; fragments and texts*. Cambridge: Polity Press, 1998.

Albrecht, Daniel, Editor. *Modernism and music: an anthology of sources*. Chicago; London: University of Chicago Press, 2004.

Albrecht, Theodore, Translator and Editor. *Letters to Beethoven and other correspondence*. Lincoln, New England: University of Nebraska Press, 3 vols., 1996.

Allsobrook, David Ian. *Liszt: my travelling circus life*. London: Macmillan, 1991.

Anderson, Christopher, Editor and Translator. *Selected writings of Max Reger*. New York; London: Routledge, 2006.

Anderson, Emily, Editor and Translator. *The letters of Beethoven*. London: Macmillan, 3 vols.,1961.

Anderson, Martin, Editor. *Klemperer on music: shavings from a musician's workbench*. London: Toccata Press, 1986.

Antheil, George. *Bad boy of music*. London; New York: Hurst & Blackett Ltd., 1945.

Appleby, David P. *Heitor Villa-Lobos: a bio-bibliography*. New York: Greenwood Press, 1988.

Aprahamian, Felix, Editor. *Essays on music: an anthology from The Listener*. London, Cassell, 1967.

Armero, Gonzalo and Jorge de Persia. *Manuel de Falla : his life & works*. London: Omnibus Press, 1999.

Arnold, Ben, Editor. *The Liszt companion*. Westport, Connecticut; London: Greenwood Press, 2002.

Arnold, Denis and Nigel Fortune, Editors. *The Beethoven companion*. London: Faber and Faber, 1973.

Ashbrook, William. *Donizetti*. London: Cassell, 1965.

Auner, Joseph Henry. *A Schoenberg reader: documents of a life*. New Haven Connecticut; London: Yale University Press, 2003.

Avins, Styra, Editor. *Johannes Brahms: life and letters*. Oxford: Oxford University Press, 1997.

Azoury, Pierre H. *Chopin through his contemporaries: friends, lovers, and rivals*. Westport, Connecticut: Greenwood Press, 1999.

Badura-Skoda, Paul. *Carl Czerny: On the Proper Performance of all Beethoven's Works for the Piano*. Universal Edition: A. G. Wien, 1970.

Bailey, Cyril. *Hugh Percy Allen*. London: Oxford University

Press, 1948.

Bailey, Kathryn. *The life of Webern*. Cambridge: Cambridge University Press, 1998.

Barenboim, Daniel. *A life in music*. London: Weidenfeld & Nicolson, 1991.

Barlow, Michael. *Whom the gods love: the life and music of George Butterworth*. London: Toccata Press, 1997.

Barrett-Ayres, Reginald. *Joseph Haydn and the string quartet*. New York: Schirmer Books, 1974.

Bartos, Frantisek. *Bedrich Smetana: Letters and reminiscences*. Prague: Artia, 1953.

Barzun, Jacques. *Pleasures of music: an anthology of writing about music and musicians*. London: Cassell, 1977.

Bauer-Lechner, Natalie. *Recollections of Gustav Mahler*. London: Faber Music, 1980.

Bazhanov, N. Nikolai. *Rakhmaninov*. Moscow: Raduga, 1983.

Beaumont, Antony, Editor. *Ferruccio Busoni: Selected letters*. London: Faber and Faber, 1987.

Beaumont, Antony, Editor. *Gustav Mahler, letters to his wife*. London: Faber and Faber, 2004.

Beecham, Thomas. *A mingled chime: an autobiography*. New York: Da Capo Press, 1976.

Bekker, Paul. *Beethoven*. London: J. M. Dent & Sons, 1925.

Bellasis, Edward. *Cherubini: memorials illustrative of his life*. London: Burns and Oates, 1874.

Bennett, James R. Sterndale. *The life of William Sterndale Bennett*. Cambridge: University Press, 1907.

Benser, Caroline Cepin. *Egon Wellesz (1885–1974): chronicle of twentieth-century musician*. New York: P. Lang, 1985.

Berlioz, Hector. *Evenings in the orchestra*. Harmondsworth: Penguin Books, 1963.

Berlioz, Hector. *The musical madhouse (Les grotesques de la musique)*. Rochester, New York: University of Rochester Press, 2003.

Bernard, Jonathan W., Editor. *Elliott Carter: collected essays and lectures, 1937-1995*. Rochester, New York; Woodbridge: University of Rochester Press, 1998.

Bernstein, Leonard. *The joy of music*. New York: Simon and Schuster, 1959.

Bertensson, Sergei. *Sergei Rachmaninoff: a lifetime in music*. London: G. Allen & Unwin, 1965.

Biancolli, Louis. *The Flagstad manuscript*. New York: Putnam, 1952.

Bickley, Nora, Editor. *Letters from and to Joseph Joachim*. London: Macmillan, 1914.

Bie, Oskar. *A history of the pianoforte and pianoforte players*. New York: Da Capo Press, 1966.

Blaukopf, Herta. *Mahler's unknown letters*. London: Gollancz, 1986.

Blaukopf, Kurt and Herta. *Mahler: his life, work and world*. London: Thames and Hudson, 1991.

Bliss, Arthur. *As I remember*. London: Thames Publishing, 1989.

Block, Adrienne Fried. *Amy Beach, passionate Victorian: the life and work of an American composer, 1867–1944*. New York: Oxford University Press, 1998.

Bloch, Ernst. *Essays on the philoso-*

phy of music. Cambridge: Cambridge University Press, 1985.

Blocker, Robert. *The Robert Shaw reader.* New Haven; London: Yale University Press, 2004.

Blom, Eric. *A musical postbag.* London: J. M. Dent, 1945.

Blom, Eric. *Beethoven's pianoforte sonatas discussed.* London: J. M. Dent, 1938.

Blom, Eric. *Classics major and minor: with some other musical ruminations.* London: J. M. Dent, 1958.

Blum, David. *The art of quartet playing: the Guarneri Quartet in conversation with David Blum.* London: Gollancz, 1986.

Blume, Friedrich. *Classic and Romantic music: a comprehensive survey.* London: Faber and Faber, 1972.

Boden, Anthony. *The Parrys of the Golden Vale: background to genius.* London: Thames Publishing, 1998.

Bonavia, Ferruccio. *Musicians on music.* London: Routledge & Kegan Paul, 1956.

Bonds, Mark Evan *After Beethoven: imperatives of originality in the symphony.* Cambridge, Massachusetts; London: Harvard University Press, 1996.

Bonis, Ferenc, Editor. *The selected writings of Zoltán Kodály.* London; New York: Boosey & Hawkes, 1974.

Bookspan, Martin. *André Previn: a biography.* London: Hamilton, 1981.

Boros, James and Richard Toop, Editors. *Brian Ferneyhough: Collected writings.* Amsterdam: Harwood Academic, 1995.

Boulez, Pierre. *Stocktakings from an apprenticeship.* Oxford: Clarendon Press, 1991.

Boult, Adrian. *Boult on music: words from a lifetime's communication.* London: Toccata Press, 1983.

Boult, Adrian. *My own trumpet.* London, Hamish Hamilton, 1973.

Boult, Adrian with Jerrold Northrop Moore. *Music and friends: seven decades of letters to Adrian Boult from Elgar, Vaughan Williams, Holst, Bruno Walter, Yehudi Menuhin and other friends.* London: Hamish Hamilton, 1979.

Bovet, Marie Anne de. *Charles Gounod: his life and his works.* London: S. Low, Marston, Searle & Rivington, Ltd., 1891.

Bowen, Catherine Drinker. *Beloved friend: the story of Tchaikowsky and Nadejda von Meck.* London: Hutchinson & Co., 1937.

Bowen, Meiron, Editor. *Gerhard on music: selected writings.* Brookfield, Vermont: Ashgate, 2000.

Bowen, Meirion. *Michael Tippett.* London: Robson Books, 1982.

Bowen, Meiron, Editor. *Music of the angels: essays and sketchbooks of Michael Tippett.* London: Eulenburg, 1980.

Bowen, Meiron, Editor. *Tippett on music.* Oxford: Clarendon Press, 1995.

Bowers, Faubion. *Scriabin: a biography.* Mineola: Dover; London: Constable, 1996.

Boyden, Matthew. *Richard Strauss.* London: Weidenfeld & Nicolson, 1999.

Bozarth, George S., Editor. *Brahms studies: analytical and historical perspectives; papers delivered at the International Brahms Conference, Washington, DC, 5-8 May 1983*. Oxford: Clarendon Press, 1990.

Brand, Juliane, Christopher Hailey and Donald Harris, Editors. *The Berg-Schoenberg correspondence: selected letters*. Basingstoke: Macmillan, 1987.

Brandenbugh, Sieghard, Editor. *Haydn, Mozart, & Beethoven: studies in the music of the classical period: essays in honor of Alan Tyson*. Oxford: Clarendon Press, 1998.

Braunstein, Joseph. *Musica Æterna, program notes for 1961–1971*. New York: Musica Æterna, 1972.

Braunstein, Joseph. *Musica Æterna, program notes for 1971–1976*. New York: Musica Æterna, 1978.

Brendel, Alfred. *Alfred Brendel on music: collected essays*. Chicago, Illinois: A Cappella Books, 2001.

Brendel, Alfred. *The veil of order: Alfred Brendel in conversation with Martin Meyer*. London: Faber and Faber, 2002.

Breuning, Gerhard von. *Memories of Beethoven: from the house of the black-robed Spaniards*. Cambridge: Cambridge University Press, 1992.

Briscoe, James R., Editor. (Brief Description): *Debussy in performance*. New Haven: Yale University Press, 1999.

Brott, Alexander Betty Nygaard King. *Alexander Brott: my lives in music*. Oakville, Ontario; Niagara Falls, New York: Mosaic Press, 2005.

Brown, Alfred Peter. *The symphonic repertoire. Vol. 2, The first golden age of the Viennese symphony: Haydn, Mozart, Beethoven, and Schubert*. Bloomington, Indiana: Indiana University Press, 2002.

Brown, Maurice John Edwin. *Schubert: a critical biography*. London: Macmillan; New York: St. Martin's Press, 1958.

Broyles, Michael. *Beethoven: the emergence and evolution of Beethoven's heroic style*. New York: Excelsior Music Publishing Co., 1987.

Brubaker, Bruce and Jane Gottlieb, Editors. *Pianist, scholar, connoisseur: essays in honor of Jacob Lateiner*. Stuyvesant, N.Y., Pendragon Press, 2000.

Buch, Esteban. *Beethoven's Ninth: a political history*. Chicago; London: University of Chicago Press, 2003.

Burk, John N., Editor. *Letters of Richard Wagner: the Burrell collection*. London: Gollancz, 1951.

Burnham, Scott G. *Beethoven hero*. Princeton, New Jersey: Princeton University Press, 1995.

Burnham, Scott G and Michael P. Steinberg, Editors. *Beethoven and his world*. Princeton, New Jersey; Oxford: Princeton University Press, 2000.

Burton, William Westbrook, Editor. *Conversations about Bernstein*. New York; Oxford: Oxford University Press, 1995.

Busch, Fritz. *Pages from a musician's life*. London: Hogarth Press, 1953.

Busch, Hans, Editor. *Verdi's Aida: the history of an opera in letters and documents*. Minneapolis:

University of Minnesota Press, 1978.

Busch, Hans, Editor. *Verdi's Falstaff in letters and contemporary reviews*. Bloomington: Indiana University Press, 1997.

Busch, Marie, Translator. *Memoirs of Eugenie Schumann*. London: W. Heinemann, 1927.

Bush, Alan Dudley. *In my eighth decade and other essays*. London: Kahn & Averill, 1980.

Busoni, Ferruccio. *Letters to his wife*. Translated by Rosamond Ley. New York: Da Capo Press, 1975.

Byron, Reginald. *Music, culture, & experience: selected papers of John Blacking*. Chicago: University of Chicago Press, 1995.

Cairns, David. *Responses: musical essays and reviews*. New York: Da Capo Press, 1980.

Cardus, Neville. *Talking of music*. London: Collins, 1957.

Carley, Lionel. *Delius: a life in letters*. London: Scolar Press in association with the Delius Trust, 1988.

Carley, Lionel. *Grieg and Delius: a chronicle of their friendship in letters*. London: Marion Boyars, 1993.

Carner, Mosco. *Major and minor*. London: Duckworth, 1980

Carner, Mosco. *Puccini: a critical biography*. London: Duckworth, 1958.

Carroll, Brendan G. *The last prodigy: a biography of Erich Wolfgang Korngold*. Portland, Oregon: Amadeus Press, 1997.

Carse, Adam von Ahn. *The life of Jullien: adventurer, showman-conductor and establisher of the Promenade Concerts in England, together with a history of those concerts up to 1895*. Cambridge England: Heffer, 1951.

Carse, Adam von Ahn. *The orchestra from Beethoven to Berlioz: a history of the orchestra in the first half of the 19th century, and of the development of orchestral baton-conducting*. Cambridge: W. Heffer, 1948.

Casals, Pablo. *Joys and sorrows: reflections by Pablo Casals as told to Albert E. Kahn*. London: Macdonald, 1970.

Casals, Pablo. *The memoirs of Pablo Casals as told to Thomas Dozier*. London: Life en Español, 1959.

Chappell, Paul. *Dr. S. S. Wesley, 1810–1876: portrait of a Victorian musician*. Great Wakering: Mayhew-McCrimmon, 1977.

Chasins, Abram. *Leopold Stokowski, a profile*. New York: Hawthorn Books, 1979.

Charlton, Davi, Editor and Martyn Clarke Translator. *E.T.A. Hoffmann's musical writings: Kreisleriana, The Poet and the Composer*. Cambridge: Cambridge University Press, 1989.

Chávez, Carlos. *Musical thought*. Cambridge: Harvard University Press, 1961.

Chesterman, Robert, Editor. *Conversations with conductors: Bruno Walter, Sir Adrian Boult, Leonard Bernstein, Ernest Ansermet, Otto Klemperer, Leopold Stokowski*. Totowa, New Jersey: Rowman and Littlefield, 1976.

Chissell, Joan. *Clara Schumann: a dedicated spirit; a study of her life and work*. London: Hamilton, 1983.

Chua, Daniel K. L. *The "Galitzin" quartets of Beethoven: Opp.127, 132, 130*. Princeton: Princeton

University Press, 1995.

Citron, Marcia, Editor. *The letters of Fanny Hensel to Felix Mendelssohn*. Stuyvesant, New York: Pendragon Press, 1987.

Clark, Walter Aaron. *Enrique Granados: poet of the piano*. Oxford, England; New York, N.Y.: Oxford University Press, 2006.

Clark, Walter Aaron. *Isaac Albéniz: portrait of a romantic*. Oxford; New York: Oxford University Press, 1999.

Clive, Peter. *Beethoven and his world*. Oxford University Press, 2001.

Closson, Ernest. *History of the piano*. Translated by Delano Ames and edited by Robin Golding. London: Paul Elek, 1947.

Cockshoot, John V. *The fugue in Beethoven's piano music*. London: Routledge & Kegan Paul, 1959.

Coe, Richard N, Translator. *Life of Rossini by Stendhal*. London: Calder & Boyars, 1970.

Coleman, Alexander, Editor. *Diversions & animadversions: essays from The new criterion*. New Brunswick, New Jersey; London: Transaction Publishers, 2005.

Colerick, George. *From the Italian girl to Cabaret: musical humour, parody and burlesque*. London: Juventus, 1998.

Coleridige, A. D. *Life of Moscheles, with selections from his diaries and correspondence by his wife*. London: Hurst & Blackett, 1873.

Colles, Henry Cope. *Essays and lectures*. London: Humphrey Milford, Oxford University Press, 1945.

Cone, Edward T., Editor. *Roger Sessions on music: collected essays*. Princeton, New Jersey: Princeton University Press, 1979.

Cone, Edward T. *The composer's voice*. Berkeley; London: University of California Press, 1974.

Cook, Susan and Judy S. Tsou, Editors. *Cecilia reclaimed: feminist perspectives on gender and music*. Urbana: University of Illinois Press, 1994.

Cooper, Barry. *Beethoven*: The master musicians series. Oxford: Oxford University Press, 2000.

Cooper, Barry. *Beethoven and the creative process*. Oxford: Clarendon Press, 1990.

Cooper, Barry. *Beethoven's folksong settings: chronology, sources, style*. Cambridge: Cambridge University Press, 1991.

Cooper, Barry. *The Beethoven compendium: a guide to Beethoven's life and music*. London: Thames and Hudson, 1991.

Cooper, Martin. *Beethoven: the last decade, 1817–1827*. London: Oxford University Press, 1970.

Cooper, Martin. *Judgements of value: selected writings on music*. Oxford; New York: Oxford University Press, 1988.

Cooper, Martin. *Ideas and music*. London: Barrie and Rockliff, 1965.

Cooper, Victoria L. *The house of Novello: the practice and policy of a Victorian music publisher, 1829–1866*. Aldershot, Hants: Ashgate, 2003.

Coover, James. *Music at auction: Puttick and Simpson (of London), 1794–1971: being an annotated, chronological list of sales of musical materials*. Warren, Michigan: Harmonie Park Press, 1988.

Copland, Aaron. *Copland on music*. London: Deutsch, 1961.

Corredor, J. Ma. *Conversations with Casals*. London: Hutchinson, 1956.

Cott, Jonathan. *Stockhausen: conversations with the composer*. London: Picador, 1974.

Cottrell, Stephen. *Professional music making in London: ethnography and experience*. Aldershot: Ashgate, 2004.

Cowell, Henry. *Charles Ives and his music*. New York: Oxford University Press, 1955.

Cowling, Elizabeth. *The cello*. London: Batsford, 1983.

Crabbe, John. *Beethoven's empire of the mind*. Newbury: Lovell Baines, 1982.

Craft, Robert. *An improbable life: memoirs*. Nashville: Vanderbilt University Press, 2002.

Craft, Robert, Editor. *Stravinsky: selected correspondence*. London: Faber and Faber, 3 Vols. 1982–1985.

Craw, Howard Allen. *A biography and thematic catalog of the works of J. L. Dussek: 1760–1812*. Ann Arbor: Michigan, 1965.

Crawford, Richard, R. Allen Lott and Carol J. Oja, Editors. *A Celebration of American music: words and music in honor of H. Wiley Hitchcock*. Ann Arbor: University of Michigan Press, 1990.

Craxton, Harold and Tovey, Donald Francis. *Beethoven: Sonatas for Pianoforte*. London: The Associated Board, [1931].

Crichton, Ronald: Editor. *The memoirs of Ethel Smyth*. New York: Viking, 1987.

Crist, Stephen A. and Roberta M. Marvin, Editors. *Historical musicology: sources, methods, interpretations*. Rochester, New York: University of Rochester Press, 2004.

Crofton, Ian and Donald Fraser, Editors. *A dictionary of musical quotations*. London: Croom Helm, 1985.

Crompton, Louis, Editor. *Shaw, Bernard: The great composers: reviews and bombardments*. Berkeley; London: University of California Press, 1978.

Csicserry-Ronay, Elizabeth, Translator and Editor. *Hector Berlioz: The art of music and other essays: (A travers chants)*. Bloomington: Indiana University Press, 1994.

Curtiss, Mina Kirstein. *Bizet and his world*. London: Secker & Warburg, 1959.

Cuyler, Louise Elvira. *The symphony*. New York: Harcourt Brace Jovanovich, 1973.

Dahlhaus, Carl. *Ludwig van Beethoven: approaches to his music*. Oxford: Clarendon Press, 1991.

Dahlhaus, Carl. *Nineteenth-century music*. Translated by J. Bradford Robinson. Berkeley; London: University of California Press, 1989.

Daniels, Robin. *Conversations with Cardus*. London: Gollancz, 1976.

Daniels, Robin. Conversations with Menuhin. London: Macdonald General Books, 1979.

Day, James. *Vaughan Williams*. London: Dent, 1961.

Davies, Peter Maxwell. *Studies from two decades*. Selected and introduced by Stephen Pruslin.

London: Boosey & Hawkes, 1979.

Dean, Winton. *Georges Bizet: his life and work*. London: J.M. Dent, 1965.

Deas, Stewart. *In defence of Hanslick*. London: Williams and Norgate, 1940.

Debussy, Claude. *Debussy on music*. London: Secker & Warburg, 1977.

Delbanco, Nicholas. *The Beaux Arts Trio*. London: Gollancz, 1985.

Demény, Janos, Editor. *Béla Bartók: letters*. London: Faber and Faber, 1971.

Dent, Edward Joseph. *Selected essays*. Edited by Hugh Taylor. Cambridge; New York: Cambridge University Press, 1979.

Deutsch, Otto Erich. *Mozart: a documentary biography*. London: Adam & Charles Black, 1965.

Deutsch, Otto Erich. *Schubert: a documentary biography*. London: J.M. Dent, 1946

Deutsch, Otto Erich. *Schubert: memoirs by his friends*. London: Adam & Charles Black, 1958.

Dibble, Jeremy. *C. Hubert H. Parry: his life and music*. Oxford: Clarendon Press, 1992.

Dibble, Jeremy. *Charles Villiers Stanford: man and musician*. Oxford: Oxford University Press, 2002.

Donakowski, Conrad L. *A muse for the masses: ritual and music in an age of democratic revolution, 1770–1870*. Chicago: University of Chicago Press, 1977.

Dower, Catherine. *Alfred Einstein on music: selected music criticisms*. New York: Greenwood Press, 1991.

Downs, Philip G. *Classical music: the era of Haydn, Mozart, and Beethoven*. New York: W.W. Norton, 1992.

Drabkin, William. *Beethoven: Missa Solemnis*. Cambridge: Cambridge University Press, 1991.

Dreyfus, Kay. *The farthest north of humanness: letters of Percy Grainger, 1901–1914*. South Melbourne; Basingstoke: Macmillan, 1985.

Dubal, David, Editor. *Remembering Horowitz: 125 pianists recall a legend*. New York: Schirmer Books, 1993.

Dubal, David. *The world of the concert pianist*. London: Victor Gollancz, 1985.

Dvorák, Otakar. *Antonín Dvorák, my father*. Spillville, Iowa: Czech Historical Research Center, 1993.

Dyson, George. *The progress of music*. London: Oxford University Press, Humphrey Milford, 1932.

Eastaugh, Kenneth. *Havergal Brian: the making of a composer*. London: Harrap, 1976.

Edwards, Allen. *Flawed words and stubborn sounds: a conversation with Elliott Carter*. New York: Norton & Company, 1971.

Edwards, Frederick George. *Musical haunts in London*. London: J. Curwen & Sons, 1895.

Ehrlich, Cyril. *First philharmonic: a history of the Royal Philharmonic Society*. Oxford: Clarendon Press, 1995.

Einstein, Alfred. *A short history of music*. London: Cassell and Company Ltd., 1948.

Einstein, Alfred. *Essays on music*. London: Faber and Faber, 1958.

Einstein, Alfred. *Mozart: his character, his work*. London: Cassell and Company Ltd., 1946.

Einstein, Alfred. *Music in the Romantic era*. London: J.M. Dent Ltd., 1947.

Ekman, Karl. *Jean Sibelius, his life and personality*. New York: Tudor Publishing. Co., 1945.

Elgar, Edward. *A future for English music: and other lectures*, Edited by Percy M. Young. London: Dobson, 1968.

Elkin, Robert. *Queen's Hall, 1893–1941*. London: Rider, 1944.

Ella, John. *Musical sketches, abroad and at home: with original music by Mozart, Czerny, Graun, etc., vocal cadenzas and other musical illustrations*. London: Ridgway, Vol. 1., 1869.

Ellis, William Ashton. *The family letters of Richard Wagner*. Edited and translated by William Ashton Ellis and enlarged with introduction and notes by John Deathridge. Basingstoke: Macmillan, 1991.

Ellis, William Ashton. *Richard Wagner's prose works: Vol. 1, The art-work of the future*. Edited and translated by William Ashton Ellis. London: Kegan Paul, Trench, Trübner, 1895.

Ellis, William Ashton. *Richard Wagner's prose works: Vol. 2, Opera and drama*. Edited and translated by William Ashton Ellis. London: Kegan Paul, Trench, Trübner, 1900.

Ellis, William Ashton. *Richard Wagner's prose works: Vol. 3, The theatre*. Edited and translated by William Ashton Ellis. London: Kegan Paul, Trench, Trübner, 1907.

Ellis, William Ashton. *Richard Wagner's prose works: Vol. 4, Art and politics*. Edited and translated by William Ashton Ellis. London: Kegan Paul, Trench, Trübner, 1895.

Ellis, William Ashton. *Richard Wagner's prose works: Vol. 5, Actors and singers*. Edited and translated by William Ashton Ellis. London: Kegan Paul, Trench, Trübner, 1896.

Ellis, William Ashton. *Richard Wagner's prose works: Vol. 6, Religion and art*. Edited and translated by William Ashton Ellis. London: Kegan Paul, Trench, Trübner, 1897.

Ellis, William Ashton. *Richard Wagner's prose works: Vol. 7, In Paris and Dresden*. Edited and translated by William Ashton Ellis. London: Kegan Paul, Trench, Trübner, 1898.

Ellis, William Ashton. *Richard Wagner's prose works: Vol. 8, Posthumous*. Edited and translated by William Ashton Ellis. London: Kegan Paul, Trench, Trübner, 1899.

Elterlein, Ernst von. *Beethoven's pianoforte sonatas: explained for the lovers of the musical art*. London: W. Reeves, 1898.

Engel, Carl. *Musical myths and facts*. London: Novello, Ewer & Co.; New York: J.L. Peters, 1876.

Eosze, László. *Zoltán Kodály: his life and work*. London: Collet's, 1962.

Etter, Brian K. *From classicism to modernism: Western musical culture and the metaphysics of order*. Aldershot: Ashgate, 2001.

Ewen, David. *From Bach to Stravinsky: the history of music by its foremost critics*. New York, Greenwood Press, 1968.

Ewen, David. *Romain Rolland's Essays on music.* New York: Dover Publications, 1959.

Fay, Amy. *Music-study in Germany: from the home correspondence of Amy Fay.* New York: Dover Publications, 1965.

Fenby, Eric. *Delius as I knew him.* London: Quality Press, 1936.

Ferguson, Donald Nivison. *Masterworks of the orchestral repertoire: a guide for listeners.* Minneapolis: University of Minnesota Press, 1954.

Fétis, François-Joseph. *Curiosités historiques de la musique: complément nécessaire de la Musique mise à la portée de tout le monde.* Paris: Janet et Cotelle, 1830.

Fifield, Christopher. *Max Bruch: his life and works.* London: Gollancz, 1988.

Fifield, Christopher. *True artist and true friend: a biography of Hans Richter.* Oxford: Clarendon Press, 1993.

Finson, Jon and R. Larry Todd, Editors. *Mendelssohn and Schumann: essays on their music and its context.* Durham, N.C.: Duke University Press, 1984.

Fischer, Edwin. *Beethoven's pianoforte sonatas: a guide for students & amateurs.* London: Faber and Faber, 1959.

Fischer, Edwin. *Reflections on music.* London: Williams and Norgate, 1951.

Fischer, Hans Conrad and Erich Kock. *Ludwig van Beethoven: a study in text and pictures.* London: Macmillan; New York, St. Martin's Press, 1972.

Fischmann, Zdenka E. *Janáček-Newmarch correspondence.* 1st limited and numbered edition. Rockville, MD: Kabel Publishers, 1986.

Fitzlyon, April. *Maria Malibran: diva of the romantic age.* London: Souvenir Press, 1987.

FitzLyon, April. *The price of genius: a life of Pauline Viardot.* London: John Calder, 1964.

Forbes, Elliot, Editor. *Thayer's life of Beethoven.* Princeton, New Jersey: Princeton University Press, 1967.

Foreman, Lewis. *Bax: a composer and his times.* London: Scolar Press, 1983.

Foreman, Lewis, Editor. *Farewell, my youth, and other writings by Arnold Bax.* Aldershot: Scolar Press, 1992.

Foster, Myles Birket. *History of the Philharmonic Society of London, 1813–1912: a record of a hundred years' work in the cause of music.* London: Bodley Head, 1912.

Foulds, John. *Music today: its heritage from the past, and legacy to the future.* London: I. Nicholson and Watson, limited, 1934.

Frank, Mortimer H. *Arturo Toscanini: the NBC years.* Portland, Oregon: Amadeus Press, 2002.

Fraser, Andrew Alastair. *Essays on music.* London: Oxford University Press, H. Milford, 1930.

Frohlich, Martha. *Beethoven's Appassionata' sonata.* Oxford: Clarendon Press, 1991.

Gal, Hans. *The golden age of Vienna.* London: Max Parrish & Co. Limited, 1948.

Gal, Hans. *The musician's world: great composers in their letters.* London: Thames and Hudson,

Galatopoulos, Stelios. *Bellini: life, times, music*. London: Sanctuary, 2002.

Garden, Edward and Nigel Gottrei, Editors. *'To my best friend': correspondence between Tchaikovsky and Nadezhda von Meck, 1876–1878*. Oxford: Clarendon Press, 1993.

Geck, Martin. Beethoven. London: Haus, 2003.

Gerig, Reginald. *Famous pianists & their technique*. Washington: R. B. Luce, 1974.

Gilliam, Bryan. *The life of Richard Strauss*. Cambridge: Cambridge University Press, 1999.

Gilliam, Bryan, Editor. *Richard Strauss and his world*. Princeton, New Jersey: Princeton University Press, 1992.

Gillies, Malcolm and Bruce Clunies Ross, Editors. *Grainger on music*. Oxford; New York: Oxford University Press, 1999.

Gillies, Malcolm and David Pear, Editors. *The all-round man: selected letters of Percy Grainger, 1914–1961*. Oxford: Clarendon Press, 1994.

Gillies, Malcolm, Editor. *The Bartók companion*. London: Faber and Faber, 1993.

Gillmor, Alan M. *Erik Satie*. Basingstoke: Macmillan Press, 1988.

Glehn, M. E. *Goethe and Mendelssohn : (1821–1831)*. London: Macmillan, 1874.

Glowacki, John, Editor. *Paul A. Pisk: Essays in his honor*. Austin, Texas: University of Texas, 1966

Gollancz, Victor. *Journey towards music: a memoir*. London: Victor Gollancz Ltd., 1964.

Good, Edwin Marshall. *Giraffes, black dragons, and other pianos: a technological history from Cristofori to the modern concert grand*. Stanford, California: Stanford University Press, 1982.

Gordon, David. *Musical visitors to Britain*. London: Routledge, 2005.

Gordon, Stewart. *A history of keyboard literature: music for the piano and its forerunners*. Schirmer Books: New York: London : Prentice Hall International, 1996.

Gorrell, Lorraine. *The nineteenth-century German lied*. Portland, Oregon: Amadeus Press, 1993.

Goss, Glenda D. *Jean Sibelius: the Hämeenlinna letters: scenes from a musical life, 1875–1895*. Esbo, Finland: Schildts, 1997.

Goss, Madeleine. *Bolero: the life of Maurice Ravel*. New York: Tudor, 1945.

Gotch, Rosamund Brunel, Editor. *Mendelssohn and his friends in Kensington: letters from Fanny and Sophy Horsley, written 1833–36*. London: Oxford University Press, 1938.

Gounod, Charles. *Charles Gounod; autobiographical reminiscences: with family letters and notes on music; from the French*. London: William Heinemann, 1896.

Grabs, Manfred, Editor. *Hanns Eisler: a rebel in music; selected writings*. Berlin: Seven Seas Publishers, 1978.

Grace, Harvey. *A musician at large*. London: Oxford University Press, H. Milford, 1928.

(La) Grange, Henry-Louis de. *Gustav Mahler*. Oxford: Oxford University Press, 1995.

Graves, Charles L. *Hubert Parry: his life and works.* London: Macmillan, 1926.

Graves, Charles L. *Post-Victorian music: with other studies and sketches.* London: Macmillan and Co., limited, 1911.

Graves, Charles L. *The life & letters of Sir George Grove, Hon. D.C.L. (Durham), Hon. LL.D. (Glasgow), formerly director of the Royal college of music.* London: Macmillan and Co., Ltd.; New York: The Macmillan Co., 1903.

Gray, Cecil. *Musical chairs, or, between two stools: being the life and memoirs of Cecil Gray.* London: Home & Van Thal, 1948.

Gregor-Dellin and Dietrich Mack, Editors. *Cosima Wagner's diaries.: Vol. 1, 1869 - 1877.* London: Collins, 1978-1980.

Griffiths, Paul. *Modern music: the avant-garde since 1945.* London: J. M. Dent & Sons Ltd., 1981.

Griffiths, Paul. *Olivier Messiaen and the music of time.* London: Faber and Faber, 1985.

Griffiths, Paul. *Peter Maxwell Davies.* London: Robson Books, 1988.

Griffiths, Paul. *The sea on fire: Jean Barraqué.* Rochester, New York: Woodbridge: University of Rochester Press, 2003.

Griffiths, Paul. *The string quartet.* London: Thames and Hudson, 1983.

Grout, Donald Jay and Claude V. Palisca, Editors. *A history of Western music.* London: J. M. Dent, 1988.

Grove, George. *Beethoven and his nine symphonies.* London: Novello, Ewer, 1896.

Grover, Ralph Scott. *Ernest Chausson: the man and his music.* London: The Athlone Press, 1980.

Grover, Ralph Scott. *The music of Edmund Rubbra.* Aldershot: Scolar Press, 1993.

Grun, Bernard. *Alban Berg: letters to his wife.* Edited and translated by Bernard Grun. London: Faber and Faber, 1971.

Gutman, David. *Prokofiev.* London: Omnibus Press, 1990.

Hadow, William Henry. *Collected essays.* London: H. Milford at the Oxford University Press, 1928.

Hadow, William Henry. *Beethoven's Op. 18 Quartets.* London: H. Milford at the Oxford University Press, 1926.

Haggin, Bernard H. *Music observed.* New York: Oxford University Press, 1964.

Hailey, Christopher. *Franz Schreker, 1878–1934: a cultural biography.* Cambridge: Cambridge University Press, 1993.

Hall, Michael. *Leaving home: a conducted tour of twentieth-century music with Simon Rattle.* London: Faber and Faber, 1996.

Hall, Patricia and Friedemann Sallis, Editors. (Brief Description): *A handbook to twentieth-century musical sketches.* Cambridge: Cambridge University Press, 2004.

Hallé, C. E. *Life and letters of Sir Charles Hallé: being an autobiography (1819–1860) with correspondence and diaries.* London: Smith, Elder & Co., 1896.

Halstead, Jill. *The woman composer: creativity and the gendered poli-*

tics of musical composition. Aldershot: Ashgate, 1997.

Hamburger, Michael, Editor and Translator. *Beethoven letters, journals, and conversations.* New York: Thames and Hudson, 1951.

Hammelmann, Hanns A. and Ewald Osers. *The correspondence between Richard Strauss and Hugo von Hofmannsthal.* London: Collins, 1961.

Hanson, Lawrence and Elisabeth Hanson. *Tchaikovsky: the man behind the music.* New York: Dodd, Mead & Co, 1967.

Harding, James. *Massenet.* London: J. M. Dent & Sons Ltd., 1970.

Harding, James. *Saint-Saëns and his circle.* London: Chapman & Hall, 1965.

Harding, Rosamond E. M. *Origins of musical time and expression.* London: Oxford University Press, 1938.

Harman, Alec with Anthony Milner and Wilfrid Mellers. *Man and his music: the story of musical experience in the West.* London: Barrie & Jenkins, 1988.

Harper, Nancy Lee. *Manuel de Falla: his life and music.* Lanham, Maryland; London: The Scarecrow Press, 2005.

Hartmann, Arthur. *'Claude Debussy as I knew him' and other writings of Arthur Hartmann.* Edited by Samuel Hsu, Sidney Grolnic, and Mark Peters. Rochester, New York; Woodbridge: University of Rochester Press, 2003.

Haugen, Einar and Camilla Cai. *Ole Bull: Norway's romantic musician and cosmopolitan patriot.* Madison: The University of Wisconsin Press, 1993.

Headington, Christopher. *The Bodley Head history of Western music.* London: The Bodley Head, 1974.

Heartz, Daniel. *Music in European capitals: the galant style, 1720–1780.* New York; London: W. W. Norton, 2003.

Hedley, Arthur, Editor. *Selected correspondence of Fryderyk Chopin: abridged from Fryderyk Chopin's correspondence.* London: Heinemann, 1962.

Heiles, Anne Mischakoff. *Mischa Mischakoff: journeys of a concertmaster.* Sterling Heights, Michigan: Harmonie Park Press, 2006.

Henderson, Sanya Shoilevska. *Alex North, film composer: a biography, with musical analyses of a Streetcar named desire, Spartacus, The misfits, Under the volcano, and Prizzi's honor.* Jefferson, N.C.; London: McFarland, 2003.

Henschel, George. *Personal recollections of Johannes Brahms: some of his letters to and pages from a journal kept by George Henschel.* Boston: R G. Badger, 1907.

Henze, Hans Werner. *Bohemian fifths: an autobiography.* London: Faber and Faber, 1998.

Henze, Hans Werner. *Music and politics: collected writings 1953–81.* London: Faber and Faber, 1982.

Herbert, May, Translator. *Early letters of Robert Schumann.* London: George Bell and Sons, 1888.

Heyman, Barbara B. *Samuel Barber: the composer and his music.* New York: Oxford University

Press, 1992.
Heyworth, Peter. *Otto Klemperer, his life and times.* Cambridge: Cambridge University Press, 2 Vols. 1983–1996.
Hildebrandt, Dieter. *Pianoforte: a social history of the piano.* London: Hutchinson, 1988.
Hill, Peter. *The Messiaen companion.* London: Faber and Faber, 1995.
Hill, Peter and Nigel Simeone. *Messiaen.* New Haven Connecticut; London: Yale University Press, 2005.
Hiller, Ferdinand. *Mendelssohn: Letters and recollections.* New York: Vienna House, 1972.
Hines, Robert Stephan. *The orchestral composer's point of view: essays on twentieth-century music by those who wrote it.* Norman: University of Oklahoma Press, 1970.
Ho, Allan B. *Shostakovich reconsidered.* London: Toccata Press, 1998.
Hodeir, André. *Since Debussy: a view of contemporary music.* New York: Da Capo Press, 1975.
Holmes, Edward. *The life of Mozart: including his correspondence.* London: Chapman and Hall, 1845.
Holmes, John L. *Composers on composers.* New York: Greenwood Press, 1990.
Hopkins, Antony. *The concertgoer's companion.* London: J.M. Dent & Sons Ltd., 1984.
Hopkins, Antony. *The seven concertos of Beethoven.* Aldershot: Scolar Press, 1996.
Holt, Richard. *Nicolas Medtner (1879–1951): a tribute to his art and personality.* London: D. Dobson, 1955.
Honegger, Arthur. *I am a composer.* London: Faber and Faber, 1966.
Hoover, Kathleen and John Cage. *Virgil Thomson: his life and music.* New York; London: T. Yoseloff, 1959.
Horgan, Paul. *Encounters with Stravinsky: a personal record.* London: The Bodley Head, 1972.
Horowitz, Joseph. *Conversations with Arrau.* London: Collins, 1982.
Horowitz, Joseph. Understanding Toscanini. London: Faber and Faber, 1987.
Horwood, Wally. *Adolphe Sax, 1814–1894: his life and legacy.* Bramley: Bramley Books, 1980.
Howie, Crawford. *Anton Bruckner: a documentary biography.* Lewiston, N.Y.; Lampeter: Edwin Mellen Press, 2002.
Hueffer, Francis. *Correspondence of Wagner and Liszt.* New York: Greenwood Press, 2 Vols.1969.
Hughes, Spike. *The Toscanini legacy: a critical study of Arturo Toscanini's performances of Beethoven, Verdi, and other composers.* London: Putnam, 1959.
Hullah, Annette. *Theodor Leschetizky.* London and New York: J. Land & Co., 1906.
Le Huray, Peter and James Day, Editors. *Music and aesthetics in the eighteenth and early-nineteenth centuries.* Cambridge: Cambridge University Press, 1988.
D'Indy, Vincent. *César Franck.* New York: Dover Publications, 1965.
Jacobs, Arthur. *Arthur Sullivan: A Victorian musician.* Aldershot: Scolar Press, 1992.

Jahn, Otto. *Life of Mozart.* London: Novello, Ewer & Co., 1882.

Jefferson, Alan. *Sir Thomas Beecham: a centenary tribute.* London: World Records Ltd., 1979.

Jezic, Diane. *The musical migration and Ernst Toch.* Ames: Iowa State University Press, 1989.

Johnson, Douglas Porter, Editor. *The Beethoven sketchbooks: history, reconstruction, inventory.* Oxford: Clarendon, 1985.

Johnson, Stephen. *Bruckner remembered.* London: Faber and Faber, 1998.

Jones, David, Wyn. *Beethoven: Pastoral symphony.* Cambridge: Cambridge University Press, 1995.

Jones, David Wyn. *The life of Beethoven.* Cambridge: Cambridge University Press, 1998.

Jones, David Wyn. *The symphony in Beethoven's Vienna.* Cambridge: Cambridge University Press, 2006.

Jones, J. Barrie, Editor. *Gabriel Fauré: a life in letters.* London: Batsford, 1989.

Jones, Peter Ward, Editor and Translator. *The Mendelssohns on honeymoon: the 1837 diary of Felix and Cécile Mendelssohn Bartholdy, together with letters to their families.* Oxford: Clarendon Press, 1997.

Jones, Timothy. *Beethoven, the Moonlight and other sonatas, Op. 27 and Op. 31.* Cambridge; New York, N.Y.: Cambridge University Press, 1999.

Kalischer, A. C., Editor. *Beethoven's letters: a critical edition.* London: J. M. Dent, 1909.

Kárpáti, János. *Bartók's chamber music.* Stuyvesant, New York: Pendragon Press, 1994.

Keefe, Simon P. *The Cambridge companion to the concerto.* Cambridge, New York, N.Y.: Cambridge University Press, 2005.

Keller, Hans. *The great Haydn quartets: their interpretation.* London: J. M. Dent, 1986.

Keller, Hans, Editor. *The memoirs of Carl Flesch.* New York: Macmillan, 1958.

Keller, Hans, and Christopher Wintle. *Beethoven's string quartets in F minor, Op. 95 and C minor, Op. 131: two studies.* Nottingham: Department of Music, University of Nottingham, 1995.

Kelly, Thomas Forrest. *First nights at the opera: five musical premiers.* New Haven: Yale University Press, 2004.

Kennedy, Michael. *Adrian Boult.* London: Hamish Hamilton, 1987.

Kennedy, Michael. *Barbirolli, conductor laureate: the authorised biography.* London: Hart-Davis, MacGibbon, 1973.

Kennedy, Michael, Editor. *The autobiography of Charles Hallé; with correspondence and diaries.* London: Paul Elek, 1972.

Kennedy, Michael. *Hallé tradition: a century of music.* Manchester: Manchester University Press, 1960.

Kennedy, Michael. *The works of Ralph Vaughan Williams.* London: Oxford University Press, 1964.

Kemp, Ian. *Tippett: the composer and his music.* London; New York: Eulenburg Books, 1984.

Kerman, Joseph. *The Beethoven quartets*. London: Oxford University Press, 1967, c1966.

Kerman, Joseph. *Write all these down: essays on music*. Berkeley, California; London: University of California Press, 1994.

Kildea, Paul, Editor. *Britten on music*. Oxford: Oxford University Press, 2003.

Kinderman, William. *Beethoven*. Oxford: Oxford University Press, 1997.

Kinderman, William. *Beethoven's Diabelli variations*. Oxford: Clarendon Press; New York: Oxford University Press, 1987.

Kinderman, William, Editor. *The string quartets of Beethoven*. Urbana, Ilinois: University of Illinois Press, 2005.

King, Alec Hyatt. *Musical pursuits: selected essays*. London: British Library, 1987.

Kirby, F. E. *Music for piano: a short history*. Amadeus Press: Portland, 1995.

Kirkpatrick, John, Editor. *Charles E. Ives: Memos*. New York: W.W. Norton, 1972.

Knapp, Raymond. *Brahms and the challenge of the symphony*. Stuyvesant, N.Y.: Pendragon Press, c.1997.

Knight, Frida. *Cambridge music: from the Middle Ages to modern times*. Cambridge, England.: New York: Oleander Press, 1980.

Knight, Max, Translator. *A confidential matter: the letters of Richard Strauss and Stefan Zweig, 1931–1935*. Berkeley; London: University of California Press, 1977.

Kok, Alexander. *A voice in the dark: the philharmonia years*. Ampleforth: Emerson Edition, 2002.

Kopelson, Kevin. *Beethoven's kiss: pianism, perversion, and the mastery of desire*. Stanford, California: Stanford University Press, 1996.

Kostelanetz, Richard, Editor. *Aaron Copland: a reader; selected writings 1923–1972*. New York; London: Routledge, 2003.

Kostelanetz, Richard. *Conversing with Cage*. New York; London: Routledge, 2003.

Kostelanetz, Richard. *On innovative musicians*. New York: Limelight Editions, 1989.

Kostelanetz, Richard, Editor. *Virgil Thomson: a reader ; selected writings, 1924–1984*. New York; London: Routledge, 2002.

Kowalke, Kim H. *Kurt Weill in Europe*. Ann Arbor, Michigan: UMI Research Press, 1979.

Krehbiel, Henry Edward. *The pianoforte and its music*. New York: Cooper Square Publishers, 1971.

Kruseman, Philip, Editor. *Beethoven's own words*. London: Hinrichsen Edition, 1948.

Kurtz, Michael. *Stockhausen: a biography*. London: Faber and Faber, 1992.

Lam, Basil. *Beethoven string quartets*. Seattle: University of Washington Press, 1975.

Lambert, Constant. *Music ho!: a study of music in decline*. London: Faber and Faber, Ltd. 1934.

Landon, H. C. Robbins. *Beethoven: a documentary study*. London: Thames and Hudson, 1970.

Landon, H. C. Robbins. *Beethoven: his life, work and world*. London: Thames and Hudson,

1992.

Landon, H. C. Robbins. *Essays on the Viennese classical style: Gluck, Haydn, Mozart, Beethoven.* London: Barrie & Rockliff The Cresset Press, 1970.

Landon, H. C. Robbins. *Haydn: chronicle and works/Haydn, the late years, 1801–1809.* Bloomington: Indiana University Press, 1977.

Landon, H. C. Robbins. *Haydn: his life and music.* London: Thames and Hudson, 1988.

Landon, H. C. Robbins. *Haydn in England, 1791–1795.* London: Thames and Hudson, 1976.

Landon, H. C. Robbins. *Haydn: the years of 'The creation', 1796–800.* London: Thames and Hudson, 1977.

Landon, H. C. Robbins. *Mozart: the golden years, 1781–1791.* New York: Schirmer Books, 1989.

Landon, H. C. Robbins. *1791, Mozart's last year.* London: Thames and Hudson, 1988.

Landon, H. C. Robbins *The collected correspondence and London notebooks of Joseph Haydn.* London: Barrie and Rockliff, 1959.

Landon, H. C. Robbins: Editor. *The Mozart companion.* London: Faber, 1956.

Landowska, Wanda. *Music of the past.* London: Geoffrey Bles, 1926.

Lang, Paul Henry. *Musicology and performance.* New Haven: Yale University Press, 1997.

Lang, Paul Henry. *The creative world of Beethoven.* New York: W. W. Norton 1971.

Laurence, Dan H., Editor. *Shaw's music: the complete musical criticism in three volumes.* London: Max Reinhardt, the Bodley Head, 1981.

Lawford-Hinrichsen, Irene. *Music publishing and patronage: C. F. Peters, 1800 to the Holocaust.* Kenton: Edition Press, 2000.

Layton, Robert, Editor. *A guide to the concerto.* Oxford: Oxford University Press, 1996.

Layton, Robert, Editor. *A guide to the symphony.* Oxford: Oxford University Press, 1995.

Lebrecht, Norman. *The maestro myth: great conductors in pursuit of power.* London: Simon & Schuster, 1991.

Lee, Ernest Markham. *The story of the symphony.* London: Scott Publishing Co., 1916.

Leibowitz, Herbert A., Editor. *Musical impressions: selections from Paul Rosenfeld's criticism.* London: G. Allen & Unwin, 1970.

Lenrow, Elbert, Editor and Translator. *The letters of Richard Wagner to Anton Pusinelli.* New York: Vienna House, 1972.

Leonard, Maurice. *Kathleen: the life of Kathleen Ferrier: 1912–1953.* London: Hutchinson, 1988.

Lesure, François and Roger Nichols, Editors. *Debussy, letters.* London: Faber and Faber, 1987.

Letellier, Robert Ignatius, Editor and Translator. *The diaries of Giacomo Meyerbeer.* Madison: Fairleigh Dickinson University Press; London: Associated University Presses, 4 Vols., 1999–2004.

Levas, Santeri. *Sibelius: a personal portrait.* London: J. M. Dent, 1972.

Levy, Alan Howard. *Edward Mac-*

Dowell, an American master. Lanham, Md. & London: Scarecrow Press, 1998.

Levy, David Benjamin. *Beethoven: the Ninth Symphony.* New Haven, Connecticut; London: Yale University Press, 2003.

Leyda, Jay and Sergi Bertensson. *The Musorgsky reader: a life of Modeste Petrovich Musorgsky in letters and documents.* New York: W.W. Norton, 1947.

Lewis, Thomas P., Editor. *Raymond Leppard on music: an anthology of critical and personal writings.* White Plains, N.Y.: Pro/Am Music Resources, 1993.

Liébert, Georges. *Nietzsche and music.* Chicago: University of Chicago Press, 2004.

Liszt, Franz. *An artist's journey: lettres d'un bachelier ès musique, 1835–1841.* Chicago: University of Chicago Press, 1989.

Litzmann, Berthold, Editor. *Clara Schumann: an artist's life, based on material found in diaries and letters.* London: Macmillan; Leipzig: Breitkopf & Härtel, 2 Vols. 1913.

Litzmann, Berthold, Editor. *Letters of Clara Schumann and Johannes Brahms, 1853–1896.* New York, Vienna House. 2 Vols. 1971.

Lloyd, Stephen. *William Walton: muse of fire.* Woodbridge, Suffolk: The Boydell Press, 2001.

Locke, Ralph P. and Cyrilla Barr, Editors. *Cultivating music in America: women patrons and activists since 1860.* Berkeley: University of California Press, 1997.

Lockspeiser, Edward. *Debussy: his life and mind.* London: Cassell. 2 Vols. 1962–1965.

Lockspeiser, Edward. *The literary clef: an anthology of letters and writings by French composers.* London: J. Calder. 1958.

Lockwood, Lewis, Editor. *Beethoven essays: studies in honor of Elliot Forbes.* Cambridge, Massachusetts: Harvard University Department of Music: Distributed by Harvard University Press, 1984.

Lockwood, Lewis and Mark Kroll, Editors. *The Beethoven violin sonatas: history, criticism, performance.* Urbana: University of Illinois Press, 2004.

Loft, Abram. *Violin and keyboard: the duo repertoire.* New York: Grossman Publishers. 2 Vols. 1973.

Longyear, Rey Morgan. *Nineteenth-century romanticism in music.* Englewood Cliffs: Prentice-Hall, 1969.

Lowe, C. Egerton. *Beethoven's pianoforte sonatas: hints on their rendering, form, etc., with appendices on definition of sonata, music forms, ornaments, pianoforte pedals, and how to discover keys.* London: Novello, 1929.

Macdonald, Hugh, Editor. *Berlioz: Selected letters.* London: Faber and Faber, 1995.

Macdonald, Malcolm, Editor. *Havergal Brian on music: selections from his journalism: Volume One, British music.* London: Toccata Press, 1986.

MacDonald, Malcolm. *Varèse: astronomer in sound.* London: Kahn & Averill, 2003.

MacDowell, Edward. *Critical and historical essays: lectures delivered at Columbia University. Edited by W. J. Baltzell. London: Elkin; Boston: A.P. Schmidt, 1912.

MacFarren, Walter. Memories: an autobiography. London: Walter Scott Publishing Co.,1905.

Mackenzie, Alexander Campbell. *A musician's narrative.* London: Cassell and company, Ltd, 1927.

McCarthy, Margaret William, Editor. *More letters of Amy Fay: the American years, 1879–1916.* Detroit: Information Coordinators, 1986.

McClary, Susan. *Feminine endings: music, gender, and sexuality.* Minneapolis: University of Minnesota Press, 1991.

McClatchie, Stephen, Editor and Translator. *The Mahler family letters.* Oxford: Oxford University Press, 2006.

McVeigh, Simon. *Concert life in London from Mozart to Haydn.* Cambridge: Cambridge University Press, 1993.

Mahler, Alma. *Gustav Mahler: memories and letters.* Enlarged edition revised and edited and with and introduction by Donald Mitchell. London: John Murray, 1968.

Mai, François Martin. *Diagnosing genius: the life and death of Beethoven.* Montreal; London: McGill-Queen's University Press, 2007.

Del Mar, Norman. *Orchestral variations: confusion and error in the orchestral repertoire.* London: Eulenburg, 1981.

Del Mar, Norman. *Richard Strauss: a critical commentary on his life and works.* London: Barrie & Jenkins. 3 Vols. 1978.

(La) Mara [pseudonym]. *Letters of Franz Liszt.* London: H. Grevel & Co., 2 Vols. 1894.

Marek, George Richard. *Puccini.* London: Cassell & Co., 1952.

Marek, George Richard. *Toscanini.* London: Vision, 1976.

(De) Marliave, Joseph. *Beethoven's quartets.* New York: Dover Publications (reprint), 1961.

Martin, George Whitney. *Verdi: his music, life and times.* London: Macmillan, 1965.

Martner, Knud, Editor. *Selected letters of Gustav Mahler.* London; Boston: Faber and Faber, 1979.

Martyn, Barrie. *Nicolas Medtner: his life and music.* Aldershot: Scolar Press, 1995.

Martyn, Barrie. *Rachmaninoff: composer, pianist, conductor.* Aldershot: Scolar, 1990.

Massenet, Jules. *My recollections.* Westport, Connecticut: Greenwood Press.1970.

Matheopoulos, Helena. *Maestro: encounters with conductors of today.* London: Hutchinson, 1982.

Matthews, Denis. *Beethoven.* London: J. M. Dent, 1985.

Matthews, Denis. *Beethoven piano sonatas.* London: British Broadcasting Corporation, 1967.

Matthews, Dennis. *In pursuit of music.* London: Victor Gollancz Ltd., 1968.

Matthews, Denis. *Keyboard music.* Newton Abbot: London David & Charles, 1972.

Mellers, Wilfrid Howard. *Caliban reborn: renewal in twentieth-century music.* London: Victor Gollancz, 1967.

Mellers, Wilfrid Howard. *The sonata*

principle (from c. 1750). London: Rockliff, 1957.

Mendelssohn Bartholdy. *Letters from Italy and Switzerland.* London: Longman, Green, Longman, and Roberts, 1862.

Mendelssohn Bartholdy, Paul. *Letters of Felix Mendelssohn Bartholdy, from 1833 to 1847.* London: Longman, Green, Longman, Roberts, & Green, 1864.

Menuhin, Yehudi and Curtis W. Davis. *The music of man.* London: Macdonald and Jane's, 1979.

Menuhin, Yehudi. *Theme and variations.* London: Heinemann Educational Books Ltd., 1972.

Menuhin, Yehudi. *Unfinished journey.* London: Macdonald and Jane's, 1977.

Messian, Olivier. *Music and color: conversations with Claude Samuel.* Portland, Oregon: Amadeus, 1994.

Miall, Antony. *Musical bumps.* London: J.M. Dent & Sons Ltd, 1981.

Michotte, Edmond. *Richard Wagner's visit to Rossini (Paris 1860): and, An evening at Rossini's in Beau-Sejour (Passy), 1858.* Chicago; London: University of Chicago Press, 1982.

Mies, Paul. *Beethoven's sketches: an analysis of his style based on a study of his sketchbooks.* New York: Johnson Reprint, 1969.

Milhaud, Darius. *My happy life.* London: Boyars, 1995.

Miller, Mina. *The Nielsen companion.* London: Faber and Faber, 1994.

Milsom, David. *Theory and practice in late nineteenth-century violin performance: an examination of style in performance, 1850–1900.* Aldershot: Ashgate, 2003.

Mitchell, Donald, Editor. *Letters from a life: the selected letters and diaries of Benjamin Britten 1913–1976.* London: Faber and Faber. 3 Vols., 1991.

Mitchell, Donald and Hans Keller, Editors. *Music survey: new series 1949–1952.* London: Faber Music in association with Faber & Faber, 1981.

Mitchell, Jon C. *A comprehensive biography of composer Gustav Holst, with correspondence and diary excerpts: including his American years.* Lewiston, New York: Edwin Mellen Press, 2001.

Moldenhauer, Hans. *Anton von Webern: a chronicle of his life and work.* London: Victor Gollancz, 1978.

Monrad-Johansen. Edvard Grieg. New York: Tudor Publishing Co., 1945.

Moore, Gerald. *Am I too loud?: memoirs of an accompanist.* London: Hamish Hamilton, 1962.

Moore, Gerald. *Farewell recital: further memoirs.* Harmondsworth: Penguin Books, 1979.

Moore, Gerald. *Furthermoore: interludes in an accompanist's life.* London: Hamish Hamilton, 1983.

Moore, Jerrold Northrop. *Edward Elgar: a creative life.* Oxford: Oxford University Press, 1984.

Moore, Jerrold Northrop. *Elgar, Edward. The windflower letters: correspondence with Alice Caroline Stuart Wortley and her family.* Oxford: Clarendon Press; New York: Oxford University Press, 1989.

Moore, Jerrold Northrop. *Elgar, Edward. Edward Elgar: letters of a lifetime.* Oxford: Clarendon Press; New York: Oxford University Press, 1990.

Moore, Jerrold Northrop. *Elgar, Edward. Elgar and his publishers: letters of a creative life.* Oxford: Clarendon, 1987.

Moreux, Serge. *Béla Bartók.* London: Harvill Press, 1953.

Morgan, Kenneth. *Fritz Reiner, maestro and martinet.* Urbana: University of Illinois Press, 2005.

Cone, Edward T., Editor. *Music, a view from Delft: selected essays.* Chicago: University of Chicago Press, 1989.

Morgan, Robert P. *Twentieth-century music: a history of musical style in modern Europe and America.* New York: Norton, 1991.

Morgenstern, Sam., Editor. *Composers on music: an anthology of composers' writings.* London: Faber & Faber, 1956.

Morrow, Mary Sue. *Concert life in Haydn's Vienna: aspects of a developing musical and social institution.* Stuyvesant, New York: Pendragon Press, 1989.

Moscheles, Felix, Editor and Translator. *Letters from Felix Mendelssohn-Bartholdy to Ignaz and Charlotte Moscheles.* London: Trübner and Co., 1888.

Mudge, Richard B., Translator. *Glinka, Mikhail Ivanovich: Memoirs.* Norman: University of Oklahoma Press, 1963.

Munch, Charles. *I am a conductor.* New York: Oxford University Press, 1955.

Mundy, Simon. *Bernard Haitink: a working life.* London: Robson Books, 1987.

Musgrave, Michael. *The musical life of the Crystal Palace.* Cambridge: Cambridge University Press, 1995.

Music & Letters. *Beethoven: special number.* London: Music & Letters, 1927.

Musical Times. *Special Issue.* John A. Fuller-Maitland London: Vol. VIII, No. 2, 1927.

Myers, Rollo H., Editor. *Twentieth-century music.* London: Calder and Boyars, 1960.

National Gallery (Great Britain). *Music performed at the National Gallery concerts, 10th October 1939 to 10th April 1946.* London: Privately printed, 1948.

Nattiez, Jean-Jacques, Editor. *Orientations: collected writings — Pierre Boulez.* London: Faber and Faber, 1986.

Nauhaus, Gerd, Editor. *The marriage diaries of Robert & Clara Schumann.* London: Robson Books, 1994.

Nectoux, Jean Michel. *Gabriel Fauré: a musical life.* Translated by Roger Nichols. Cambridge: Cambridge University Press, 1991.

Nettl, Paul. *Beethoven handbook.* Westport, Connecticut: Greenwood Press, 1975.

Neumayr, Anton. *Music and medicine.* Bloomington, Illinois: Medi-Ed Press, 1994–1997

Newbould, Brian. *Schubert and the symphony: a new perspective.* Surbiton: Toccata Press, 1992.

Newlin, Dika. *Schoenberg remembered: diaries and recollections (1938–76).* New York: Pendragon Press, 1980.

Newman, Ernest. *From the world of*

Newman, Ernest. *music: essays from 'The Sunday Times'*. London: J. Calder, 1956.

Newman, Ernest. *Hugo Wolf*. New York: Dover Publications, 1966.

Newman, Ernest, Annotated and Translated. *Memoirs of Hector Berlioz from 1803 to 1865, comprising his travels in Germany, Italy, Russia, and England*. New York: Knopf, 1932.

Newman, Ernest. *More essays from the world of music: essays from the 'Sunday Times'*. London: John Calder, 1958.

Newman, Ernest. *Musical studies*. London; New York: John Lane, 1910.

Newman, Ernest. *Testament of music: essays and papers*. London: Putnam, 1962.

Newman, Richard. *Alma Rosé: Vienna to Auschwitz*. Portland, Oregon: Amadeus Press, 2000.

Newman, William S. *The sonata in the classic era*. Chapel Hill: University of North Carolina Press 1963.

Newman, William S. *The sonata in the Classic era*. New York; London: W.W. Norton, 1983.

Newmarch, Rosa Harriet. *Henry J. Wood*. London & New York: John Lane, 1904.

Nicholas, Jeremy. *Godowsky: the pianists' pianist; a biography of Leopold Godowsky*. Hexham: Appian Publications & Recordings, 1989.

Nichols, Roger. *Debussy remembered*. London: Faber and Faber, 1992.

Nichols, Roger. *Mendelssohn remembered*. London: Faber and Faber, 1997.

Nichols, Roger. *Ravel remembered*. London: Faber and Faber, 1987.

Niecks, Frederick. *Robert Schumann*. London: J. M. Dent, 1925.

Nielsen, Carl. *Living music*. Copenhagen, Wilhelm Hansen, 1968.

Nielsen, Carl. *My childhood*. Copenhagen, Wilhelm Hansen, 1972.

Nikolska, Irina. *Conversations with Witold Lutoslawski, (1987–92)*. Stockholm: Melos, 1994.

Nohl, Ludwig. *Beethoven depicted by his contemporaries*. London: Reeves, 1880.

De Nora, Tia. *Beethoven and the construction of genius: musical politics in Vienna, 1792–1803*. Berkeley: University of California Press, 1997.

Norton, Spencer, Editor and Translator. *Music in my time: the memoirs of Alfredo Casella*. Norman: University of Oklahoma Press, 1955.

Nottebohm, Gustav. *Two Beethoven sketchbooks: a description with musical extracts*. London: Gollancz, 1979.

Oakeley, Edward Murray. *The life of Sir Herbert Stanley Oakeley*. London: George Allen, 1904.

Lucas, Brenda and Michael Kerr. *Virtuoso: the story of John Ogdon*. London: H. Hamilton, 1981.

Oliver, Michael, Editor. *Settling the score: a journey through the music of the twentieth century*. London: Faber and Faber, 1999.

Olleson, Philip. *Samuel Wesley: the man and his music*. Woodbridge: Boydell Press, 2003.

Olleson, Philip, Editor. *The letters of Samuel Wesley: professional and social correspondence, 1797–1837*. Oxford; New York: Oxford University Press, 2001.

Olmstead, Andrea. *Conversations with Roger Sessions.* Boston: Northeastern University Press, 1987.

Orenstein, Arbie, Editor. *A Ravel reader: correspondence, articles, interviews.* New York: Columbia University Press, 1990.

Orenstein, Arbie. *Ravel: man and musician.* New York: Columbia University Press, 1975.

Orledge, Robert. *Charles Koechlin (1867–1950): his life and works.* New York: Harwood Academic Publishers, 1989.

Orledge, Robert. *Gabriel Fauré.* London: Eulenburg Books, 1979.

Orledge, Robert. *Satie remembered.* London: Faber and Faber, 1995.

Orledge, Robert. *Satie the composer.* Cambridge: Cambridge University Press, 1990.

Orlova, Alexandra. *Glinka's life in music: a chronicle.* Ann Arbor: UMI Research Press, 1988.

Orlova, Alexandra. *Musorgsky's days and works: a biography in documents.* Ann Arbor: UMI Research Press, 1983.

Orlova, Alexandra. *Tchaikovsky: a self-portrait.* Oxford: Oxford University Press, 1990.

Osborne, Charles, Editor and Translator. *Letters of Giuseppe Verdi.* London: Victor Gollancz, 1971.

Osmond-Smith David, Editor and Translator. *Luciano Berio: Two interviews with Rossana Dalmonte and Bálint András Varga.* New York; London: Boyars, 1985.

Ouellette, Fernand. *Edgard Varèse.* London: Calder & Boyars, 1973.

Paderewski, Ignacy Jan and Mary Lawton. *The Paderewski memoirs.* London: Collins, 1939.

Page, Tim: Editor. *The Glenn Gould reader.* London: Faber and Faber, 1987.

Page, Tim. *Music from the road: views and reviews, 1978–1992.* New York; Oxford: Oxford University Press, 1992.

Page, Tim and Vanessa Weeks, Editors. *Selected letters of Virgil Thomson.* New York: Summit Books, 1988.

Page, Tim. *Tim Page on music: views and reviews.* Portland, Oregon: Amadeus Press, 2002.

Palmer, Christopher. *Herbert Howells, (1892–1983): a celebration.* London: Thames, 1996.

Palmer, Christopher, Editor. *Sergei Prokofiev: Soviet diary 1927 and other writings.* London: Faber and Faber, 1991.

Palmer, Fiona M. *Domenico Dragonetti in England (1794–1846): the career of a double bass virtuoso.* Oxford: Clarendon, 1997.

Palmieri, Robert, Editor. *Encyclopedia of the piano.* New York: Garland, 1996.

Panufnik, Andrzej. *Composing myself.* London: Methuen, 1987.

Parsons, James, Editor. *The Cambridge companion to the Lied.* Cambridge: Cambridge University Press, 2004.

Paynter, John, Editor. *Between old worlds and new: occasional writings on music by Wilfrid Mellers.* London: Cygnus Arts, 1997.

Pestelli, Giorgio. *The age of Mozart and Beethoven.* Cambridge: Cambridge University Press, 1984.

Peyser, Joan. *Bernstein: a biography: revised & updated.* New York: Billboard Books, 1998.

Phillips-Matz, Mary Jane. *Verdi: a biography.* Oxford: Oxford University Press, 1993.

Piggott, Patrick. *The life and music of John Field, 1782–1837: creator of the nocturne.* London: Faber and Faber, 1973.

Plantinga, Leon. *Beethoven's concertos: history, style, performance.* New York: Norton, 1999.

Plantinga, Leon. *Clementi: his life and music.* London: Oxford University Press, 1977.

Plantinga, Leon. *Romantic music: a history of musical style in nineteenth-century Europe.* New York; London: Norton, 1984.

Plaskin, Glenn. *Horowitz: a biography of Vladimir Horowitz.* London: Macdonald, 1983.

Pleasants, Henry, Editor and Translator. *Hanslick, Eduard: Music criticisms, 1846–99.* Baltimore: Penguin Books, 1963.

Pleasants, Henry, Editor and Translator. *Hanslick's music criticisms.* New York: Dover Publications, 1988.

Pleasants, Henry, Editor and Translator. *The music criticism of Hugo Wolf.* New York: Holmes & Meier Publishers, 1978.

Pleasants, Henry, Editor and Translator. *The musical journeys of Louis Spohr.* Norman: University of Oklahoma Press, 1961.

Pollack, Howard. *Aaron Copland: the life and work of an uncommon man.* New York: Henry Holt, 1999.

Poulenc, Francis. *My friends and myself.* London: Dennis Dobson, 1978.

Powell, Richard, Mrs. *Edward Elgar: memories of a variation.* Aldershot, Hants, England: Scolar Press; Brookfield, Vermont, USA: Ashgate Publishing. Co., 1994.

Poznansky, Alexander, Editor. *Tchaikovsky through others' eyes.* Bloomington: Indiana University Press, 1999.

Praeger, Ferdinand. *Wagner as I knew him.* London; New York: Longmans, Green, 1892.

Previn, Andre. *Antony Hopkins. Music face to face.* London, Hamish Hamilton, 1971.

Prieberg, Fred K. *Trial of strength: Wilhelm Furtwängler and the Third Reich.* London: Quartet, 1991.

Procter-Gregg, Humphrey. *Beecham remembered.* London: Duckworth, 1976.

Prokofiev, Sergey. *Prokofiev by Prokofiev: a composer's memoir.* London: Macdonald and Jane's, 1979.

Rachmaninoff, Sergei. *Rachmaninoff's recollections told to Oskar von Riesemann.* London: George Allen & Unwin, 1934.

Radcliffe, Philip. *Beethoven's string quartets.* Cambridge: Cambridge University Press, 1978.

Radcliffe, Philip. *Piano Music in: The Age of Beethoven, The New Oxford History of Music, Vol. VIII.* Gerald Abraham, (Editor), 1988, p. 340.

Ratner, Leonard G. *Romantic music: sound and syntax.* New York: Schirmer Books, 1992.

Raynor, Henry. *A social history of music: from the middle ages to Beethoven.* London: Barrie & Jenkins, 1972.

Rees, Brian. *Camille Saint-Saëns: a life.* London: Chatto & Windus, 1999.

Reich, Willi, Editor. *Anton Webern: The path to the new music.* London; Bryn Mawr: Theodore Presser in association with Universal Edition, 1963.

Reid, Charles. *John Barbirolli: a biography.* London, Hamish Hamilton, 1971.

Reid, Charles. *Malcolm Sargent: a biography.* London: Hamilton, 1968.

Rennert, Jonathan. *William Crotch (1775–1847): composer, artist, teacher.* Lavenham: Terence Dalton, 1975.

Rice, John A. *Antonio Salieri and Viennese Opera.* Chicago, Illinois: University of Chicago Press, 1998.

Rice, John A. *Empress Marie Therese and music at the Viennese court, 1792–1807.* Cambridge: Cambridge University Press, 2003.

Richards, Fiona. *The Music of John Ireland.* Aldershot: Ashgate, 2000.

Rigby, Charles. *Sir Charles Hallé: a portrait for today.* Manchester: Dolphin Press, 1952.

Ringer, Alexander, Editor. *The early Romantic era: between Revolutions; 1789 and 1848.* Basingstoke: Macmillan, 1990.

Roberts, John P.L. and Ghyslaine Guertin, Editors. *Glenn Gould: Selected letters.* Toronto; Oxford: Oxford University Press, 1992.

Robertson, Alec. *More than music.* London: Collins, 1961.

Robinson, Harlow, Editor and Translator. *Selected letters of Sergei Prokofiev.* Boston: Northeastern University Press, 1998.

Robinson, Harlow. *Sergei Prokofiev: a biography.* London: Hale, 1987.

Robinson, Paul A. *Ludwig van Beethoven, Fidelio.* Cambridge: Cambridge University Press, 1996.

Robinson, Suzanne, Editor. *Michael Tippett: music and literature.* Aldershot: Ashgate, 2002.

Rochberg, George. *The aesthetics of survival: a composer's view of twentieth-century music.* Ann Arbor, Michigan: University of Michigan Press, 2004.

Rodmell, Paul. *Charles Villiers Stanford.* Aldershot: Ashgate, 2002.

Roeder, Michael Thomas. *A history of the concerto.* Portland, Oregon: Amadeus Press, 1994.

Rohr, Deborah Adams. *The careers of British musicians, 1750–1850: a profession of artisans.* Cambridge: Cambridge University Press, 2001.

Rolland, Romain. *Goethe and Beethoven.* New York; London: Blom, 1968.

Rolland, Romain. *Beethoven and Handel.* London: Waverley Book Co., 1917.

Rolland, Romain. *Beethoven the creator.* Garden City, New York: Garden City Pub., 1937.

Roscow, Gregory, Editor. *Bliss on music: selected writings of Arthur Bliss, 1920–1975.* Oxford: Oxford University Press, 1991.

Rosen, Charles. *Beethoven's piano sonatas: a short companion.* New Haven, Connecticut: London: Yale University Press, 2002.

Rosen, Charles. *Critical entertainments: music old and new.* Cambridge, Massachusetts; London: Harvard University Press, 2000.

Rosen, Charles. *The classical style: Haydn, Mozart, Beethoven.* London: Faber and Faber, 1976.

Rosen, Charles. *The romantic generation.* Cambridge, Massachusetts: Harvard University Press, 1995.

Rosenthal, Albi. *Obiter scripta: essays, lectures, articles, interviews and reviews on music, and other subjects.* Oxford: Offox Press; Lanham: Scarecrow Press, 2000.

Rostal, Max. *Beethoven: the sonatas for piano and violin; thoughts on their interpretation.* London: Toccata Press, 1985.

Rostropovich, Mstislav and Galina Vishnevskaya. *Russia, music, and liberty.* Portland, Oregan: Amadeus Press, 1995.

Rubinstein, Arthur. *My many years.* London: Jonathan Cape, 1980.

Rubinstein, Arthur. *My young years.* London: Jonathan Cape, 1973.

Rumph, Stephen C. *Beethoven after Napoleon: political romanticism in the late works.* Berkeley; London: University of California Press, 2004.

Rye, Matthew Rye. *Notes to the BBC Radio Three Beethoven Experience, Friday 10 June 2005,* www.bbc.co.uk/radio3/Beethoven.

Sachs, Harvey. *Toscanini.* London: Weidenfeld and Nicholson, 1978.

Sachs, Joel. *Kapellmeister Hummel in England and France.* Detroit: Information Coordinators, 1977.

Saffle, Michael, Editor. *Liszt and his world: proceedings of the International Liszt Conference held at Virginia Polytechnic Institute and State University, 20–23 May 1993.* Stuyvesant, New York: Pendragon Press, 1998.

Safránek, Milos. *Bohuslav Martinu, his life and works.* London: Allan Wingate, 1962.

Saint-Saëns, Camille. *Outspoken essays on music.* Westport, Connecticut: Greenwood Press, 1970.

Saussine, Renée de. *Paganini.* Westport, Connecticut: Greenwood Press, 1976.

Sayers, W. C. Berwick. *Samuel Coleridge-Taylor, musician: his life and letters.* London; New York: Cassell and Co., 1915.

Schaarwächter, Jürgen. *HB: aspects of Havergal Brian.* Aldershot: Ashgate, 1997.

Schafer, R. Murray. *E.T.A. Hoffmann and music.* Toronto: University of Toronto Press, 1975.

Schafer, R. Murray, Editor. *Ezra Pound and music: the complete criticism.* London: Faber and Faber, 1978.

Schat, Peter. *The tone clock.* Chur, Switzerland; Langhorne, Pa.: Harwood Academic Publishers, 1993.

Schenk, Erich. *Mozart and his times.* Edited and Translated by Richard and Clara Winstin. London: Secker & Warburg, 1960.

Schindler, Anton Felix. *Beethoven as I knew him.* Edited by Donald W. MacArdle and Translated by Constance S. Jolly from the German edition of 1860 London: Faber and Faber, 1966.

Schlosser, Johann. *Beethoven: the first biography, 1827.* Edited by Barry Cooper. Portland, Oregon: Amadeus Press, 1996.

Schnabel, Artur. *My life and music.*

London: Longmans, 1961.

Schnittke, Alfred. *A Schnittke reader.* Bloomington: Indiana University Press, 2002.

Scholes, Percy Alfred. *Crotchets: a few short musical notes.* London: John Lane, 1924.

Schonberg, Harold C. *The great pianists.* London: Victor Gollancz, 1964.

Schrade, Leo. *Beethoven in France: the growth of an idea.* New Haven; London: Yale University Press, H. Milford, Oxford University Press, 1942.

Schrade, Leo. *Tragedy in the art of music.* Cambridge, Massachusetts: Harvard University Press, 1964.

Schuh, Willi. *Richard Strauss: a chronicle of the early years 1864–1898.* Cambridge: Cambridge University Press, 1982.

Schuh, Willi, Editor. *Richard Strauss: Recollections and reflections.* London; New York: Boosey & Hawkes, 1953.

Schuller, Gunther. *Musings: the musical worlds of Gunther Schuller.* New York: Oxford University Press, 1986.

Schumann, Robert. *Music and musicians: essays and criticisms.* London: William Reeves, 1877.

Schuttenhelm, Editor. *Selected letters of Michael Tippett.* London: Faber and Faber, 2005.

Schwartz, Elliott. *Music since 1945: issues, materials, and literature.* New York: Schirmer Books, 1993.

Scott, Marion M. *Beethoven: (The master musicians).* London: Dent, 1940.

Scott-Sutherland, Colin. *Arnold Bax.* London: J. M. Dent, 1973.

Searle, Muriel V. *John Ireland: the man and his music.* Tunbridge Wells: Midas Books, 1979.

Secrest, Meryle. *Leonard Bernstein: a life.* London: Bloomsbury, 1995.

Seeger, Charles. *Studies in musicology II, 1929–1979.* Edited by Anne M. Pescatello. Berkeley; London: University of California Press, 1994.

Selden-Goth, Gisela, Editor. *Felix Mendelssohn: letters.* London: Paul Elek Publishers Ltd, 1946.

Senner, Wayne M., Robin Wallace and William Meredith, Editors. *The critical reception of Beethoven's compositions by his German contemporaries.* Lincoln: University of Nebraska Press, in association with the American Beethoven Society and the Ira F. Brilliant Center for Beethoven Studies, San José State University, 1999.

Seroff, Victor I. *Rachmaninoff.* London: Cassell & Company, 1951.

Sessions, Roger. *Questions about music.* Cambridge, Massachusetts: Harvard University Press, 1970.

Sessions, Roger. *The musical experience of composer, performer, listener.* New York: Atheneum, 1966, 1950.

Seyfried, Ignaz von. *Louis van Beethoven's Studies in thoroughbass, counterpoint and the art of scientific composition.* Leipzig; New-York: Schuberth and Company, 1853.

Sharma, Bhesham R. *Music and culture in the age of mechanical reproduction.* New York: Peter Lang, 2000.

Shaw, Bernard. *How to become a musical critic.* London: R. Hart Davis, 1960.

Shaw, Bernard. *London music in 1888–89 as heard by Corno di Bassetto (later known as Bernard Shaw): with some further autobiographical particulars.* London: Constable and Company, 1937.

Shaw, Bernard. *Music in London, 1890–1894.* London: Constable and Company Limited, 3 Vols., 1932.

Shedlock, John South. *Beethoven's pianoforte sonatas: the origin and respective values of various readings.* London: Augener Ltd., 1918.

Shedlock, John South. *The pianoforte sonata: its origin and development.* London: Methuen, 1895.

Shepherd, Arthur. *The string quartets of Ludwig van Beethoven.* Cleveland: H. Carr, The Printing Press, 1935.

Sheppard, Leslie and Herbert R. Axelrod. *Paganini: containing a portfolio of drawings by Vido Polikarpus.* Neptune City, New Jersey: Paganiniana Publications, 1979.

Short, Michael. *Gustav Holst: the man and his music.* Oxford: Oxford University Press, 1990.

Shostakovich, Dmitry. *Dmitry Shostakovich: about himself and his times.* Moscow: Progress Publishers, 1981.

Simpson, John Palgrave. *Carl Maria von Weber: the life of an artist, from the German of his son Baron, Max Maria von Weber.* London: Chapman and Hall, 1865.

Simpson, Robert. *Beethoven symphonies.* London: British Broadcasting Corporation, 1970.

Sipe, Thomas. *Beethoven: Eroica symphony.* Cambridge: Cambridge University Press, 1998.

Sitwell, Sacheverell. *Mozart.* Edinburgh: Peter Davies Limited, 1932.

Skelton, Geoffrey. *Paul Hindemith: the man behind the music; a biography.* London: Victor Gollancz, 1975.

Smallman, Basil. *The piano trio: its history, technique, and repertoire.* Oxford: Clarendon Press; Oxford; New York: Oxford University Press, 1990.

Smidak, Emil. *Isaak-Ignaz Moscheles: the life of the composer and his encounters with Beethoven, Liszt, Chopin, and Mendelssohn.* Aldershot, Hampshire, England: Scolar Press; Brookfield, Vermont, USA: Gower Publishing Co., 1989.

Smith, Barry. *Peter Warlock: the life of Philip Heseltine.* Oxford: Oxford University Press, 1994.

Smith, Joan Allen. *Schoenberg and his circle: a Viennese portrait.* New York: Schirmer Books, London: Collier Macmillan, 1986.

Smith, Richard Langham, Editor. *Debussy on music: the critical writings of the great French composer Claude Debussy.* London: Secker & Warburg, 1977.

Smith, Ronald. *Alkan.* London: Kahn and Averill, 1976.

Snowman, Daniel. *The Amadeus Quartet: the men and the music.* London: Robson Books, 1981.

Solomon, Maynard. *Beethoven.* New York: Schirmer, 1977.

Solomon, Maynard. *Beethoven*

essays. Cambridge, Massachusetts; London: Harvard University Press, 1988.

Solomon, Maynard. *Late Beethoven: music, thought, imagination.* Berkeley; London: University of California Press, 2003.

Solomon, Maynard. *Mozart: a life.* London: Hutchinson, 1995.

Sonneck, Oscar George Theodore. *Beethoven: impressions of contemporaries.* London: Oxford University Press, 1927.

Spalding, Albert. *Rise to follow: an autobiography.* London: Frederick Muller Ltd., 1946.

Spohr, Louis. *Louis Spohr's autobiography.* London: Longman, Green, Longman, Roberts, & Green, 1865.

Stafford, William. *Mozart myths: a critical reassessment.* Stanford, California: Stanford University Press, 1991.

Stanford, Charles Villiers. *Interludes: records and reflections.* London: John Murray, 1922.

Stanley, Glenn, Editor. *The Cambridge companion to Beethoven.* Cambridge; New York: Cambridge University Press, 2000

Stedman, Preston. *The symphony.* Englewood Cliffs, New Jersey; London: Prentice-Hall, 1979.

Stedron, Bohumír, Editor and Translator. *Leos Janácek: letters and reminiscences.* Prague: Artia, 1955.

Stein, Erwin, Editor. *Arnold Schoenberg: letters.* London: Faber and Faber, 1964.

Stein, Erwin. *Orpheus in new guises.* London: Rockliff, 1953.

Stein, Jack Madison. *Poem and music in the German lied from Gluck to Hugo Wolf.* Cambridge, Massachusetts: Harvard University Press, 1971.

Stein, Leonard, Editor. *Style and idea: selected writings of Arnold Schoenberg.* London: Faber and Faber, 1975.

Steinberg, Michael P. *Listening to reason: culture, subjectivity, and nineteenth-century music.* Princeton, New Jersey: Princeton University Press, 2004.

Steinberg, Michael. *The concerto: a listener's guide.* New York: Oxford University Press, 1998.

Steinberg, Michael. *The symphony: a listener's guide.* Oxford; New York: Oxford University Press, 1995.

Sternfeld, Frederick William. *Goethe and music: a list of parodies and Goethe's relationship to music; a list of references.* New York: Da Capo Press, 1979.

Stivender, David. *Mascagni: an autobiography compiled, edited and translated from original sources.* New York: Pro/Am Music Resources; London: Kahn & Averill, 1988.

Stone, Else and Kurt Stone, Editors. *The writings of Elliott Carter: an American composer looks at modern music.* Bloomington: Indiana University Press, 1977.

Stowell, Robin. *Beethoven: violin concerto.* Cambridge: Cambridge University Press, 1998.

Stowell, Robin: Editor. *The Cambridge companion to the cello.* Cambridge: Cambridge University Press, 1999.

Stowell, Robin: Editor. *The Cambridge companion to the string quartet.* Cambridge: Cambridge University Press, 2003.

Stratton, Stephen Samuel. *Men-

delssohn. London: J.M. Dent & Co.; New York: E.P. Dutton & Co., 1901.

Straus, Joseph N. *Remaking the past: musical modernism and the influence of the tonal tradition.* Cambridge, Massachusetts: Harvard University Press, 1990.

Stravinsky, Igor. *An autobiography.* London: Calder and Boyars, 1975.

Stravinsky, Igor. *Themes and conclusions.* London: Faber and Faber, 1972.

Stravinsky, Igor and Robert Craft. *Conversations with Igor Stravinsky.* London: Faber and Faber, 1959.

Stravinsky, Igor and Robert Craft. *Dialogues and a diary.* London: Faber and Faber 1968.

Stravinsky, Igor and Robert Craft. *Memories and commentaries.* London: Faber and Faber, 2002.

Strunk, Oliver. *Source readings in music history, 4: The Classic era.* London: Faber and Faber 1981.

Sullivan, Blair, Editor. *The echo of music: essays in honor of Marie Louise Göllner.* Warren, Michigan: Harmonie Park Press, 2004.

Sullivan, Jack, Editor. *Words on music: from Addison to Barzun.* Athens: Ohio University Press, 1990.

Symonette, Lys and Kim H. Kowalke, Editors and Translators. *Speak low (when you speak love): the letters of Kurt Weill and Lotte Lenya.* London: Hamish Hamilton, 1996.

Swalin, Benjamin F. *The violin concerto: a study in German romanticism.* New York, Da Capo Press, 1973.

Szigeti, Joseph. *With strings attached: reminiscences and reflections.* London: Cassell & Co. Ltd, 1949.

Tanner, Michael, Editor. *Notebooks, 1924–1954: Wilhelm Furtwängler.* London: Quartet Books, 1989.

Taylor, Robert, Editor. *Furtwängler on music: essays and addresses.* Aldershot: Scolar, 1991.

Taylor, Ronald. *Kurt Weill: composer in a divided world.* London: Simon & Schuster, 1991.

Tchaikovsky, Peter Ilich. *Letters to his family: an autobiography.* Translated by Galina von Meck. London: Dennis Dobson, 1981.

Tertis, Lionel. *My viola and I: a complete autobiography; with, 'Beauty of tone in string playing', and other essays.* London: Paul Elek, 1974.

Thayer, Alexander Wheelock. *Salieri: rival of Mozart.* Edited by Theodore Albrecht. Kansas City, Missouri: Philharmonia of Greater Kansas City, 1989.

Thomas, Michael Tilson. *Viva voce: conversations with Edward Seckerson.* London: Faber and Faber 1994.

Thomson, Andrew. *Vincent d'Indy and his world.* Oxford: Clarendon Press, 1996.

Thomson, Virgil. *The musical scene.* New York: Greenwood Press, 1968.

Thomson, Virgil. *Virgil Thomson.* London: Weidenfeld & Nicolson, 1967.

Tillard, Françoise. *Fanny Mendelssohn.* Amadeus Press: Portland, 1996.

Tilmouth, Michael, Editor. *Donald Francis Tovey: The classics of* music: talks, essays, and other writings previously uncollected. Oxford: Oxford University Press, 2001.

Tippett, Michael. *Moving into Aquarius*. London: Routledge and Kegan Paul, 1959.

Tippett, Michael. *Those twentieth century blues: an autobiography*. London: Hutchinson, 1991.

Todd, R. Larry, Editor. *Nineteenth-century piano music*. New York; London: Routledge, 2004.

Todd, R. Larry, Editor. *Schumann and his world*. Princeton: Princeton University Press, 1994.

Tommasini, Anthony. *Virgil Thomson: composer on the aisle*. New York: W.W. Norton, 1997.

Tortelier, Paul. *A self-portrait: in conversation with David Blum*. London: Heinemann, 1984.

Tovey, Donald Francis. *A Companion to Beethoven's Pianoforte Sonatas*. Revised by Barry Cooper. London: The Associated Board, [1931], 1998.

Tovey, Donald Francis. *Beethoven*. London: Oxford University Press, 1944.

Tovey, Donald Francis. *Essays and lectures on music*. London: Oxford University Press, 1949.

Tovey, Donald Francis. *Essays in musical analysis*. London: Oxford University Press, H. Milford, 7 Vols., 1935–41.

Tovey, Donald Francis. *The forms of music: musical articles from The Encyclopaedia Britannica*. London: Oxford University Press, 1944.

Toye, Francis. *Giuseppe Verdi: his life and works*. London: William Heinemann Ltd., 1931.

Truscott, Harold. *Beethoven's late string quartets*. London: Dobson, 1968.

Tyler, William R. *The letters of Franz Liszt to Olga von Meyendorff, 1871–1886, in the Mildred Bliss Collection at Dumbarton Oaks*. Translated by William R. Tyler. Washington: Dumbarton Oaks, Trustees for Harvard University; Cambridge, Massachusetts: distributed by Harvard University Press, 1979.

Tyrrell, John. *Janácek: years of a life. Vol. 1, (1854–1914) The lonely blackbird*. London: Faber and Faber, 2006.

Tyrrell, John, Editor and Translator. *My life with Janácek: the memoirs of Zdenka Janácková*. London: Faber and Faber, 1998.

Tyson, Alan, Editor. *Beethoven studies 2*. Cambridge: Cambridge University Press, 1977.

Tyson, Alan, Editor. *Beethoven studies 3*. Cambridge: Cambridge University Press, 1982.

Tyson, Alan. *Mozart: studies of the autograph scores*. Cambridge, Massachusetts; London: Harvard University Press, 1987.

Tyson, Alan. *The authentic English editions of Beethoven*. London: Faber and Faber, 1963.

Underwood, J. A., Editor. *Gabriel Fauré: his life through his letters*. London: Marion Boyars, 1984.

Vechten, Carl van, Editor. *Nikolay, Rimsky-Korsakov: My musical life*. London: Martin Secker & Warburg Ltd., 1942.

Vinton, John. *Essays after a dictionary: music and culture at the close of Western civilization*. Lewisburg: Bucknell University Press, 1977.

Volkov, Solomon, Editor. *Testimony: the memoirs of Dmitri Shostakovich. London: Faber and Faber, 1981.

Volta, Ornella, Editor. *A mammal's notebook: collected writings of Erik Satie.* London: Atlas Press, 1996.

Wagner, Richard. Beethoven: *With [a] supplement from the philosophical works of A. Schopenhauer.* Translated by E. Dannreuther. London: Reeves, 1893.

Wagner, Richard. *My life.* London: Constable and Company Ltd., 1911.

Walden, Valerie. *One hundred years of violoncello: a history of technique and performance practice, 1740–1840.* Cambridge: Cambridge University Press, 1998.

Walker, Alan. *Franz Liszt. Volume 1, The virtuoso years: 1811–1847.* New York: Alfred A. Knopf, 1983.

Walker, Alan. *Franz Liszt. Volume 2, The Weimar years: 1848–1861.* London: Faber and Faber, 1989.

Walker, Alan. *Franz Liszt. Volume 3, The final years, 1861–1886.* London: Faber and Faber, 1997.

Walker, Bettina. *My musical experiences.* London: Richard Bentley and Son, 1890.

Walker, Ernest. *Free thought and the musician, and other essays.* London; New York: Oxford University Press, 1946.

Walker, Frank. *Hugo Wolf: a biography.* London: J. M. Dent, 1951.

Walker, Frank. *The man Verdi.* London: Dent, 1962.

Wallace, Grace, [Lady Wallace]. *Beethoven's letters (1790–1826): from the collection of Dr. Ludwig Nohl . Also his letters to the Archduke Rudolph, Cardinal-Archbishop of Olmutz, K.W., from the collection of Dr. Ludwig Ritter Von Kolchel.* London: Longmans, Green, 2 Vols., 1866.

Wallace, Robin. *Beethoven's critics: aesthetic dilemmas and resolutions during the composer's lifetime.* Cambridge; New York: Cambridge University Press, 1986.

Walter, Bruno. *Theme and variations: an autobiography.* London: H. Hamilton, 1948.

Warrack, John Hamilton. *Writings on music.* Cambridge: Cambridge University Press, 1981.

Wasielewski, Wilhelm Joseph von. *Life of Robert Schumann: with letters, 1833–1852.* London: William Reeves, 1878.

Watkins, Glenn. *Proof through the night: music and the Great War.* Berkeley: University of California Press, 2003.

Watkins, Glenn. *Pyramids at the Louvre: music, culture, and collage from Stravinsky to the postmodernists.* Cambridge, Massachusetts; London: Belknap Press of Harvard University Press, 1994.

Watkins, Glenn. *Soundings: music in the twentieth century.* New York: Schirmer Books London: Collier Macmillan, 1988.

Watson, Derek. *Liszt.* London: J. M. Dent, 1989.

Weaver, William, Editor. *The Verdi-Boito correspondence.* Chicago; London: University of Chicago Press, 1994.

Wegeler, Franz. *Remembering Beethoven: the biographical*

notes of Franz Wegeler and Ferdinand Ries. London: Andre Deutsch, 1988.

Weingartner, Felix. *Buffets and rewards: a musician's reminiscences.* London: Hutchinson & Co., 1937.

Weinstock, Herbert. *Rossini: a biography.* New York: Limelight, 1987.

Weiss, Piero and Richard Taruskin. *Music in the Western World: a history in documents.* New York: Schirmer; London: Collier Macmillan, 1984.

Weissweiler, Eva *The complete correspondence of Clara and Robert Schumann.* New York: Peter Lang, 2 Vols., 1994.

Whittaker, William Gillies. *Collected essays.* London: Oxford University Press, 1940.

Whittall, Arnold. *Exploring twentieth-century music: tradition and innovation.* Cambridge; New York: Cambridge University Press, 2003.

Whittall, Arnold. *Music since the First World War.* London: J. M. Dent, 1977.

Whitton, Kenneth S. *Lieder: an introduction to German song.* London: Julia MacRae, 1984.

Wightman, Alistair, Editor. *Szymanowski on music: selected writings of Karol Szymanowski.* London: Toccata Press, 1999.

Wilhelm, Kurt. *Richard Strauss: an intimate portrait.* London: Thames and Hudson, 1999.

Will, Richard James. *The characteristic symphony in the age of Haydn and Beethoven.* Cambridge: Cambridge University Press, 2002.

Willetts, Pamela J. *Beethoven and England: an account of sources in the British Museum.* London: British Museum, 1970.

Williams, Adrian, Editor and Translator. *Liszt, Franz: Selected letters.* Oxford: Clarendon Press, 1998.

Williams, Adrian. *Portrait of Liszt: by himself and his contemporaries.* Oxford: Clarendon Press, 1990.

Williams, Ralph Vaughan. *Heirs and rebels: letters written to each other and occasional writings on music.* London; New York: Oxford University Press, 1959.

Williams, Ralph Vaughan. *Some thoughts on Beethoven's Choral symphony: with writings on other musical subjects.* London; Oxford University Press, 1953.

Williams, Ralph Vaughan. *The making of music.* Ithaca, New York: Cornell University Press, 1955.

Williams, Ursula Vaughan. *R.V.W.: a biography of Ralph Vaughan Williams.* London: Oxford University Press, 1964.

Wilson, Conrad. *Notes on Beethoven: 20 crucial works.* Edinburgh: Saint Andrew Press, 2003.

Wilson, Elizabeth. *Shostakovich: a life remembered.* Princeton, New Jersey: Princeton University Press, 1994.

Winter, Robert, Editor. *Beethoven, performers, and critics: the International Beethoven Congress, Detroit, 1977.* Detroit: Wayne State University Press, 1980.

Winter, Robert. *Compositional origins of Beethoven's opus 131.* Ann Arbor, Michigan: UMI Research Press, 1982.

Winter, Robert and Robert Martin,

Editors. *The Beethoven quartet companion.* Berkeley: University of California Press, 1994.

Wolf, Eugene K. and Edward H. Roesner, Editors. *Studies in musical sources and style: essays in honor of Jan LaRue.* Madison, Wisconsin: A-R Editions, 1990.

Wolff, Christoph and Robert Riggs. *The string quartets of Haydn, Mozart and Beethoven: studies of the autograph manuscripts: a conference at Isham Memorial Library, March 15–17, 1979.* Cambridge, Massachusetts: Department of Music, Harvard University, 1980.

Wolff, Konrad. *Masters of the keyboard: individual style elements in the piano music of Bach, Haydn, Mozart, Beethoven, Schubert, Chopin, and Brahms.* Bloomington: Indiana University Press, 1990.

Wörner, Karl Heinrich. *Stockhausen: life and work.* London: Faber, 1973.

Wright, Donald, Editor. *Cardus on music: a centenary collection.* London: Hamish Hamilton, 1988.

Wyndham, Henry Saxe. *August Manns and the Saturday concerts: a memoir and a retrospect.* London and Felling-on-Tyne, New York, The Walter Scott Publishing Co., Ltd., 1909.

Yastrebtsev, V.V. Edited and Translated by Florence Jonas. *Reminiscences of Rimsky-Korsakov.* New York: Columbia University Press, 1985.

Yates, Peter. *Twentieth century music: its evolution from the end of the harmonic era into the present era of sound.* London: Allen & Unwin Ltd., 1968.

Young, Percy M. *Beethoven: a Victorian tribute based on the papers of Sir George Smart.* London: D. Dobson, 1976.

Young, Percy M. *George Grove, 1820–1900: a biography.* London: Macmillan, 1980.

Young, Percy M. *Letters of Edward Elgar and other writings.* London: Geoffrey Bles, 1956.

Young, Percy M., Editor. *Letters to Nimrod: Edward Elgar to August Jaeger, 1897–1908.* London: Dennis Dobson, 1965.

Young, Percy M. *The concert tradition: from the middle ages to the twentieth century.* London: Routledge and Kegan Paul, 1965.

Young, Rob, Editor. *(Brief Description): Undercurrents: the hidden wiring of modern music.* London; New York, N.Y.: Continuum, 2002.

Yourke, Electra Slonimsky, Editor. *Nicolas Slonimsky: writings on music.* New York, N.Y.; London: Routledge, 4 Vols. 2003-2005.

Slonimsky, Nicolas. *The great composers and their works.* Edited by Electra Slonimsky Yourke. New York: Schirmer Books, 2 Vols. 2000.

Ysaÿe, Antoine. *Ysaÿe: his life, work and influence.* London: W. Heinemann, 1947.

Zamoyski, Adam. *Paderewski.* London: Collins, 1982.

Zegers, Mirjam, Editor. *Louis Andriessen: The art of stealing time.* Todmorden: Arc Music, 2002.

Zemanova, Mirka, Editor. *Janácek's uncollected essays on music.* London: Marion Boyars, 1989.

INDEX

Index to: String Quartets Op. 59, Nos. 1-3; String Quartet, Op. 74; and String Quartet, Op. 95. Incorporating a Beethoven time-line of significant musical and related events.

The order adopted for the listing of the individual entries in this index, for each of the string quartets under consideration, is chronological — according to the sequential unfolding of events under discussion. Thereby, the reader is provided with both a guide to the contents discussed in the main text and a timeline of the principal events bearing on Beethoven's life and work.

STRING QUARTETS, OP. 59, NOS. 1–3 PP. 1-50
Wilhelm von Lenz, estimation
Rebecca Clarke, estimation
Beethoven's new compositional outlook
Standing of string quartet
Haydn and Mozart, contributions to quartet writing
Wenzel Krumpholz, recollections of Beethoven
Beethoven's new style of expression
Op. 59 perceived as quartet-symphonies

Breitkopf and Härtell, Beethoven's negotiations with
Beethoven's resolve to compose string quartets
Departure from salon-style compositions
Expansion of structure characteristic of Beethoven's 'heroic period'
Beethoven's growing popularity in Vienna
Demand as a piano teacher
Attention from music publishers
Beethoven in portraiture
Johann Friedrich Reichardt, impression of Beethoven
Illness, views of Anton Neumayr
Kaspar Karl (Caspar Carl), role in Beethoven's business affairs
Gottfried Christoph Härtel, Beethoven's negotiations with
Count Andrey Razumovsky
Schuppanzigh's String Quartet
Razumovsky's String Quartet
Archduke Trio, Op. 97, first performance
Recollections of Schuppanzigh style of playing
Karl Möser, Beethoven pioneer
Razumovsky's commissioning of Op. 59
Russian folk melodies, incorporation of
Ivan Pratsch, collection of Russian themes
1806, period of creative self-confidence
Breitkopf and Härtel, publication negotiations with
Count Franz Brunsvik
1807, significant meeting with Muzio Clementi
Negotiations for publication of Beethoven's works in England
Johann Baptist Cramer, role of in England
Baron Ignaz von Gleichenstein, service to Beethoven
Grasnick 20b Sketchbook
Eroica Symphony and Beethoven's expanding stylistic tendencies
Expanded performing time of string quartet
Diversity of expression in Razumovsky Quartets
Demands made on players and listeners
Muzio Clement, London publication negotiations
Nikolaus Simrock, revised publication dealings with
Camille Pleyel, putative negotiations with
Kunst und Industrie-Comptoir — Bureau des Arts et d'Industrie, publication of Op. 59
Title Page publication announcement
Allgemeine musikalische Zeitung, review of Op. 59 (March 1807)
Bleak public reaction to Op. 59 Quartets
Adalbert Gyrowetz, recollections of
Rossini, views of
Clementi's London publication
Thomas Appleby, recollections of
Felix Radicati, recollections of
George Thomson, Beethoven's dealings with
Joseph de Marliave, Beethoven's reception in France
François Antoine Habeneck, pioneering admirer of Beethoven
Review musicale, critical assessment of Op. 59 (March 1832)
Franco-Mendès String Quartet
Pierre-François-Alexandre Chevillard and foundation of Société des Quatuors de Beethoven
Estimations of contemporary authorities: Joseph Kerman, Paul Bekker, Maynard Solomon, Igor Stravinsky

STRING QUARTET, OP. 59, NO. 1
PP. 56-76

Autograph, text inscription
Allgemeine musikalische Zeitung, review
Norbert Brainin, recollections of
Eroica Symphony, affinities with
Pastoral Symphony, affinities with
New scale of Op. 59
Beethoven's craftsmanship
Matured and deepened powers of expression'
Joseph Linke, influence of
Imagery of 'inspired spirituality'
Beethoven's constructional procedures
First movement
Mozart's C major Quintet, K 515, influence of
thème russe
One of greatest Beethoven openings
Counterpoint evermore contrapuntal
Joseph Haydn and Johann Albrechtsberger, influence of
Dika Newlin, Schoenberg anecdote
Second movement
Scherzo-like character
Robert Schumann, 'most wonderful utterance'
'Orchestral' sound
An astonishingly original conception
Signal masterpiece of second period
First performance
Count Soltikoff (Soltykow)
Bernhard Romberg
Privy Councillor Lwoffin
Spirit of dance
Artur Rubinstein, anecdote
Gerald Abraham, estimation of
Adagio most inscrutable
Donald Tovey, views of
Shakespeare's Twelfth Night, allusion to
Florestan's soliloquy, affinities with
Franz Georg Beethoven
Ivan Pratsch, Russian folk melodies
Final movement
Russian folksong, influence of
Beethoven's assimilation of Slav folk song
Elegiac character
Beethoven's sketches

STRING QUARTET, OP. 59, NO. 2
PP. 79-91

Beethoven's manner to explore contrast
Character, tenser, darker in colour
tenser, darker in colour
Monotonic composition, E minor
Depths of dark mystery of music
First movement
High drama
Silence, significance of
Beethoven's construction
Ensemble, challenge of
Second movement
Choral-like opening
Third movement
Quartet's scherzo
Beethoven's jeux d'esprit
Expressive dance form
Trio section, thème russe
Modest Mussorgsky Boris Godunov
Parodistic fugal medley
Fourth movement
Boisterous finale
Symphonic conception

STRING QUARTET, OP. 59, NO. 3
PP. 93-112

Berliner Allgemeine musikalische Zeitung
Adoption of C major
Mozart's K. 465, influence of
Alan Tyson
Ivan Pratsch, Russian collection
Allgemeine musikalische Zeitung
Count Razumovsky
Piano arrangement
First movement
Haydn and Mozart, parallels with

Beethoven's originality
Mozart's Dissonance Quartet, K. 465
Atmosphere of mystery and suspense
Marion Scott, Shakespearian parallels
Fourth Symphony, affinities with
Gesellschaft der Musikfreunde
Second movement
Russian folksong, suggestion of
Sketch origins
Performance restraint required
Third movement
Minuet, glance back to past
jeu d'esprit
Fourth movement
Ebullient power'
Greatest quartet finale so far
Initiation of fugal finale – fugal style
Hans von Bülow
Beethoven's construction
Review musicale
Johann Georg Albrechtsberger, pedagogical studies
Mozart's K. 387

STRING QUARTET OP. 74 PP. 115-169

Nickname, origins of
French occupation of Vienna
Beethoven's debt to Haydn
Key of E flat, particular significance for Beethoven
Beethoven's creativity
Haydn, death of
Johann Georg Albrechtsberger, death of
Johann Adam Schmidt death of
Franz Gerhard Wegeler, support of
Beethoven's loss of hearing
Für Elise
Beethoven's personal circumstances
Wiener Zeitung
French occupation of Vienna
Archduke Rudolph, study with Beethoven
Beethoven's resolve to leave Vienna

Jérôme Bonaparte, offer of appointment
Beethoven's patrons: Archduke Rudolph, Prince Ferdinand Kinsky and Count Franz Joseph Lobkowitz.
Beethoven's Annuity Contract
1809, compositional origins
Four-movement structure
Landsberg 5 sketchbook
Autograph
Ernst von Mendelssohn-Bartholdy, sketch sources
Breitkopf and Härtell, publisher
Nikolaus Zmeskall von Domanovecz, assistance from
Royal Institute of Science and Fine Arts, Amsterdam, honour from
Gottfried Härtell, role of publisher
Pirate publishers, challenge of
Monetary inflation
Allgemeine musikalische Zeitung
Publication, Title Page
Muzio Clementi, meeting with Beethoven
English edition
William Frederick Collard, reactions of
AmZ review
First movement
Mozart's K428, affinities with
Expressive nature of movement
Quartet's pizzicato opening
AmZ reception
Beethoven's chromaticism
Philip Radcliffe
Coda
French quatuor brilliant
Second movement
Sketch origins
AmZ response
Romanticism anticipated
Nineteenth century sentimentality
Lyrical nature of music
Schubert's Das Wirsthuas
Third movement

Schubert's Quartettsatz
Beethoven's construction
Goethe's Rastlose Liebe, affinities with
Adolph Bernhard Marx, expression of enthusiasm
Workmanship, feathery lightness
Trio
Ignaz Pleyel, incident concerning
Rebecca Clarke, challenge to performers
Fourth movement
Theme and variations
Haydn influence, String Quartet, Op. 76, No. 6
Deeply expressive feeling
Wiener Vaterländische Blätter, Beethoven's interest in metronome
Sketch origins
Variations, construction
Coda, conclusion
Summation: a work of consolidation

STRING QUARTET OP. 95 PP. 176-229

Beethoven's expansive scale
Character, implicit in title
An exploration of seriousness
1810, Beethoven's personal circumstances
Therese Malfatti, affection for
Loss of hearing, influence of
Johann Friedrich Reichardt, recollections of
Invasion of Vienna, impact of
Goethe's Werthe, parallels with
Beethoven's audiences
Beethoven's caution regarding public performance
Last quartets anticipated
Beethoven's F minor phase
Nineteenth-century reception
Benito Mussolini, reference to
Benjamin Britten, youthful admiration of Beethoven
Aaron Copland and The Distinguished Lecture Series
Nicholas Zmeskall von Domanovez (Domanovecz), relationship with Beethoven
Sketchbook sources: Landsberg 11 sketchbook
Title Page
1810, creation origins
Carl Maria von Weber, critical views of
Leonora-Fidelio, progress with
Beethoven's interest in future opera projects
Beethoven's health, hydrotherapy
Karl August von Ense, recollections of
Johann Wolfgang von Goethe, meeting with Beethoven
Nannette and Andreas Streicher, Franz Klein commission for plaster cast
1814, Congress of Vienna
Beethoven's celebrity
Trio in B-flat major, Beethoven's last public performance as pianist
Allgemeine musikalische Zeitung, estimation of Beethoven
Louis Letronne, portrait of Beethoven
Sir George Smart, recollections of
Charles Neate, London negotiations with
Sigmund Anton Steiner & Co., role of publishing house
Joseph Mähler and Johann Christoph Heckel, portraits of Beethoven
1815, freedom of city conferred
Dr. Karl von Bursy, impressions of Beethoven
Title Page
Clementi & Co., English publication
1816, Wiener Zeitung and Wiener Vaterländische Blätter publication announcement

Prince Nikolay Galitzin, admiration of
1899, Gustav Mahler orchestral transcription
First movement: compression
Parallels with other works
Impassioned music
Aphoristically abbreviated theme structures
Donald Tovey, views of
Arnold Schoenberg, views of
Second movement
Lyrical expression linked with intellectual precision
Prominence of cello
Bach's Chromatic Fantasia and Fugue, influence of
Song and fugue combined
Affinities with passages in Seventh and Eighth Symphonies
Fugal exposition, anticipations of Beethoven's later pre-occupation with fugue
Third movement, scherzo-like
Character of march
Mendelssohnian flavour
Challenge to performers
Fourth movement
Moment of reflection'
Recollections of La Melancholia in Op. 18, No.6
Character, mood of anguish
Donald Tovey, views of
Mozart's C minor Piano Concerto, affinities with
Shakespearian-like tragedy
Piano Sonata Op. 31, No. 2, parallels with
Mendelsohn, influence upon
Stravinsky, admiration of
Vincent d'Indy, critical views of
Beethoven's rare adoption of ppp
Romain Rolland, expression of enthusiasm
Joseph Kerman, summative words

ABOUT THE AUTHOR

Terence M. Russell graduated with first class honours in architecture and was a nominee for the coveted Silver Medal of the Royal Institute of British Architects. He is a Fellow of the Royal Incorporation of Architects in Scotland (retired), was formerly Reader in the School of Arts, Culture and Environment at the University of Edinburgh, a Fellow of the British Higher Education Academy, and Senior Assessor to the Scottish Higher Education Funding Council. Alongside his professional work in the field of architecture – embracing practice, teaching and research – he has maintained a lifetime's interest in the music and musicology of Beethoven. He has an equal admiration for the work of Franz Schubert and was for many years an active member of the Schubert Institute, UK. His book writings in the field of architecture include the following:

The Built Environment: A Subject Index, Gregg Publishing (1989):
- Vol. 1: Town planning and urbanism, architecture, gardens and landscape design
- Vol. 2: Environmental technology, constructional engineering, building and materials
- Vol. 3: Decorative art and industrial design, international exhibitions and collections, recreational and performing arts
- Vol. 4: Public health, municipal services, community welfare

Architecture in the Encyclopédie of Diderot and D'Alemebert: The Letterpress Articles and Selected Engravings, Scolar Press (1993)

The Encyclopaedic Dictionary in the Eighteenth Century: Architecture, Arts and Crafts, Scolar Press (1997):
- Vol. 1: John Harris, Lexicon Technicum
- Vol. 2: Ephraim Chambers, Cyclopaedia
- Vol. 3: The Builder's Dictionary
- Vol. 4: Samuel Johnson, A Dictionary of the English Language
- Vol. 5: A Society of Gentlemen, Encyclopaedia Britannica

Gardens and Landscapes in the Encyclopédie of Diderot and D'Alemebert: The Letterpress Articles and Selected Engravings, 2 Vols., Ashgate (1999)

The Napoleonic Survey of Egypt: The Monuments and Customs of Egypt, 2 Vols., Ashgate (2001)

The Discovery of Egypt: Vivant Denon's Travels with Napoleon's Army, History Press (2005)

www.ingramcontent.com/pod-product-compliance
Lightning Source LLC
Chambersburg PA
CBHW011956090526
44590CB00023B/3749